HUNGARY

ROMANIA

Erdut

ukovar

Danube R.

Belgrade

SERBIA

Drina R.

A

Kragujevac

vo

MONTENEGRO

Pristina

KOSOVO

Podgorica

Skopje

MACEDONIA

BULGARIA

ALBANIA

GREECE

# THE BUTCHER'S TRAIL

# THE BUTCHER'S TRAIL

## How the Search for Balkan War Criminals
## Became the World's Most Successful Manhunt

Julian Borger

Other Press
New York

Maps on endpapers and page 11 by Valerie Sebestyen.

Production editor: Yvonne E. Cárdenas
Text designer: Julie Fry
This book was set in Freight and Franklin Gothic.

1  3  5  7  9  10  8  6  4  2

Library of Congress Cataloging-in-Publication Data
Borger, Julian.
The butcher's trail : how the search for Balkan war criminals
became the world's most successful manhunt / by Julian Borger.
pages cm
Includes bibliographical references and index.
ISBN 978-1-59051-605-8 (hardback : acid-free paper) —
ISBN 978-1-59051-606-5 (e-book)
1. Karadžić, Radovan V., 1945–  2. Mladić, Ratko. 3. Gagović, Dragan, 1960–
4. Milošević, Slobodan, 1941–2006. 5. Yugoslav War, 1991–1995 — Atrocities.
6. War crimes investigation — History — 20th century. 7. International Tribunal
for the Prosecution of Persons Responsible for Serious Violations of
International Humanitarian Law Committed in the Territory of the Former
Yugoslavia since 1991. 8. Yugoslav War, 1991–1995 — Biography.
9. War criminals — Former Yugoslav republics — Biography. 10. Fugitives
from justice — Former Yugoslav republics — Biography. I. Title.
DR1313.7.A85B66 2016
341.6'90268 — dc23
2015016962

*For Benji*

# CONTENTS

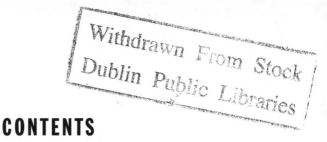

# AUTHOR'S NOTE

## ON LANGUAGE, SPELLING, AND ETHNICITY

WORDS MATTER, and they matter doubly in the countries that emerged from Yugoslavia. The majority Yugoslav language used to be known as Serbo-Croat, but that hyphenated term now offends most people in the three principal nations that speak it: Bosnia and Herzegovina, Croatia, and Serbia. They individually refer to it as Bosnian, Croatian, and Serbian, and I have tended to follow suit depending on the geographical context. The Hague Tribunal uses the abbreviation BCS, which is a safe enough umbrella, yet hardly evocative.

I have used the terms Serbian, Croatian, and Bosnian to denote citizenship of the post-Yugoslav states, while Serb, Croat, and Bosniak describe ethnicity. For example, a Bosnian Serb is a Serb living in Bosnia. As for ethnic Albanians in Kosovo, I have generally used their preferred term, Kosovar.

I have not anglicized names except for a couple that entered into English usage in the Second World War. I write Ustasha instead of Ustaša for the wartime Croatian fascist movement, and Chetnik rather than Četnik for the Serb ultranationalists. Otherwise I have left in place the Latin version of the alphabet, with all its special characters, again with one niggling exception. I think the letter Đ is so strange for most English-language readers that it would be a distraction, so I have used Dj for that soft consonant instead.

# INTRODUCTION
# THE ECHO OF NUREMBERG

"The Security Council thought we would never become
operational. We had no budget. We had nothing. Zero."
—*Antonio Cassese, first president of the International
Criminal Tribunal for the former Yugoslavia*

**THE TRAIL CAME TO A HALT** in a forest clearing. A man emerged
from the trees at the agreed time, but the friend he had come to
meet was nowhere to be seen. The man waited, feeling increasingly out of place. It was a burning hot day in late July, and he was
flabby and pale from years spent in colder climes.

He regretted having come home, but he had no real choice.
By the summer of 2011, the man had spent seven years as a fugitive, most recently in Russia, and was out of money. The only
people on earth prepared to help him were here, in Serbia, where
he could surely still count on a handful of true believers from the
old days of national struggle. But where were they now?

As the appointed hour came and went, the only sounds in the
forest were birdsong and the wind in the leaves. But the man was
not alone. All along the path as it wound through the trees, he had
been watched intently. As he emerged into the clearing, the illusion of solitude lasted just a few more moments before explod-
ing with shouts and a blur of movement. In an instant, there were

men all around him in white T-shirts and black knitted masks, pointing guns, gripping him by the wrists and shoulders.

One of the men, a police officer, began a recitation: "Goran Hadžić, we are arresting you..."

It was a name that had scarcely been heard for years. Even its owner had stopped using it, in favor of a string of aliases. But two decades earlier, Goran Hadžić had been a name to reckon with in this corner of the Balkans. He had been a president, albeit of a trumped-up little statelet with jagged edges — a bite taken out of one reborn country, Croatia, to be chewed and swallowed by another, Serbia, its covetous neighbor.

When the exhausted federal experiment that was Yugoslavia collapsed, its constituent republics were left to fight over its corpse. Serbia was the biggest and most predatory, spurred on by the most ruthless leader. Slobodan Milošević truly was a man for all seasons — a Socialist turned banker turned nationalist despot and unflinching war criminal. His preference was for a Serb-dominated Yugoslavia, but if he could not have that, he would carve out a Greater Serbia at the expense of his neighbors.

Hadžić was Milošević's puppet, but the sort of puppet that belongs in a horror film, a bloodied ventriloquist's dummy. He helped preside over the first large-scale slaughter of innocent civilians in Europe since the Nazi era. From August to November 1991, the early days of Yugoslavia's dismemberment, the baroque Croatian town of Vukovar, which had sat comfortably by the Danube for centuries, was razed to the ground by Serb artillery.

Once the town had fallen, some three hundred Croat men and teenage boys, many of them wounded, were taken from a hospital to a nearby farm where they were beaten and tortured by Serb soldiers and paramilitary volunteers serving with the Yugoslav army. They were driven away at night in trucks, ten to twenty at a time, taken to a wooded ravine, and executed. Only a handful escaped. In all, 263 men and boys were killed, the youngest aged sixteen. There was also one woman among the victims. Their bodies were dumped in a mass grave and covered by a bulldozer.

In Western capitals, it seemed beyond comprehension that wholesale slaughter was being committed once more in the heart of Europe. In the early nineties, it was a continent preoccupied with harmonizing food safety standards and the many other intricate chores of building a closer union. The dark past, two generations earlier, was buried under layer upon layer of democracy, diplomacy, and bureaucracy, or so it seemed from Brussels. The return of mass murder was deeply shocking. An entire town was pulverized, and its surviving Croats and minorities driven out with the goal of creating a swath of territory that would be home only to Serbs.

The process was called "ethnic cleansing," a turn of phrase beyond George Orwell's darkest satire. Like all the most effective propaganda, it worked by inversion. It took an act that was inherently dirty and gore-spattered and made it sound like a salutary rite of purification. It was a "cleansing" that left a permanent stain on everyone and everything it touched.

The "purified" mini-state was named the Republic of Serbian Krajina (Republika Srpska Krajina, or RSK), and Hadžić became its despot. He was thirty-three years old, a former warehouseman for an agro-industrial company in Vukovar who had been a leading light in the local League of Communists in his youth. He was picked for the role of the RSK's warlord because he had made the same ideological swerve to nationalism as Milošević. He had plenty of ambition and no evident scruples. He was perfect.

Twenty years on, Hadžić was isolated and abandoned. His realm, the RSK, had been swept away, and Milošević had been dead for more than five years. In an effort to help him make ends meet, one of Hadžić's childhood friends tried to sell a plundered artwork, but the intended favor only helped corner him. It was a painting attributed to the Italian artist Amedeo Modigliani, taken as booty during the Croatian war. The art market was awash with such looted treasure, real and fake, but it was also thick with informers and spies. The French external intelligence service, the General Directorate for External Security (Direction Générale de la Sécurité Extérieure, or DGSE), had a particularly strong presence. One of its officers was even given a special award for extended service undercover in the Balkan art world.[1] The French alerted Serbian intelligence, who monitored Hadžić's friend and set a trap. In the wooded hills of Fruška Gora National Park near the Serbian-Croatian border, he was cornered and captured like the last grizzled specimen of a once ferocious breed.

The masked policemen turned him toward a camera to capture the moment. Surprise had given way to realization and resentment on Hadžić's hangdog face. By now he was fifty-two years old. The warrior's beard was gone, leaving a graying mustache and sagging jowls. The only familiar features left from his glory days were the angry eyes and the sneer, which once looked at home with his camouflage fatigues but now jarred with the baby-blue T-shirt he had chosen for his meeting.

The pathetic scene at the end of the forest trail marked the culmination of a long and extraordinary history. Hadžić was the last fugitive to be caught in a fifteen-year manhunt, involving the pursuit, arrest, or surrender of all those indicted for war crimes, crimes against humanity, and genocide by a special court created by the United Nations in The Hague, the International Criminal Tribunal for the former Yugoslavia (ICTY).

# INTRODUCTION

The ICTY, or the Hague Tribunal as it came to be popularly known, was established in 1993 as an experiment in international justice. It was the first time in the history of conflict that a truly global court had been created to pursue war criminals. It embodied the conviction that a universal sense of humanity could and should be upheld in the face of mass atrocities, transcending national jurisdiction.

The dramatic landmark trials at The Hague have been the subject of several books and countless articles. But those trials would never have taken place if the defendants had not been tracked down, arrested, and brought to court. That pursuit itself was a historic achievement. It took a very long time, but by 2011 all 161 people on the ICTY list of indictees faced justice one way or another. Former prison camp guards and ex-presidents all stood before the same tribunal. More than half the suspects were tracked down and captured. Others gave themselves up rather than lie awake every night wondering whether masked, armed men were about to storm into their bedroom. Two committed suicide. Others decided they would rather die in a blaze of gunfire and explosives than be taken alive. Two of them got their wish.

The individuals and agencies who pursued the suspects were many and various, but most did their work in the shadows, their successes never acknowledged. This account is based on interviews with more than two hundred of these people — former soldiers, intelligence officials, investigators, data analysts, diplomats, and officials from a dozen nations who were directly involved in the manhunt, most of them speaking about their actions for the first time. A majority agreed to talk only on the promise of anonymity, as the arrest operations are still classified in their home countries. Part of the narrative is also based on a trove of previously secret British government documents, declassified by the Foreign and Commonwealth Office in response to a request under the Freedom of Information Act.

Special forces from six countries took part in the hunt, the biggest special operations deployment anywhere in the world before 9/11. Polish commandos made history by becoming the first soldiers to carry out an arrest on behalf of the tribunal—to the surprise of many, including their own government. Britain's Special Air Service (SAS), who carried out NATO's first manhunting missions in Bosnia, brought techniques learned in Northern Ireland. The participation of a newly formed German special forces unit in an arrest operation, at the cost of some serious injuries, marked the first time that country's soldiers had gone into action since 1945. And the skills acquired in the Balkan manhunt by America's elite soldiers in Delta Force and SEAL Team Six would soon be applied to the looming war on terror and to another manhunt—for Osama bin Laden and al-Qaida's leaders.

An alphabet soup of Western spy agencies, including the CIA, NSA, Britain's MI6 and GCHQ (Government Communications Headquarters), and France's DGSE, conducted a parallel manhunt in the shadows with varying degrees of success. Despite the millions spent, none proved as effective as a small, secretive tracking unit inside the Hague Tribunal, which hugely enhanced the clout of the once-derided court.

From time to time, this multinational array of soldiers, spies, and sleuths acted in concert, following a trail that led from the Balkans west to the Canary Islands and Buenos Aires, and east as far as St. Petersburg and the Black Sea resort of Sochi. Just as often, they tripped over one another in their pursuit of conflicting national and institutional interests. That helps explain why the manhunt took so long.[2] The story of the manhunt's success contains within it many stories of failure. To survivors and families of victims waiting for justice, it did not feel like a triumph at the time. It is only now, when it is all over, that it stands out. There has been nothing quite like it in history.

The ICTY did not just complete its mission, rare enough for a UN operation and all the more striking in view of the patchy and ambivalent support it received from the major powers. The relentless pursuit of the indictees also made legal history. It led to the arrest and trial of Milošević, the first sitting head of state ever to be charged with war crimes by an international court. At the time of writing, the two men who presided over the worst of the atrocities in Bosnia — Radovan Karadžić, the Bosnian Serbs' political leader, and his military commander, Ratko Mladić — are on trial for genocide, war crimes, and crimes against humanity. The trail of blood was followed, not just to the immediate perpetrators of the mass atrocities but all the way to the orchestrators, the master butchers themselves.

Along the way, the ICTY defined mass rape for the first time as a crime against humanity in international law, as a result of atrocities committed by Bosnian Serb forces in the town of Foča. It was a legal breakthrough that would have meant little without the actions of German and French special forces, who tracked down the rapists and brought them to The Hague.

Before the ICTY's creation, there was no institutional framework for judging war crimes and crimes against humanity. There was an attempt to put Napoleon Bonaparte's commanders on trial for treason in 1815, but the effort collapsed. More than a century later, the British government sought to prosecute Kaiser Wilhelm for war crimes but failed to persuade Holland, where the Kaiser had taken refuge, to hand him over.[3]

After the Second World War, the question loomed once more of what to do with leaders, officials, and soldiers responsible for mass atrocities, and it was by no means inevitable they would be put on trial. Winston Churchill, Joseph Stalin, and Franklin Delano Roosevelt initially approved a plan for summary executions of top Nazis, lest their survival help rally their followers.[4] The trials in the ruined city of Nuremberg were something of a last-minute decision.

Meanwhile, in Tokyo a parallel tribunal was established for Japanese war crimes suspects, but Emperor Hirohito and members of the imperial family were exempted. Neither Tokyo nor Nuremberg succeeded in drawing a line in human history, despite the hopeful mantra of "never again." More than forty-five years later, mass murder returned to the modern, industrialized world.

Genocide and other mass atrocities challenge our idea of what it is to be human. The acts perpetrated against innocent victims are so grotesque and disturbing, we recoil from their contemplation. We prefer them to be either far away or long ago. When Yugoslavia began to fall apart, the rest of Europe started to distance itself, like neighbors of a dying household. Shutting their doors, they convinced themselves that if they looked the other way, they would never catch the disease. Western politicians diagnosed "ancient ethnic hatreds" let loose by the fall of Communism as the cause of the bloodshed.[5] It was one of a litany of excuses for not getting involved, but it explained nothing.

The history of the ethnic communities that made up Yugoslavia had indeed been marked by sporadic bouts of violence but those eruptions had been interspersed by long periods of peaceful coexistence. The same could be said of most regions in Europe's diverse and turbulent continent.

Yugoslavia marched into hell because its leaders took it there. When Communist dogma lost its already tenuous hold on people's minds with the fall of the Iron Curtain, the more ideologically flexible and unscrupulous of the fading Communist elite, led by Milošević, switched to nationalism. The leaders packaged it as a new emotional certainty in the face of the chaos and fear left by the collapse of the old order. The challenges of converting a totalitarian state into a democracy, or turning a command economy into a free market, were waved away with colorful flags, hazy nostalgia, and folk music. Political power at the breakup of Yugoslavia depended on the ability to weave myths, wield arms, and manipulate reality.

No one was better at this than Milošević, but he was not alone. His Croatian counterpart was another rebranded Communist, the former Partisan officer turned nationalist Franjo Tudjman. In Bosnia and Herzegovina,* Alija Izetbegović, a paler and frailer version of the national strongman, unfurled his party's green flag and offered his people a sense of Muslim identity. It was a defensive nationalism, however. Bosnia's Muslims generally did not nurse irredentist ambitions, but they were afraid that the revival of backward-looking nationalism among their neighbors would once more mark them as prey. Izetbegović was playing a dangerous game, waving a green banner with little to defend it.

His neighbors Milošević and Tudjman did not make the same mistake. As Yugoslavia collapsed, they armed their foot soldiers. Milošević had access to a near-bottomless arsenal thanks to Serb domination of the Yugoslav National Army (Jugoslavenska Narodna Armija, or JNA), once one of the largest militaries in Europe. The Croats took a smaller share of the JNA arms

---

* This is the full name of the Socialist Republic and then the independent nation, which will mostly be referred to simply as Bosnia for the rest of the book, for the sake of brevity.

stockpile and as war approached they smuggled in weaponry to narrow the gap.

Milošević and Tudjman drew up maps expressing their dreams for a Greater Serbia and a Greater Croatia, aspirations that left little if any room for Bosnia. Neither of these despots regarded the Muslims — known as Bosniaks* — as a distinct ethnic group, viewing them respectively as renegade Serbs or Croats who had converted to Islam.

The new nationalist maps were clear and simple, filled with solid blocks of color. The reality of Yugoslavia on the other hand was uncommonly messy. It was pockmarked and spattered by more than a thousand years of human interaction, mingling Croats and Serbs with Illyrians, Romans, Goths, Asiatic Huns, Iranian Alans, and Avars.

The mix was stirred repeatedly by outside powers and rival empires — Roman, Frankish, Byzantine, Habsburg, and Ottoman — who scattered its constituent parts, occasionally adding new ingredients. Religion and ethnicity were intertwined throughout, creating both harmony and discord. The people of the western Balkans largely converted to Catholicism under the sway of the Franks and Habsburgs. Those in the east followed the Orthodox Christianity of Byzantium. Caught in between, many of the mountain people of central Bosnia converted to Islam after the Ottomans arrived from the east in the fifteenth century.

Mixing, migration, and intermarriage intensified during the two incarnations of Yugoslavia, as a monarchy in between the interwar period and as a Socialist federal republic after the

---

* Bosnian Muslims formally adopted the term "Bosniaks" to describe themselves in 1993.

Second World War. The mingling was made all the easier by the fact that the three biggest communities — Serbs, Croats, and Bosnian Muslims — shared a common language.*

The result was a complicated country that looked nothing like the simple ethnic maps being circulated in the death throes of Yugoslavia. Making allowances for ethnic nuance would have robbed the nationalist message of its simplicity and power. Rather than change their maps, the nationalist leaders sought to force change on the flesh and blood of the region, creating ethnically pure territories, by terror when necessary. Whether they were nationalists or not, one community after another was confronted by the brutal violence unleashed by a deceptively simple question: Why should I be a minority in your country, when you could be a minority in mine?[6]

Yugoslavia unraveled in a succession of increasingly ferocious wars. The first in Slovenia was little more than a prelude. After ten days of skirmishes with Slovene separatists in the early summer of 1991, the JNA withdrew. There were hardly any Serbs in the renegade republic, and Milošević let it go. He was conserving his strength for the next battle.

Croatia, which had a sizable Serb population,† had declared independence on the same day as Slovenia. Milošević and Tudjman may have seen eye to eye on the division of Bosnia but they had very different maps of Croatia. Milošević wanted the Serb-inhabited area, the Krajina, for a Greater Serbia, while Tudjman's map of Croatia was all one color. His independence constitution downgraded the new nation's Serbs, about one in nine of the

---

*Known in Yugoslav days as Serbo-Croat, it now known as Bosnian-Croatian-Serbian (BCS). Apart from a handful of differences in vocabulary, the only major distinction is that the Serbs use the Cyrillic alphabet.

† About 11 percent of Croatia identified as Serb.

population, from a constituent people to one of many minorities. His rhetoric played into Milošević's hands. Belgrade television had been stoking local Serb fears with reminders of what happened the last time Croatia had been officially independent. It had been a Nazi puppet state, run by the fascist Ustasha movement that committed genocide against Jews, Serbs, and Roma in Croatia and Bosnia. Memories of the death camps may have faded in Western Europe, but they were kept fresh in the Balkans by the propaganda of resurgent nationalism.

As soon as he was confident he had secured the Serb enclaves in Croatia, Milošević turned his attention to Bosnia. The techniques were the same. Proxies were armed, under the direction of Karadžić, a psychiatrist and poet from Sarajevo. In Bosnia, regular Yugoslav units simply swapped insignia and declared themselves to be the Bosnian Serb army, commanded by Mladić, a veteran JNA officer.

With Milošević's support, Karadžić and Mladić would go on to oversee the ethnic cleansing of Serb territory, the siege of Sarajevo, and ultimately the massacre of Srebrenica. The embryonic Muslim-led army organized by Izetbegović was no match for Serb forces, and in 1993 it was forced to fight on two fronts when the Bosnian Croats, egged on by Tudjman, turned on their Bosniak neighbors.

An estimated twenty thousand people died in the Croatian war. About a hundred thousand were killed in Bosnia. The much higher death toll in Bosnia reflects its greater ethnic diversity — more territory to be cleansed — and the relative defenselessness of the Bosniak population. More than 80 percent of the civilians killed were Bosniak.[7] Overall across the region, two civilians were killed for every three soldiers who died in battle. The whole conflict was characterized by random brutality. Psychopaths were made masters of the life and death of their former neighbors. Their barbarity was invariably sanctified by the nationalist leaders as self-defense against an enemy depicted in grotesque terms, as either Nazi Ustasha, wild-eyed Islamic fundamentalists, or Serb Chetnik* marauders.

The genocide of the Nazi era had set a precedent for mass killing that was never erased, only half buried under Tito's slogan "Brotherhood and Unity." Half a century later, the ghosts of Yugoslavia's past arose and nationalism once more cut like a hacksaw through the human bonds that had held diverse communities together, unleashing murder. In the name of the nation, everything would be allowed.

The Serbs were by no means alone in committing mass atrocities. Croatia was also responsible for the ethnic cleansing of Serbs from its territory, as well as Muslims from the parts of Bosnia that Croatian nationalists coveted. The Muslim-led Bosnian army carried out serious crimes, running a small but appalling prison camp just southwest of Sarajevo, for example. The Kosovo Liberation Army carried out brutal reprisals against Serb civilians. Members of all these groups were brought before the ICTY for judgment. But Serbs were responsible for most of the mass atrocities and accordingly Serb names made up the majority of The Hague's wanted list.

Faced with such an enormous moral challenge at a time of volcanic upheaval across the whole of Europe, Western leaders dithered. Neither they nor their armies were equipped doctrinally or intellectually to halt the Balkan atrocities in 1992. A newly

---

*Chetniks were Serb bands who harried the Turks during the Ottoman era and during the Second World War were revived as a royalist resistance movement that fought first against then for the Nazi-backed regimes in Zagreb and Belgrade.

united Europe failed its first great test. Its troops had rehearsed fighting as junior members of an alliance against a massed Warsaw Pact offensive on the German plains. They had not been trained to parachute into an ethnic conflict.

Meanwhile, the American military was still recovering from the trauma of Vietnam. Colin Powell, who was the chairman of the Joint Chiefs of Staff when Yugoslavia collapsed, had gone to fight in Indochina as a young officer and then spent much of his military career trying to ensure his country did not repeat the mistake. His eponymous doctrine stipulated that the United States should only go to war if it could deploy overwhelming force for clearly defined national interests with broad public support. Bosnia ticked between one and zero of those boxes.

On the campaign trail in 1992, Bill Clinton had promised to use American military might to stop the mass killing in Bosnia,[8] but once he was in office that promise was quickly forgotten. The young president, who had avoided serving in Vietnam, did not have the confidence to take on the military.

Unwilling to intervene to stop the slaughter, the UN Security Council took two initiatives to try to mitigate it. It sent in peacekeepers to safeguard deliveries of humanitarian aid, and it established the ICTY to prosecute war crimes in the hope of deterring further atrocities.

Blue-helmeted UN troops were sent into the thick of the war, but they arrived shackled with restrictive rules of engagement that allowed them to open fire only to defend themselves, not to protect the civilian victims falling like mown grass around them. By escorting aid convoys, the UN Protection Force (UNPROFOR) could stop Bosnians from starving, but not from being shot or blown apart. They became passive witnesses to genocide. At times their compliance with Serb intimidation went to the very edges of complicity.

So when the UN Security Council gathered in February 1993 to vote the Hague Tribunal into life,* the global powers already owed a huge debt to the victims of Yugoslavia, and the rhetoric of the occasion made weighty promises of what the new court would achieve.

"There is an echo in this Chamber today," declared Madeleine Albright, the American envoy to the UN and a former refugee from genocide herself. "The Nuremberg Principles have been reaffirmed . . . this will be no victors' tribunal. The only victor that will prevail in this endeavor is the truth."[9]

In reality, the court came into being as an exercise in penance and distraction, the unstable product of high ideals and low politics. For the world powers at the UN Security Council it was a gesture toward justice in lieu of military intervention. The mass atrocities would not be prevented, but they would be judged after the victims were dead. This is how the ICTY was born: as a substitute. It represented the promise of justice tomorrow in place of salvation today for the people of Yugoslavia.

Most of the nations who brought this new judicial creature into being had no expectation that it would ever function properly. It was initially so short of money it could not afford to lease a court building, and it took eighteen months to find a chief prosecutor. No one of the right caliber wanted to do the job. The judges found themselves presiding over an empty theater of justice, without prosecutors or anyone to prosecute. Antonio Cassese, an Italian professor of international law appointed as

---

* Resolution 808 called for a tribunal in general. Resolution 827 of May 25, 1993, set out the specific framework for the ICTY.

the tribunal's first president, complained: "The Security Council thought we would never become operational. We had no budget. We had nothing. Zero."[10]

Cassese's judges were paid on an ad hoc basis. The UN granted them just enough money for a handful of computers and two weeks' rent on a suite of offices in The Hague's Peace Palace. Looking for more space, Cassese heard that the insurance company Aegon was only using part of its faded Art Deco building on Churchillplein. He decided to rent it, but squeezing money out of the UN was so hard that the tribunal was unable to put down a deposit on a long-term lease before the summer of 1994. Prosecutors and investigators shared a cafeteria with Aegon's actuaries and account managers, which meant they could never discuss cases at lunch, for security reasons. And they only had enough room for a single court, a converted conference room. But what good was a court anyway, without defendants?

Just at the point when the judges were considering mutiny or resignation, Nelson Mandela kept the tribunal alive by helping to persuade Richard Goldstone, a South African lawyer and veteran anti-apartheid campaigner, to take the chief prosecutor's job in July 1994.[11] In the eighteen months it had taken to find someone suitable, thousands of people had died in Bosnia and Herzegovina. And the tribunal was still far from functional. There was no one willing to carry out arrests. Goldstone's staff scrambled to piece together a string of indictments wherever there was evidence to do so, but the overwhelming majority of the seventy-four indictments issued in the Goldstone era concerned small fry—camp guards who had tortured their former neighbors and who could be readily identified by survivors. The urgency to demonstrate the tribunal was operational left no time to build more sophisticated cases against the master butchers.

The court's first defendant was a perfect example of this "low-hanging fruit" syndrome. Duško Tadić had been a particularly sadistic guard at two notorious Bosnian Serb prison camps, Omarska and Keraterm. He fled to Germany after the war but was spotted in a benefits office in Munich by camp survivors, who called the local police. In November 1994, Tadić arrived in The Hague to become the world's first war crimes defendant for two generations. Yet for all the tribunal's attempts to play up the echoes of Nuremberg, it was clear this brutal turnkey was no Hermann Göring or Joseph Goebbels. Most of the other names on Goldstone's indictment list were similarly inconsequential. Their pictures were printed on posters distributed among UNPROFOR battalions, who tacked them up on their barracks notice boards and ignored them.

The international community was finally shocked out of its indecision and half measures by the worst single massacre of the Bosnian war, the murder of more than eight thousand men and boys by Serb forces after the fall of the Muslim enclave at Srebrenica in July 1995. A handful survived the mass executions, acting dead and climbing out of mass graves over the bodies of their friends and relatives. It was impossible for the world to ignore their testimony, but the most chilling account of all was to come from one of the killers.

Dražen Erdemović was a Bosnian Croat locksmith married to a Serb. In a country that was falling apart, with its people forced to choose sides according to ethnicity, Erdemović belonged nowhere. At different points in the swirling conflict he had served in the Croat, Bosnian, and Serb armies, trying to survive in noncombat jobs. But in July 1995, when he was twenty-three, he was dragooned into a Serb execution squad at Srebrenica, where he witnessed things he would never be able to forget. The awful scenes were lodged deep in his brain.

Eight months later, Erdemović started looking for someone to confess to. He called the US embassy in Belgrade but was turned away, so he went to the press.[12] The police, who tapped journalists' phones as a matter of course, picked him up but it was too late. His story was all over the world, and the Milošević regime had little choice but to hand him over to The Hague.[13]

Erdemović became the first person since Nuremberg to be sentenced by an international tribunal for crimes against humanity. But he will be remembered mostly for the excruciating testimony he gave on the events of July 16, 1995, when 1,200 men and boys were killed at a single site.

> *They would bring out groups of ten people out of the bus and, of course, they were looking into the ground. Their heads were bent downwards and their hands were tied and they were blindfolded... They took them to the meadow. So we started shooting at those people. I do not know exactly. To be honest, ... I simply felt sick.*[14]

NATO intervention and a Croatian ground offensive forced a peace treaty, signed in November 1995 by Milošević, Tudjman, and Izetbegović at an air force base in Dayton, Ohio. But Milošević was not quite done with war. In a brutish epilogue to his decade of misrule, he sent troops into Kosovo in 1998 to crush a fledgling insurgency by the province's Albanians. Like his earlier adventures, it left a mountain of corpses — more than ten thousand dead — and backfired totally. NATO intervened again in March 1999 with a bombing campaign that forced Milošević to withdraw his troops three months later. Kosovo declared independence in 2008.

Once more, Western intervention only came after the dead were already in their graves.[15] Justice arrived even later. The Dayton Accords did indeed stop the killing in Bosnia, but the divisions created by ethnic cleansing were frozen in place. The persistent influence of Karadžić, Mladić, and Milošević meanwhile threatened to render Dayton meaningless and make the Hague Tribunal a colossal farce.

Yet by 2011, the ICTY manhunters had crossed off all the names on their indicted list. As this book goes to press, the last trials are under way. Karadžić and Mladić are in the dock facing the very people they tried to obliterate. Witness testimony is streamed live online. Millions of documents have been analyzed and saved. Transcripts are posted online. The buried crimes of the past are dug up and laid in the open for all those who can bring themselves to look.

It was a more substantial endeavor than the hunt for Nazis after World War II. The US-led investigators at Nuremberg had the advantage that most of their suspects had already been captured or had surrendered. The prosecutors mostly chose defendants according to the prisoners of war they already had in their cells, rather than according to the scale of their crimes. Only one prominent Nazi was tried in absentia because he could not be found—Hitler's private secretary, Martin Bormann, whose remains were identified in 1998.[16] The real precursor to the ICTY manhunt was the US Department of Justice's Office of Special Investigations, established in 1979. Over the next quarter century, OSI "Nazi hunters" tracked down and prosecuted more than a hundred war criminals who had tried to hide in the United States.[17]

Whereas the Nuremberg and Tokyo tribunals never escaped the taint of "victors' justice," the ICTY represented the first genuine attempt at an international reckoning for war crimes on all sides in a conflict. The judges and prosecutors were drawn from around the world, and the defendants came from four fledgling nations — Serbia, Croatia, Bosnia, and Kosovo.[18] The effort to bring them to justice was long, uneven, and mired with mistakes, but it ultimately emerged as the most successful manhunt in history and an extraordinary testament to the tenacity of a remarkably small group of people. This book tells their story.

# THE BUTCHER'S TRAIL

# 1.

# OPERATION AMBER STAR

The unbearable timidity of the United States and its European
allies to rapidly strategize and then implement an effective means
of apprehending indicted fugitives from justice in the former
Yugoslavia constituted an abdication of responsibility that will haunt
the legacies of these governments and those who led them.
—*David Scheffer, former US war crimes envoy*[1]

**ON MAY 27, 1997,** the leaders of the NATO alliance and Russia
gathered at the Élysée Palace in Paris to bury the Cold War amid
the fin de siècle splendor of a hundred crystal chandeliers and a
thousand bottles of vintage champagne.

In retrospect, the signing ceremony for the Founding Act on
Mutual Relations, Cooperation and Security marked a brief flowering of amity and goodwill before a return to the dangerous
mutual contempt of the Vladimir Putin era.

That Parisian spring, however, everything seemed possible.
Boris Yeltsin was still Russia's president and at his gregarious
best. High on geopolitics and fine wine, he bestowed heartfelt
kisses on the cheeks of Western leaders.

"You have good eyes, a bright mind, the right age, good experience. So I believe Great Britain is in good hands," Yeltsin told a

blushing Tony Blair, the United Kingdom's freshly elected forty-four-year-old prime minister.[2]

Bill Clinton was hobbling around with a cane after a knee operation and facing a sexual harassment suit back home,[3] but even he seemed revived and animated by the general spirit of euphoria, saying that "the veil of hostility between East and West has lifted."[4]

The French president Jacques Chirac, who was hosting the event, aimed even higher. "The Paris accord does not shift the divisions created in Yalta. It does away with them once and for all," he promised.[5]

As a prediction, it has not stood the test of time, but it was not true even then. As Chirac spoke that evening in Paris, the foundations of a new east-west divide were being dug. When the leaders gathered for a banquet, Clinton, Blair, and Chirac formed a brief huddle to discuss a pressing concern, imminent joint military action to arrest war criminals in Bosnia and Herzegovina, starting with Radovan Karadžić, the Bosnian Serbs' wartime leader, who had presided over the wholesale ethnic cleansing of his territory.

This was something that could not be shared with Moscow, the Serbs' longstanding and most powerful ally. So when Yeltsin found the group and asked his new friends what they were talking about, they swiftly dropped the subject.

"Nothing, Boris. Come and join us," Clinton beckoned, beaming.[6]

The secret the Western leaders were guarding was new and fragile. They had only recently agreed to pursue war crimes suspects, after furious debates within their governments which had pitted civilians against soldiers. In the eyes of the generals, chasing criminals was a job for the police.

After all the blood spilled in Afghanistan and Iraq, it is striking to look back on the extreme caution of the US military and its NATO allies about deployment to Bosnia in December 1995. They had delayed intervening in the Balkan slaughter for years but once a peace had been signed, the world's most powerful alliance arrived in force. More than sixty thousand soldiers were garrisoned in a country smaller than West Virginia with a population of less than four million. The NATO-led Implementation Force (IFOR) — rechristened the Stabilization Force (SFOR) after its first year[7] — was one of the most intensive peacekeeping missions in history. You could not drive more than a few miles along the country's rutted, potholed roads without encountering a NATO patrol or checkpoint. And this mighty armed presence faced no real military opposition. The paramilitary bands who had been so effective at killing civilians and intimidating the UN's blue helmets during the Bosnian war had withdrawn to the shadows with scarcely a shot fired in defiance.

Even in this relatively unchallenging environment, the force's American commanders were reluctant to confront the war crimes suspects roaming openly in their new domain. More than seventy of these suspects had been identified by the Hague Tribunal, and the NATO peacekeepers were provided with their names and pictures. But they were not a priority. Far from it. The soldiers were under orders that the fugitives should be arrested only if they were encountered in the normal conduct of NATO duties. In practice, that meant never.

This timidity was shaped by history. Three years earlier, during a humanitarian relief mission in Somalia, the US military launched an operation to arrest local militia leaders who were hampering the delivery of food supplies. On October 3, 1993, a force of US Rangers, Delta Force soldiers, and Navy SEALs were sent into Mogadishu to seize two lieutenants of the Somali warlord Mohamed Farrah Aidid. The outcome was a disaster. Two Black Hawk helicopters were shot down by militiamen, eighteen US servicemen were killed, and seventy-three were wounded. It was the bloodiest battle America had fought since Vietnam.

The experience was seared into the collective memory of the US officer corps. The operation had been approved by the chairman of the Joint Chiefs of Staff, Colin Powell, as one of his last acts in office. He left the job three days before the Mogadishu raid was launched, and his successor, General John Shalikashvili, had to clear up the mess. The video footage of the corpse of an American soldier being dragged through the streets was being shown on television when Shalikashvili was sworn in. The general never tired of reminding civilians of that when they came to the Pentagon trying to persuade him to send American troops on the hunt for war crimes suspects in Bosnia. It was not an experience he was in a hurry to repeat. He was the living embodiment of the "Mogadishu syndrome," the intense risk aversion that dominated American military thinking throughout the Balkan episode and which lasted until September 11, 2001.

It was not just a psychological hangover. The US generals deployed in Bosnia firmly believed that their chance of winning an extra star depended heavily on their ability to achieve zero casualties on their watch. The overwhelming priority was force protection. American troops were under orders to don full body armor when they left their bases, and whenever possible to stay in their vehicles.

American self-defense measures may have been the most pronounced, but none of the NATO contingents in IFOR (and later SFOR) were keen on chasing war criminals. In Prijedor, an epicenter of mass killing during the war, the British garrison bought takeout pizzas from a restaurant run by one of the suspects. The guidelines coming down the chain of command were clear: there would be no "mission creep," and no arrests.

As Charles Crawford, the British ambassador in Sarajevo at the time, recalls: "The rules of engagement said in effect: 'Don't pick him up, unless you actually trip over him.' Anything that involved going off the road even ten yards was regarded as 'not being in the course of your normal duties.' "[8]

It was not a sustainable policy either for Bosnia or for NATO. Once the fugitives became convinced of their impunity, they went about making the country unmanageable. Meanwhile NATO's credibility was corroding daily under the caustic derision of the world press, which delighted in portraying the grand alliance as hapless and cowardly.

The first impetus toward a change in policy came in the spring of 1996 from the Dutch. The Netherlands was haunted by the failure of its army to protect the people of Srebrenica from slaughter the previous summer. The small Dutch UN garrison in the Muslim enclave had been overwhelmed by the Serb attack and had been provided only token and belated air support from UN headquarters. The garrison capitulated and handed over Muslim civilians who had taken refuge in the Dutch compound under the UN flag. In so doing, they sent thousands of men and boys to their death. Nearly a year later, the Dutch were keenly aware that no one had been held accountable. The ICTY had been established in their capital, The Hague, but it had hardly any defendants in its cells. They were as empty as the international community's promises of justice.

The Dutch government set about lobbying Washington for a change in NATO's approach, and the Clinton White House agreed to review the matter. But in reality the administration had no interest in doing anything practical, at least not until after the presidential elections in November of that year. Clinton's pollster, Dick Morris, had surveyed voters when American soldiers were first deployed to Bosnia and found that, of all the challenges facing the military, the "arrest of war criminals was the one Americans opposed most."[9] And Karadžić only had 20 percent name recognition. Most Americans had no idea who these people were. Politically, there were far more reasons to do nothing than to act.

The White House nonetheless commissioned a study. Robert Gelbard, the assistant secretary of state for International Narcotics and Law Enforcement, was told to put together an assessment of whether a manhunt in Bosnia was militarily and politically feasible. Gelbard was as qualified as anyone in Foggy Bottom to venture an opinion. He had firsthand experience of a manhunt operation in Latin America. In 1989, during his stint as the ambassador to Bolivia, he had masterminded the capture of one of the country's most feared figures, Colonel Luis Arce Gómez.

As the interior minister in a military junta in the early eighties, Arce Gómez ran death squads that abducted and executed dissidents. He hired a fugitive Nazi war criminal, Klaus Barbie, as an adviser and staged an armed takeover of the narcotics trade. He was unofficially known as "the minister for cocaine." When the junta fell and was replaced by a democratically elected government in La Paz, Arce Gómez went on the run to avoid narco-trafficking charges in Bolivia and the United States. He remained at large for six years.

In early December 1989, US intelligence was told that the fugitive would be visiting his family ranch near Santa Cruz for a party, so Ambassador Gelbard made an approach to the Bolivian government and offered three options: "We do nothing, you get him, or we get him together." The government chose the third, and on December 11 a joint team of three dozen Navy SEALs and Bolivian special police raided the Santa Cruz ranch and seized Arce Gómez. The next day he was on a plane to Florida to stand trial, where he was sentenced to spend almost twenty years in jail.

With that experience behind him, Gelbard's instinct was that it was eminently feasible for America to track down war criminals in Bosnia. It was just a question of political will. He set about writing a proposal with the help of Andrew Bair, a young American diplomat Gelbard had recruited from the UN ranks in Sarajevo. They circulated their feasibility study on detention operations in the ex-Yugoslavia in the fall of 1996, arguing that the effort would have to include the British, Dutch, and French as well as the Germans, because operations would probably have to be run out of US bases in Germany. As for which agency should take the lead, Gelbard and Bair laid out a range of options, including US Army Special Forces, Navy SEALs, the CIA, the FBI, and the Drug Enforcement Administration.

"There was clear high-level interest at the State Department, and from Madeleine Albright [the ambassador to the UN] but strong opposition from any entity that would have to be asked to actually do it," Gelbard recalled.[10]

Louis Freeh, the FBI director, was furious the bureau had even been included as a candidate for what he viewed as a wild-goose chase in a far-off country. Gelbard and Bair faced even stiffer resistance from the Pentagon. To Secretary of Defense William Cohen, and to Shalikashvili, the whole manhunt idea smelled of mission creep. They argued strenuously that their soldiers had been sent to Bosnia with a single task, to keep the peace, and manhunting was not part of that mandate. It would bog down their forces in a sideshow that was not essential to American national security and could easily cause casualties.

On the other side of the argument stood the determined figure of Albright, who was weeks away from becoming secretary of state. She maintained that Bosnia would be ungovernable as long as the top war criminals continued to enjoy impunity. The policy battle was fought all the way to the White House, and the breakthrough came only after Clinton won reelection in November 1996. The victory released him from the fear that American casualties in Bosnia might derail his ambition to be a two-term president.

At a White House principals meeting a few days after the election, Clinton listened to objections from Secretary Cohen, General Shalikashvili, and the director of Central Intelligence, John Deutch, before overruling all of them. He declared the United States was duty-bound to pursue the arrests. Vice President Al Gore backed him enthusiastically. It was the moral course of action, Gore said.

Once his commander in chief had spoken, Shalikashvili had little choice. Since a decision had been made, the general said, the country should use the best tool for the job — US Army Special Forces. Cohen looked dismayed. Albright turned around in her seat and shook Gelbard's hand. It was a victory in principle, but there were still months of bureaucratic wrangling ahead before the first arrest would be made.

Early in 1997, however, the wheels began to turn. David Scheffer, the State Department's first ambassador at large for war crimes, went to Europe in the first week of February to sell the idea to the allies, with mixed results. The British, Dutch, and Germans were more open to the idea than the French. The Americans stressed to their counterparts in Paris that they would not be making a commitment in blood. They were simply being invited inside the planning loop with no obligation to contribute troops to any operation. According to Scheffer, that did not seem to make the idea any easier to digest: "The French looked as if they were experiencing collective constipation. They were pained with our legal explanations and had difficulty with their own domestic legal authorities. For them, the risks included failure, the taking of hostages, the consequences for the peace process, the lack of secrecy, and the fear that French soldiers would be the first victims of any Serb retaliation."[11]

The French officials delayed a decision until Albright made her first trip to Paris as secretary of state at the end of February. Another few weeks were lost, but ultimately Paris agreed at least to talk about the initiative.

From the end of February, a committee began to convene regularly in The Hague, chaired by the Dutch and bringing together representatives of five nations: the United States, the United Kingdom, the Netherlands, France, and Germany. It convened in total secrecy. Gelbard and Bair did not go through the arrivals lounge when they flew in for meetings but were picked up by a black limo on the tarmac at Schiphol Airport in Amsterdam and driven straight to The Hague.

In Dutch government offices, the five countries wrestled over the law and terminology that would underpin the manhunt. No one liked the term "rendition," and all the defense officials in the room were nervous about their soldiers carrying out civilian arrests, which was normally the constitutional role of the police. It did not help that the 1995 Dayton Accords provided no direct mandate for such operations, despite the effort of the State Department to get the language written into the text. The American diplomats at the talks barely managed to fend off Serb demands for a war crimes amnesty to be included in the final treaty.[12] That would have rendered the Hague Tribunal pointless at a stroke.

In the absence of clear wording in the treaty, the State Department and its allies in European foreign ministries pieced together a legal case for NATO arrests from a combination of documents. They argued the Dayton Accords and three UN Security Council Resolutions — establishing the ICTY in 1993, implementing the Dayton Accords in 1995, and then establishing SFOR at the end of 1996[13] — together created a legal framework that empowered the military to use all necessary means to uphold the peace and enforce the will of the tribunal.

A formula was developed to get around legal qualms, involving a complex minuet of interlocking moves. When an arrest plan was ready, SFOR would request assistance from NATO member states to ensure fulfillment of its mission. At the same time, the ICTY prosecutor would request assistance in making arrests. The NATO secretary-general would order SFOR troops to cooperate with the prosecutor. Special forces would be dispatched from their home country with the mandate to act on SFOR's request to assist in the performance of the mission, which would include detention of indicted fugitives "if the circumstances and tactical situation permitted." The special forces would then find and detain the suspect, delivering him within hours to tribunal lawyers whose job it was to perform the actual arrest.[14] It was an elaborate and somewhat fragile legal contraption that, to the relief of the lawyers who put it together, was never comprehensively challenged at the tribunal.

The military preparations were straightforward by comparison. A secret joint planning operation was established at the European headquarters of US Special Operations Command at

# POST-DAYTON BOSNIA

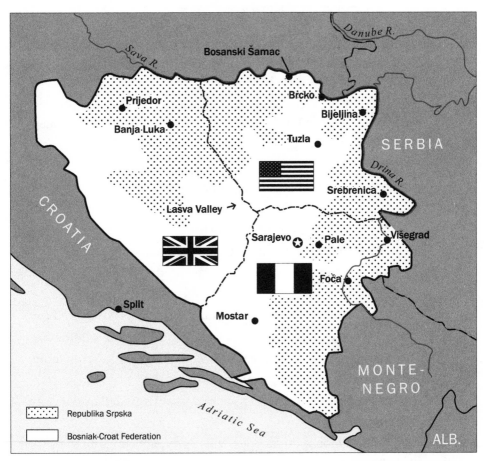

Bosnia in the aftermath of war, split by the Dayton Accords into two halves, the Republika Srpska and a Bosniak-Croat Federation, and then divided by NATO into three military zones, run by the British, Americans, and French.

Patch Barracks near Stuttgart, which had been a German Panzer base during the Second World War. The operation was code-named Amber Star and included special forces, intelligence agencies, and police officials from the five countries involved.[15]

**THE FIRST HURDLE** for Amber Star was to write up a feasibility study, laying out various tactical options and rating the risk involved in each.[16] But from the very beginning there were deep differences of opinion on how to go about the task. Three basic variants were on offer: Amber Star could start by pursuing the top targets; it could begin with more junior war crimes suspects who had less protection, the low-hanging fruit, and work its way up; or it could try to do both, going for a single sweep that caught as many indictees as possible at the same time.

In general, the bigger the prize the harder the pursuit. Ratko Mladić, the Bosnian Serb commander who orchestrated the siege of Sarajevo and the capture of Srebrenica, was wanted for genocide and crimes against humanity. Catching him would have been a coup, but he had withdrawn to a mountain stronghold befitting a Bond villain, a nuclear bunker Tito had built at Han Pijesak, in eastern Bosnia. There he was surrounded by concentric rings of bodyguards.

Mladić's mountain hideout, Villa Javor, appeared on the surface to be a modest hunting lodge, but a heavy metal door inside its garage hid a shaft that led deep into the rock.[17] The bunker was equipped with fresh water supplies, air filtration systems, and a command center. The quarters were spartan but there was a double bed for the general and a cot outside the door for his most trusted guard, his last line of defense. Risk-averse and highly disciplined, Mladić hunkered down at Han Pijesak until the summer of 1997, when he decided that even Tito's nuclear shelter was not secure enough and slipped across the Drina River into Serbia.

There, Mladić could rely for protection on the man who did more than any other to unleash war in Yugoslavia, Slobodan Milošević. In 1997, Milošević had yet to be indicted, in part because Western capitals still viewed him as the guarantor of the Dayton peace deal and consequently withheld intelligence from the ICTY that would have incriminated him directly. He was only charged in May 1999, after he had started his fourth war, in Kosovo. He became the first sitting head of state to be indicted by an international tribunal.

In the spring of 1997, Milošević's Croatian counterpart, President Franjo Tudjman, was also under investigation for his role in the ethnic cleansing of Muslims in central Bosnia and the murder of Serb civilians in the wake of a major offensive across the Croatian Krajina in the summer of 1995. But Tudjman died in December 1999 while those investigations were still under way.

At the time Amber Star was launched, Karadžić was the only feasible target among Yugoslavia's wartime leaders. Only he was under indictment and potentially within reach. Although he had been forced by Washington to step down from his formal party and government functions in 1996, he continued to wield influence behind the scenes and traveled around Bosnia with impunity. There was no mistaking his gray pompadour hairstyle, his large retinue of bodyguards, and his distinctive Audi A8. But no one sought to challenge him, let alone arrest him.

Outside Sarajevo, a detachment of Italy's famous Garibaldi Bersaglieri Brigade, with their magnificent cockades of black wood-grouse feathers in their helmets, manned a critical junction near the Bosnian Serb wartime capital in Pale. When Karadžić's motorcade approached the crossing, the plumed soldiers would turn their backs to the road and face Sarajevo, choosing not to encounter the wanted man in the "normal course" of their duties.

Yet despite an outward show of nonchalance, Karadžić was deeply anxious about his future and even more frightened than NATO of the Serb gunmen assigned to protect him. Some of them worked for Milošević's security apparatus, and Milošević had no wish to see his former protégé testify before the tribunal. William Stuebner, a former US soldier and diplomat recruited as a special adviser to the Hague Tribunal, was struck by Karadžić's air of vulnerability in the spring of 1996, when he visited his office at the Famos car-parts factory in Pale: "He was nervous. He had bitten his nails. Every time a helicopter went over he went to the window. He said, 'If they come for me, there will be blood on carpet.' I said, 'I know these people. It will be your blood.' We talked for two hours. He was very interested in turning himself in. It was the first time I realized just how very scared he was of his own guards. He knew Milošević had people around him ready to kill him."[18]

Stuebner tried to persuade Karadžić to hand himself in, telling him The Hague would offer an opportunity to present his case on the world stage. Karadžić appeared to be convinced, asking his Cambridge-educated aide, Jovan Zametica, to make the arrangements. "He said Jovan will be the intermediary. He would have been lifted by helicopter, and would have gone to a US aircraft carrier to make a broadcast saying how he was going to defend the honor of the Serbs...Radovan's dream was going to The Hague with smart lawyers and winning, becoming a national hero and eclipsing Milošević."[19]

Had the plan succeeded, a twelve-year multimillion-dollar manhunt would have been averted. But at the eleventh hour,

Karadžić balked, most likely out of fear of assassination. Then as the months went by after NATO's arrival, with no sign that the alliance had any interest in making arrests, he started to think that he might not only survive if he stayed put; he might even have a political future.

In February 1997, Karadžić staged a comeback tour intended to demonstrate he was still a force to be reckoned with. Pointedly, he went to Banja Luka, the biggest town in the west of the Republika Srpska (the Serb-run half of Bosnia) and the political base of his former deputy and chief rival, Biljana Plavšić, a biology professor who believed in the genetic superiority of the Serbs. She was an enthusiast for ethnic cleansing and would be indicted by the Hague Tribunal for genocide three years later. But in 1997 the West backed Plavšić as a lesser evil than Karadžić. She had agreed to allow Bosniaks and Croats to return to their villages in the Republika Srpska, while Karadžić's activists sought to sabotage any such resettlement effort.

On the stump, Karadžić publicly derided the Hague Tribunal as "ridiculous." Less than a year earlier he had been fretting over whether to turn himself in. Now he dismissed the very notion as absurd. "It is not a court or a tribunal," he said. "It is a form of lynching for the whole nation."[20]

Simply by showing up in Banja Luka, Karadžić was directly challenging Western efforts to reshape Bosnia, while underlining the impotence of both the ICTY and NATO. To cross the Republika Srpska from Pale, his motorcade had breezed past SFOR troops, including an American patrol.

"His Audi A8 and escort went straight past a US Humvee column," General Montgomery "Monty" Meigs, the US commander at the time, recalled with regret. "The chairman of the Joint Chiefs of Staff just didn't want to get involved. Mission creep is a legitimate concern, but we missed an opportunity to break up the old leadership structure."[21]

Ultimately, Karadžić's brazen defiance helped swing support in Western capitals behind an arrest strategy in 1997. The Amber Star talks in The Hague and Stuttgart eventually led to a provisional agreement to pursue him and thirty-five more-junior suspects of all ethnicities. The lesser targets would be divided among the various NATO contingents according to which zones they lived in. The exception would be the capture of Karadžić. That great endeavor would be shared, in a flagship joint operation that would show the alliance at its best.[22] At least, that was the plan.

The Karadžić snatch operation was to rely more on brute force than guile, much to the anxiety of the British who worried that the Americans would ask them to demonstrate their commitment to Amber Star by taking part in a mission they had no hand in planning. Officials from the Foreign and Commonwealth Office (FCO) nervously reported back to London from the Amber Star talks:

> On military channels, we understand that it is a large scale conventional military operation to surround Pale and fight their way into the point at which Karadžić is presumed to be hiding. This is not the way UK forces would approach the problem…[The Americans] may ask for UK participation in a "Sarajevo cell"…to pursue planning on Karadžić. The Defence Secretary is likely to take a cautious line until we have more answers on the nature of any operation.[23]

Kim Darroch, the head of the FCO's Eastern Adriatic Department at the time,[24] warned in June 1997 that there was "a strong

chance" that the Americans and French would ask British soldiers to participate in the Karadžić assault.

> *This would present us with a difficult choice. There are*
> *obvious political and bilateral arguments for a positive*
> *response. But there would also be good reasons for caution.*
> *An operation against Karadžić, however carefully planned,*
> *will be highly hazardous...The question is hypothetical*
> *for the moment. No proposition has been put to us. Were such*
> *an approach made, military factors would need to weigh*
> *heavily in any response. Political factors cannot sensibly be*
> *viewed in isolation.*[25]

The British had their own plans to consider. For several
weeks they had been preparing a separate operation in their sector in western Bosnia. It involved simultaneously detaining three
provincial Bosnian Serb officials — the former mayor, police
chief, and hospital director — who had run the notorious concentration camps around the town of Prijedor.* The Hague had
delivered sealed indictments against the "Prijedor Three," and
the British military command could not wait to be rid of them.
They ran much of the organized crime in the zone, while using
intimidation and terror tactics to prevent the return of Muslim
refugees.

However, the Prijedor operation had to be put on hold until
Washington and the Stuttgart cell could make a decision about
Karadžić and the other Amber Star targets. In a memo on June 17,
Darroch noted: "If they decide to put Karadžić on hold for the
moment — and depending on how quickly they wish to mount a

---

* See chapter 3.

wider operation against lesser indictees—they may be happy for the UK to go ahead separately with an operation on the Prijedor Three. They have asked for two weeks grace to consider the Prijedor issue."[26]

However, time was slipping away. The British military had wanted to carry out the Prijedor operation by the end of June, nervous that operational secrecy would be blown if they waited too long. Yet the Amber Star committee was talking about six more weeks for "tactical planning, training and rehearsal, subject to political agreement from the capitals of the countries involved."[27]

All that preparatory work and committee discussion would last well into September 1997, which is when municipal elections were supposed to take place across Bosnia. Organizing the vote was a priority for the international community, and substantial resources were being provided in the hope that the poll would diminish the nationalist parties and reshape the political landscape.

A controversial military operation just before the election could entrench Serb national resentment and work in favor of Karadžić's hardline Serb Democratic Party (Srpska Demokratska Stranka, or SDS). That meant that if there was to be a grand Amber Star operation it would most likely have to be put off until October or later.

In the event, it never happened at all. The idea of large-scale joint arrest operations by the five allied armies, sweeping up Karadžić and nearly three dozen other suspects, was a hugely ambitious scheme, but it was brought crashing down by a single twenty-eight-year-old French officer, Hervé Gourmelon. The Gourmelon affair, as it came to be known, would not only eclipse Amber Star but also sour Franco-American military cooperation in Bosnia for years to come.

GOURMELON, a French army major stationed in Sarajevo since 1995, was instructed by his French superiors in SFOR to liaise with the Bosnian Serb leadership. Short, blond, and charming, Gourmelon did not seem to be subject to normal military rules. He lived in an apartment in town rather than in the French barracks. He was a highly cultured aesthete who seemed to have hours to spare for drinking coffee and discussing literature and fine art. He was a fervent admirer of the British romantic painter J. M. W. Turner, and he usually had a small drawing pad and pencils in his pocket to knock off quick sketches in idle moments.

Gourmelon would beguile the Bosnian women working at SFOR headquarters, bringing them pastries and showing them pictures of an idyllic life back in the French countryside, complete with a blond wife and three blond children, an old manor house with extensive grounds, and a collection of vintage cars.

His rank was an infantry *chef de bataillon*, equivalent to commandant or major, but he seemed more like a French James Bond, a cultured spy. It was never clear which intelligence agency, if any, he worked for. When things turned sour, French intelligence, both military and civilian, disowned him. But for a regular infantry major, he was given some surprisingly sensitive jobs. As one of the very few French officers who had been in Sarajevo during the war for the UN and then stayed on under NATO, Gourmelon was better connected in Pale than anyone else in SFOR. He had talked his way into Karadžić's confidence, meeting with the separatist leader at least once a month. He sent reports of these encounters with the man he code-named Teddy all the way up the French chain of command to the director of military intelligence, Lieutenant General Bruno Elie.

The CIA was suspicious of Gourmelon's striking success and his apparently cozy relationship with the Bosnian Serb hierarchy. The Sarajevo station put the urbane Frenchman under surveillance and came to the conclusion the flow of intelligence was mostly going the wrong way. Gourmelon appeared to be giving away more valuable information than he was receiving. Every time an SFOR security sweep through Pale was planned, the French major would drive up the road from Sarajevo in his Volkswagen Golf to visit Serb officials on the other side of the front lines. After rummaging through Gourmelon's apartment and searching his car, the CIA believed it had proof that he had been leaking classified cables.

The evidence was sent to Langley and quickly landed on the desk of General Wesley Clark, the commander of US forces and NATO in Europe, at his headquarters in Mons, Belgium. Clark immediately took the documents to his French counterparts. "You have a spy in your midst!" he yelled at them.

The French reaction could best be described as a shrug. Gourmelon was called back to Paris for interviews, some of which US intelligence officers were allowed to observe. The French argument to the Americans was that it was Gourmelon's job to win Karadžić's confidence even if he perhaps used "questionable" tactics on occasion. And to demonstrate Paris's faith in its man, he was sent back to Sarajevo in the fall of 1997 to take up his previous duties.

The CIA was furious but finally comprehended what had been going on under its nose in Sarajevo. Gourmelon was not a rogue or a traitor. He had simply been carrying out the French version of force protection. Rather than sending out lots of heavily armed soldiers on every fact-finding or liaison mission, Gourmelon simply let the Serb leadership know what SFOR was doing and where its patrols were going. The idea was no one would be taken by surprise and there would be no chance of a spontaneous shootout. Forty-five French soldiers had been killed over the course of the war, more than any other UN contingent, and Paris did not want to lose any more lives in a "misunderstanding" with Karadžić's bodyguards.

There was little Washington could do about the French policy, but the CIA was ultimately able to get rid of Gourmelon. In December 1997, a Bosnian teenage girl appeared at the central Sarajevo police station claiming she had been assaulted and named her attacker as Hervé Gourmelon. Soon afterward the CIA station chief received a copy of the girl's testimony from a police contact along with some vivid pictures of her injuries, including a bite mark on her thigh. He showed them to his French counterpart, and within hours Gourmelon was on a plane out of the country, so fast in fact his clothes and personal possessions were left behind in his apartment and had to be sent on later by his colleagues. French officials told journalists asking for an explanation of the sudden disappearance of a popular figure that there had been a "murky sex scandal." [28]

Female colleagues at SFOR described Gourmelon as sometimes impatient and emotional, but insisted his attitude toward women, though flirtatious, was always courteous and respectful. He could have had a hidden dark side, or he could have been set up by either Bosnian or US intelligence services, both of whom had been irritated to see him return to Sarajevo. He was certainly never prosecuted for the alleged assault. Whatever the truth, the French military was not about to get itself mired in a scandal that would inevitably become public.*

---

*I was not able to track Gourmelon down. He does not have a listed address or phone number, and former military colleagues said they thought he did not want to be found.

Officially at least, the top brass stuck by their man. Gour-melon was never subjected to disciplinary action and was eventually promoted to lieutenant colonel.[29] Franco-American cooperation in Bosnia, on the other hand, never recovered. The joint plan to grab Karadžić went no further than the drawing board in Stuttgart. The French kept liaison officers at Patch Barracks who continued to attend Amber Star meetings, but intelligence sharing and joint planning with the Americans was dead from that moment on. British diplomats reported that while France "has favoured continuing efforts against lesser indictees in their sector," General Clark was "apparently determined to concentrate on Karadžić only."[30]

But on both fronts, the FCO report noted, there had been "little progress towards workable plans." From the point of view of Scheffer, the whole episode provided American officialdom a pretext to dodge involvement in the manhunt: "Unfortunately the [Gourmelon] affair scared off the Pentagon from coordinating any Karadžić operations for a long time thereafter and gave the cynics within the Washington bureaucracy plenty of reasons to back away from arrest strategies."[31]

The United States had its own Karadžić-hunting operation, code-named Green Light, but it existed largely as a tasking order for the CIA and DIA (Defense Intelligence Agency) to keep an eye out for the fugitive. They failed to track him down, and the military was clearly unprepared to commit large resources to the operation, especially while relations with the French in Bosnia were so dysfunctional.

By late May 1998, Scheffer described the arrest strategy as "dead in the water...The British remained supportive, but the French appeared to have shut down, no doubt still chastened by the [Gourmelon] affair. There was no real operation against

Karadžić or Mladić...Karadžić might have been located within days if a full-court press were applied to the challenge."

Secretary of Defense Cohen remained adamantly opposed to the whole project and continued to insist until his last days in office that detentions were not in the SFOR mandate. He and the generals played a waiting game until even Albright seemed to lose her stamina.

Scheffer, the most persistent advocate for the pursuit of the war criminals, was told in November 1999 that Albright no longer wanted him involved in the Karadžić pursuit. He would henceforward be excluded from all meetings on the subject.[32] He never learned if he was squeezed out because of pressure from the Pentagon, the intelligence agencies, or the French. His determination to go after Karadžić had made him plenty of enemies.

For all the champagne-fueled triumphalism in Paris in May 1997, Operation Amber Star was rendered virtually meaningless before it could get off the ground, hobbled by the Gourmelon affair, Franco-American distrust, and the ingrained resistance of the Western military establishments. British officials noted as early as 1997 that the focus for planning was shifting away from Stuttgart. It was gravitating instead toward General Clark's NATO headquarters in Mons. Decisions were also devolving to individual capitals.

Each of the five nations involved in Amber Star ultimately took action to arrest second-tier war crimes suspects in their zones, and the Stuttgart meetings were used for "deconfliction," ensuring national special forces units did not pursue the same quarry at the same time and stumble into a shootout with one another. It was a banal end for such an ambitious and expensive undertaking.

The initiative that finally broke the paralysis surrounding war crimes arrests was everything Amber Star was not: cheap, improvised, and unexpected. As would happen again and again in the course of the Balkan manhunt, a small operation by a few determined individuals succeeded where the grandiose plans of military juggernauts failed.

# 2.
# OPERATION LITTLE FLOWER

You don't send a Ferrari to import coal.

—*Jacek, a Polish special forces officer*

**IN LATE 1995,** Jacques Paul Klein, a political adviser to the US military command in Europe, received a call out of the blue from a senior official at the State Department, with a somewhat unusual question: "Are you still some kind of general?"

Klein was a career diplomat but he had been seconded to the Pentagon in the 1980s and stayed in the Air Force Reserve, rising to the rank of major general with a Distinguished Service Medal and a Bronze Star. So the short answer to the question was: Yes. Once a general always a general. He could be called back to service at any time.

This was all the State Department needed to hear. It happened to have a diplomatic job only a general could perform. Croatia's bristling, autocratic president, Franjo Tudjman, had vowed never to have another UN mission on his territory. To him, the presence of blue helmets was an offense to the country's hard-won sovereignty. Tudjman's US-backed offensive four months earlier had brought the wars in Croatia and Bosnia to an end, and had also emptied Croatia of most of its Serb minority. They had either fled or been driven out, except in a small northern enclave known as Eastern Slavonia. In the tense postwar period, the traumatized villages of the area still required peacekeepers. So after a good deal of American cajoling, Tudjman granted an exception. There could be a UN mission in Eastern Slavonia, but only on the condition it was run by a US general. So Washington went looking for a general it could spare.

Klein had been born in France, in the old European battleground of Alsace, and was fiercely proud of both his Alsatian and American identities. He was a boisterous storyteller in both English and French and a bon vivant, fond of good cuisine, cognac, and cigars. Some of the military can-do attitude had rubbed off on him from his days at the Pentagon, but he had not been there long enough to become a slave to the chain of command. Klein was decidedly his own man, and was looking to make a mark in his new fiefdom.

His appointment presented an opportunity for the struggling ICTY and its new chief prosecutor, Louise Arbour. When Klein passed through Brussels in January 1996 to see NATO officials before taking up his post, Arbour went to meet him with an American prosecutor, Clint Williamson, who knew as well as anyone the situation Klein would be walking into. Williamson had been investigating wartime massacres in Vukovar, an eastern Croatian town where the true scale of the savagery being unleashed by the collapse of Yugoslavia first became clear in late 1991. Large parts of a provincial town in the heart of Europe were systematically demolished by Serb forces. Hundreds of Croats — soldiers and civilians; men, women, and children — had been killed, and twenty thousand were driven from their homes in the name of cleansing a new Serb statelet being hewn out on orders from Belgrade.

By this time, Arbour and Williamson had become accustomed to demurral and excuses from American officials on the issue of arresting war criminals, so Klein took them by surprise. He was not just willing; he was eager. He was already well aware of the atrocities committed at Vukovar, including the executions of more than two hundred wounded Croatian soldiers and civilians at Ovčara in November 1991.

The Serb officers and soldiers involved in the massacre had mostly melted away across the border into Serbia where they were being sheltered by the Yugoslav army. However, Slavko Dokmanović, the former Serb mayor of Vukovar who was identified by two witnesses as being at Ovčara at the time the executions were committed, had been spotted on the Croatian side of the border, in Klein's UN-administered territory.

"He was one of the few people who had been in a civilian leadership role and who had been linked directly to the site of the killings," Williamson said. Dokmanović, charged in a sealed indictment in March 1996, would be the first target of a UN arrest operation.

Klein made a call to the UN legal counsel in New York who told him that he was not only authorized to carry out such arrests but was under an obligation to do so. He felt no need to check with Washington on the grounds that he been appointed a representative of the UN, not of the US government. "Let's do it," he told Arbour and Williamson. For the first time since its creation, the ICTY had an international figure with real authority in the region willing to carry out an arrest.

Arbour recalled that Klein was "particularly keen to embarrass NATO," which had sixty-five thousand troops in Bosnia but had hitherto been reluctant to risk carrying out war crimes detentions for fear of casualties. By comparison, Klein had a tiny force at his disposal, drawn from an untried unit — Poland's brand-new special forces, known as the Operational Mobile Response Group (Grupa Reagowania Operacyjno-Manewrowego, or GROM, Polish for "thunderclap"). On first impression, it seemed an unlikely scenario: a reserve American general leading the cream of the Polish army into action. But beneath the surface, there was something appropriate about the pairing. GROM owed its genesis to the Americans.

The unit was conceived as a result of a peculiar incident in Iraq. When Saddam Hussein invaded Kuwait in 1990, six CIA agents were trapped behind Iraqi lines. Washington appealed to the Polish for help because they still had construction contractors in the country. The Poles dispatched a senior intelligence official to Iraq who found the six American agents and brought them to a Polish building site. They were provided with Polish passports and, to comply with a national stereotype, given hard liquor to drink with the idea they would blend in with other Polish workers as they traveled by bus across the Iraqi border with Turkey. The crossing attempt came close to foundering from a piece of bad luck — there was an Iraqi border guard on duty who happened to speak Polish. But the quick-thinking bus driver leaped out of his cabin to embrace him like an old friend and plant a Slavic triple kiss on the Iraqi's cheeks. He offered to show the guard all the passengers' passports but the Iraqi would have none of it, waving him along and saying, "No problem. You are friends, you can go."[1]

In gratitude for the rescue operation, the George H. W. Bush administration asked Poland what it wanted from Washington in return. After some reflection, the Poles requested American money and know-how to establish an elite unit modeled on Delta Force and Britain's Special Air Service (SAS).

The request was granted. The new Polish recruits, drawn from regular army regiments, were flown to the United States for training, but while the American instructors were ready to teach, they were not quite ready to trust. After all, both sides had been prepared over the previous half century to fight each other to oblivion in a third world war, and the habits of suspicion take time to break down. The Polish soldiers were not told where they were being trained. They were forbidden from taking photographs and in some cases the blinds were drawn in their lecture rooms to prevent them from seeing their surroundings. Only by climate and occasional landmarks were they able to guess they were in the Shenandoah mountains and then in Florida.

The Polish recruits trained with America's best soldiers and then with the SAS at its base in Herefordshire. They were armed with modern guns and equipment. But when they were deployed to Croatia they were sent as a mere gendarmerie force. For budget and political reasons, GROM had been made part of Poland's Ministry of the Interior, and so the UN Department of Peacekeeping Operations assumed it was a glorified police unit. For the proud officers of an elite unit, the whole situation was intensely irritating.

"I was upset to be designated like that. We were an excellent unit, an elite force. You don't send a Ferrari to import coal," complained Jacek,[2] GROM's first squadron commander who arrived in Croatia as a major. "Just in case, I brought all our equipment. You never know."

His caution paid off. Conditions in Eastern Slavonia were more febrile than the UN realized. At Christmas 1996, Major Jacek was told to take two teams, about twenty men, equipped only with batons, to protect a group of two dozen elderly Croats who were going to attend Catholic mass in Ilok. It would be the first time the Croats had visited their church since being ethnically cleansed from the area five years before. Jacek took all the men he had and all his equipment, including sniper rifles, just in case.

In the event, the major needed everyone and everything he had brought with him. The church visit soon escalated into the most violent incident the area had witnessed since the war. A crowd of two hundred angry Serbs gathered at Ilok, furious to discover the Croats had been smuggled into the Catholic church through a back entrance. The mob rushed the outer rings of UN peacekeepers, under-equipped Pakistanis and Jordanians, who turned and bolted. As the crowd reached the Poles, pelting them with bricks, Major Jacek ordered his men to throw flash grenades and pull back inside the churchyard, but a handful of Serb protesters had managed to get around the cordon and throw a live grenade into the church. The Poles chased them out and Jacek called for his interpreter. He had a message for the crowd. "I now have the right to kill you and I will," he shouted through a megaphone and got the translator to repeat it while he pointed to his men in sniper positions around the churchyard. This is not how UN officers normally spoke or behaved. The crowd hushed and withdrew from the churchyard.

Later, when Klein arrived at the scene, GROM put up a protective cordon around him. The American was impressed. From that point on, GROM provided close protection for him and any other visiting VIPs. And a few months later, the Polish soldiers would make history, making the UN's first war crimes arrest when they captured Dokmanović.

The team assembled to catch the ex-mayor was an oddball mix of the sort only the UN could throw together. At its core was Williamson, a slim, bespectacled, intense American attorney, whose drive to make the arrest was informed by his experience digging up corpses at Ovčara with their hands still tied behind their backs.

Working alongside him was Kevin Curtis, a ginger-haired mustachioed British detective sergeant, from Shakespeare's birthplace, Stratford-on-Avon, who had been partnered at the ICTY with Vladimir Dzuro, a Czech homicide detective from Prague. Along with the Polish soldiers and the American prosecutor, the team embodied the highest aspirations of the post–Cold War world, an unlikely posse united in pursuit of international justice. It was Williamson who came up with the code name for the operation: Little Flower, the affectionate nickname of Fiorello La Guardia, one of New York's most famous sons and a mayor like Dokmanović.

After the war, Dokmanović had settled in the Serbian town of Sombor, but it was thought that he occasionally crossed into Croatia to visit friends and family. Spotters were put on the border bridge to look out for him but he never showed up. The trail went cold and could very well have stayed cold had it not been for a chance encounter at a Christmas party in The Hague.

One of the ironic weaknesses of the Hague investigative arm was that, just like the suspects it was supposed to track down, it divided the world according to ethnicity rather than geography. There was not one team investigating all the war crimes around Vukovar but two teams: one focusing on Serb war criminals, the other on crimes committed by Croats. They largely operated independently of each other.

Thus when Dokmanović met an official from the ICTY's Belgrade office in late October 1996 and offered to provide testimony on alleged Croat war crimes, the official initially had no idea this new witness was himself under indictment.[3] It was only two months later when Dzuro happened to meet this official in The Hague at a Christmas celebration that he realized that his unit's most wanted man had just become a star witness in another Hague investigation. Dokmanović had even handed over his telephone number in Sombor.

Thomas Osorio, the operations officer from the tribunal's office in Zagreb who spoke Serbo-Croatian, was given the job of coaxing the ex-mayor over the border on the pretext of seeking help with the inquiry into Croat crimes. Dokmanović seemed receptive in the exploratory phone conversations, but two days before a proposed rendezvous in late January 1997, his mood changed markedly and he canceled the meeting. He would not come across the border.[4]

But Dokmanović did not rule out an ICTY visit to his home in Sombor. So over the next couple of months, the tribunal investigators met with Klein and Captain David Jones, his American military adviser, to come up with a new plan in which the tribunal team would cross into Serbia to lure Dokmanović back over the border into UN-run territory.

There was a delay of another six weeks when the fugitive mayor did not answer his phone.

Time was running out. In early July, the Croatian government was due to start exerting direct control over Eastern Slavonia, and Klein's authority as the UN administrator would come to an end. Finally Dokmanović picked up a call on his home telephone and a meeting was arranged at his house for June 24. The day before, Williamson and Dzuro went to Sombor to look around and find a spot where Dokmanović's house could be put under surveillance.

Meanwhile, back in Erdut, on the Croatian side of the frontier, Major Jacek faced a lonely choice. The Polish interior minister had told him he could make his own decisions in the field, but he was well aware that if he consulted his immediate superior officers in Warsaw, they would veto any participation in Little Flower. Asking for advice would be equivalent to canceling the mission.

"It was a dilemma. It would be good experience for the men, and it was at a time when politicians in Warsaw were talking about cutting the unit, to save money," he said. "Success would save the unit. Failure would mean its disbandment for sure. I had sleepless nights thinking about it. I knew one mistake would ruin GROM and I would be done for."

Jacek decided to gamble and embarked on preparations with Captain Jones. The GROM troops set up a surveillance point at the border and sniper positions around the Erdut UN base. A helicopter would be on standby with a rapid reaction squad should reinforcements be needed. The plan was for Curtis to drive Dokmanović in a UN Land Rover from the border on the pretense of taking him to Klein's office, but when the car went past the Polish base at Erdut, it would veer suddenly through an entrance concealed by a tarpaulin and into a dead end surrounded by blast walls. The vehicle would crash into a bank of sandbags, so that Dokmanović would be thrown forward and disoriented. To that end, his seat belt would be disabled beforehand, and his door lock broken so GROM soldiers could easily wrench him out of the vehicle. Curtis was to roll under the chassis, to get out of the way should bullets start flying.[5]

Little Flower was rehearsed again and again on June 22 and 23, and was tweaked along the way. After budget officers had expressed irritation at the costly damage to the Land Rover in early dry runs, it was replaced by a Chevrolet Suburban, and it was decided that a sharp application of the brakes would be good enough to throw the target off-balance. Curtis, a heavy smoker of stout build, also pointed out that the idea of him nimbly slipping under the car was unrealistic. Jacek agreed. One of his men would do the driving instead.

On a whiteboard in a UN briefing room, Jacek listed the various scenarios in which the operations could go wrong. Some of them ended in gunfire. His men would not hesitate to shoot to defend the lives of UN civilians or themselves if any of the Serbs in the car pulled a gun, the Polish officer said. Klein signed the authority for lethal force, shrugging off the anxiety of some of his advisers. That evening, in a characteristically relaxed pose behind his desk, he nursed a brandy and waved his cigar in the air declaring: "If he pulls a gun, shoot him, drop him in a ditch, and put up a sign saying: Don't Mess with the ICTY."

It was time to go to see Dokmanović. On Tuesday, June 24, Dzuro had found a café from where he could watch the suspect's house and installed himself in the window with a cup of coffee. Curtis and Osorio drove across the bridge and arrived at Dokmanović's front door.

Apart from a couple of Rottweilers going beserk in a cage by the front door, the ex-mayor was alone and invited his guests inside as expected. But from then on, the plan collapsed. Before Curtis could even raise the subject, Dokmanović announced he would not be crossing into Croatia. Curtis hid his disappointment and kept to his cover story, offering instead to take pictures of suspected war crimes sites and bring them back to Sombor to show the former mayor for verification. Dokmanović agreed, and then for the next five hours set about presenting his version of events in wartime Vukovar.

As Curtis took notes, Dzuro was beginning to wear out his welcome in the café across the road. After drinking a couple of cups of coffee, he went out for a walk and then returned for yet more caffeine. The waitress grew curious and asked if there was anything or anyone he was waiting for, prompting the Czech policeman to improvise a tale of romantic love and a Serb girl for whom he had fallen back in Prague. But the faithless girl had distressingly failed to turn up for a long-planned tryst in Sombor. Suspicions allayed, Dzuro was able to spend another couple of hours nursing a coffee and staring expectantly out of the window. His impatience and nerves fit the cover story perfectly.

Toward the end of the interview, just as Curtis was beginning to despair of persuading Dokmanović to leave Serbia, the Serb's daughter and granddaughter dropped by. As he introduced them, the former mayor waxed nostalgic about the old Yugoslav days and their family home in the village of Trpinja,[6] which they had been forced to abandon. Curtis seized on the opening. "Have you thought about talking to Jacques Klein about compensation?" he asked.

"He felt he had once been mayor and had been somebody, and now he was nothing and he was finding it hard to adjust," Curtis recalled. Here was some leverage the British policeman could use. "Maybe you could negotiate about all Serb houses, not just your own," he suggested.

Dokmanović instantly took to the idea and the British policeman promised he would raise the matter with Klein on his return. Curtis and Osorio came back the next day and said that if he wanted to visit Klein, they could guarantee there was no risk of arrest by the Croatian police. The guarantee was technically true though somewhat incomplete. Curtis said nothing about arrest by the Polish commandos under a UN flag. Dokmanović took the bait and agreed to cross the border that Friday, June 27. He even offered to have dinner ready for Curtis and Osorio when they returned from the trip.

On Friday afternoon, the ICTY team was waiting in an office overlooking the chosen arrest site, anxiously listening to the radio communications from the Poles. At 2:50 they received confirmation that Dokmanović had crossed the border near Erdut but he had not come alone. He was with a burly friend, Milan Knežević. They had both climbed inside the white armored Chevrolet being driven by a Polish soldier. Jacek was in the front passenger seat. As soon as they drove off, other UN troops set up a vehicle checkpoint behind them, delaying any other cars from traveling along the same route.

As the Chevrolet drew level with the Polish base at Erdut, traveling at forty miles an hour, a truck pulled out abruptly from a side road in front of them. It was also driven by a GROM soldier, with the aim of forcing the Chevy to make a sharp left turn into the base. At precisely 3:04, the white SUV made the turn, screeching to a halt as rehearsed. GROM soldiers rushed at it from both sides, pulling Dokmanović out from the right rear passenger seat and Kneževic´ from the left. To an untrained eye it looked like a perfectly executed operation, but Jacek later pilloried one of his men for momentarily missing his grip on the left rear door. The slip could have cost lives, Jacek thundered. The delay was only a fraction of a second and is only noticeable when the UN video of the arrest is played in slow motion. Later events, however, would prove once more that Jacek's paranoia was entirely justified.

Dokmanović had come with a leather attaché case that had been left behind in the car when he was grabbed. One of the Polish soldiers picked it up and left it on the gravel as another slipped a hood over Dokmanović's head and walked him away from the vehicle to a white Portakabin. The hood was then taken off so that he could hear Dzuro and a translator perform the first direct arrest in the ICTY's four-year history.

"Mr. Dokmanović. My name is Vladimir Dzuro, I am an investigator with the Office of the Prosecutor of the International Criminal Tribunal for Yugoslavia. You are charged in an indictment and named in an arrest warrant of the International Criminal Tribunal for Yugoslavia. You are charged with grave breaches of the Geneva Convention, crimes against humanity, violation of the law and customs of war, for your role in the beating and killing that occurred in Ovčara farm, near Vukovar in 20 November 1991. Do you understand?" Dzuro asked.

"I understand but it's not true," Dokmanović replied.

The detainee insisted he had come on the invitation of Klein and demanded Dzuro call him right away, seemingly oblivious to the possibility that Klein was party to his capture. The hood was put back on Dokmanović's head and he was guided into another UN armored car. This took him to a small airfield at Čepin, near the Croatian town of Osijek, where Klein's plane, a two-engine turboprop Merlin provided by the Belgian military, was waiting on the tarmac.

Before going up the steps, Williamson signed a form transferring custody to the ICTY while UN doctors gave Dokmanović a quick medical examination and discovered he had an irregular heartbeat. He was given some pills to keep it under control, and after twenty minutes the medics gave approval for the flight.

The delay nearly torpedoed Operation Little Flower at its final hurdle. Just as Dokmanović and his captors were climbing aboard, the control tower withdrew permission for takeoff, querying the flight manifest and a Croatian police car sped across the tarmac toward them. The officers demanded to know what the UN employees were doing hustling a hooded man into a foreign-registered aircraft.

The moment of the first arrest, June 27, 1997, as Polish soldiers seize Slavko Dokmanović. Photograph provided by Col. David Jones, US Army.

For a few minutes, the operation teetered on the line between triumph and fiasco. There was nothing to stop the Croatian police from seizing Dokmanović themselves. It would have been a career-crowning coup for them, and a triumph for Tudjman, to capture one of the most hated men in the country. Croatian sovereignty would have been shown to trump the jurisdictional claims of this UN court in a foreign capital, which would at the same time have appeared both sneaky and incompetent. Not for the first or last time, the manhunt was in danger of disaster before it had a chance to get off the ground. In The Hague, Arbour and her prosecutors had been getting updates relayed through Klein's office and had been about to start celebrating. But suddenly the news from Čepin had petered out with no explanation, leaving them bewildered and knotted with tension.

On the baking-hot runway at Čepin, a stilted and surreal conversation ensued between Williamson and a Croatian police officer. The latter demanded to know who was on the plane. Williamson spelled out the names of the UN staff on board and adding as an afterthought, "And one other person."

There was a pause. "Another person?"

"Yes, another person."

The question ping-ponged to and fro in various forms, without the policeman ever asking straight out for the mystery passenger's name, perhaps assuming such a direct question might break some opaque UN protocol he was unaware of. On the other hand, the exchange did not seem to be bringing the policeman any closer to allowing the plane to leave.

Williamson gambled, offering to call Croatian officials in Zagreb, and was lucky enough to get Deputy Prime Minister Ivica Kostović on the line. He had dealt with Kostović before on war crimes issues, and the Croatian appreciated Williamson's dedication to unearthing the truth from the mass graves at Ovčara. Without troubling to ask who else was on the plane, he ordered the policeman to allow it to take off.

At 4:09 the Merlin left the ground,[7] and it took another few minutes for the aircraft to clear Croatian airspace. The radio message from the cockpit signaled that Operation Little Flower was accomplished, and the tribunal in The Hague was still in business. In fact, it was better than that. The court had unexpectedly grown some teeth and used them. If the Western nations were content to let mass murderers off the hook, the ICTY had demonstrated it was capable of delivering justice independently.

The sense of relief spread through Williamson's team on the plane as they reached The Hague, somewhat prematurely as it turned out. They had no idea they were again just one small slip from potential disaster.

After takeoff, Williamson presented Dokmanović with the indictment against him, and the detainee once more denied any wrongdoing, asking for his attaché case so that he could put the document away for later study. The case had been picked up by the Poles from Erdut and was on board, but Williamson refused to hand it over, saying he would hold on to the paperwork for the prisoner.

Dokmanović then asked if he could smoke, and when permission was granted by the Belgian pilots, he said he wanted his own brand, which were in the attaché case. Again the ICTY investigators refused, and Curtis offered some of his own cigarettes instead. Dokmanović accepted, gracelessly.

The plane landed at Valkenburg Naval Air Base near The Hague, and the party drove from there to Scheveningen prison on the North Sea coast, where cells had been set aside for the ICTY's use. The bag traveled along with them, passing through the X-ray machines at security. It was only when Dokmanović's personal possessions were being unpacked on a prison table that Curtis stuck his hand into the case and pulled out a loaded Magnum revolver.

"If Dokmanović had been able to get the gun, he would have been the only armed man on the plane," Dzuro pointed out later. "He could have done anything. He could have forced the pilots to turn around and land in Belgrade."

In retrospect, Dokmanović's dramatic voyage to The Hague was an early version of rendition. Superficially at least, it bore some of the hallmarks of the CIA's later abductions during the war on terror—the black hood on the captive, the executive jet at the obscure airfield. But in one crucial respect it was entirely different. The UN was legally entitled, even obliged, to carry out the arrest under the Hague Tribunal's statutes. The renditions that were to follow early in the new century were on the outer edges of the law, arguably far beyond.

Knežević, who had accompanied Dokmanović on his ill-advised trip across the border, had been one of the mayor's wartime associates but there was no warrant for his arrest. Klein ordered his release soon after the plane was airborne, promising not to publicize his involvement in the detention, as long as Knežević was equally discreet.

Within hours, however, Knežević gave a series of increasingly fanciful interviews to the Belgrade press, portraying the detention as a forcible abduction on sovereign Serbian territory. Klein immediately called him and threatened to publish a fulsome letter thanking Knežević for his assistance in his friend's capture. Klein read out a draft of the letter, relishing the flowery language in which the international community would express its debt. Without him, the arrest of war crimes suspect Dokmanović would never have taken place. Klein was threatening to frame Knežević as a traitor.

"You can't publish this! You'll kill me!" Knežević cried.

"No," Klein replied. "*They'll* kill you."

From that moment on, Knežević stopped talking in public about the arrest.

In The Hague, Dokmanović's lawyers issued a more formal challenge to the manner of their client's capture, describing it as a kidnapping. However, in a critical early battle for the tribunal, the judges presiding over the hearing—an American, a Costa Rican, and a Pakistani—ultimately sided with the prosecution. They accepted the argument that Dokmanović had not been detained until he was at Erdut, in Croatian territory, and ruled that the ruse was acceptable to bring about the arrest, particularly in view of the scale of the crimes. The Trial Chamber declared that Klein's UN team in Eastern Slavonia, "in discharging its obligation to cooperate with the International Tribunal and enforcing its Chapter VII mandate, is assuring the effectiveness of the Tribunal and thus contributing to the maintenance of international peace and security, as it is intended to do."[8]

In Serbia and the Serb enclaves in Croatia, the UN braced for a backlash, but it never came. On the weekend after the arrest, a grenade exploded near a UN vehicle in Eastern Slavonia, but on further investigation it turned out to have been detonated during a particularly boisterous Serb wedding, where the discharge of firearms and other weapons was common, even obligatory.

For the Operation Little Flower team, Dokmanović's arrest was a high-wire act. For Klein and Jacek in particular, it could have been career-ending. They had acted as mavericks, deciding not to seek permission from their own governments. Despite its success, both men received a dressing-down. Jacek's commander only found out about the operation at a diplomatic reception in Warsaw, where he suffered the humiliation of being told what his elite soldiers had been up to by an American military attaché. Jacek could have been disciplined had Klein's glowing report on GROM's performance not landed on President Clinton's desk, significantly easing Poland's entry into NATO. Not long after, Jacek was promoted to lieutenant colonel.

Klein received a furious call from an American general in Bosnia, who asked him, "What the hell are you playing at?" The US military had been trying to fend off pressure to carry out arrests, and now Klein — one of their own — had shown them up. The White House was pointing to Operation Little Flower as proof that war criminals could be captured with guile and minimal risk, a worrisome precedent as far as the Pentagon was concerned. Klein shrugged off the criticism. The president was happy and Klein felt he had done the right thing. That was all that mattered.

Klein was summoned to Belgrade a few days later to see Slobodan Milošević, who — Klein was warned by Serbian government officials — was fuming over the Dokmanović affair. When Klein arrived in the Serbian capital and walked into the presidential office, Milošević looked up from his desk and spat out: "General, I will not tolerate this bullshit." For a man who had spent more than four years trying to cleave Croatia and Bosnia in two, he was highly sensitive about Serbian territorial integrity.

Klein, figuring Milošević would have read only Serb press accounts of the affair, had taken the precaution of bringing some photographs with him showing Dokmanović and Knežević walking over the bridge at the Croatian border voluntarily and unaccompanied. He had not been abducted from Serbian soil as the Belgrade press had reported. He had crossed in pursuit of real estate and personal gain.

"He did this on his own?" an incredulous Milošević asked. Klein nodded. "Then he was stupid," Milošević pronounced, and never mentioned the subject again.

One year later, on June 29, 1998, a week before a verdict was to be issued on Dokmanović's role in organizing the Ovčara slaughter, the defendant found a way of short-circuiting the lights in his cell. By the time the fuse had been replaced, the lights turned back on, and his cell opened just after midnight, Dokmanović was dead. Despite regular surveillance triggered by concerns over his depression, he had managed to hang himself by attaching his tie to a hinge on his cell door and knotting it around his throat.[9] He had made sure he would not be the first Serb to be convicted of war crimes. That particular dishonor would fall to someone else.

# 3.
# A HIGH EXPECTATION OF VIOLENCE:
# THE SAS IN BOSNIA

If World War Three is going to start, it's about to start now.
—*Bob Reid, ICTY chief of operations, prosecutor's office*

You're hunting a very rare beast that knows its environment
much better than you do... You've got to be a step ahead.
—*SAS officer in Bosnia*

**IT IS THE MORNING** of July 10, 1997, in western Bosnia. The sun is up and it is already warm. At a reservoir outside of Prijedor, the town's burly semi-retired police chief, Simo Drljača, has stripped down to his underwear and taken a boat out fishing, leaving his seventeen-year-old son and his brother-in-law to sleep off their breakfast on the shore.

At the same time, Milan Kovačević, an old wartime buddy of Drljača's, is beginning his day at Prijedor's hospital, where he is the director. At fifty-six, with a jutting brow and graying walrus mustache, he has a lugubrious air that usually gets gloomier as the day wears on. He keeps a bottle of homemade plum brandy in a filing cabinet for visitors and for solace in his darker moments.[1]

Not far away, Milomir Stakić is still in his car on the way to his job as the head of Prijedor's health center. He is also heavyset, with a black goatee and polished bald head like the front end of a torpedo. Running late because of the traffic, he turns into the clinic's parking lot to find his usual space already taken and has to drive around to find an alternative spot.

These three men, all starting their day in different ways, are bound together by a shared past they would like to stay buried. Together they form a triangle at the core of the town's troubled identity. It is largely due to them that Prijedor has earned a place in history as a byword for inhumanity. And they have something else in common of which even they are unaware: They have all been indicted for war crimes and are the targets, that summer morning, of NATO's first arrest operation in Bosnia.

Drljača, Kovačević, and Stakić were the driving force in the Serb "crisis staff" that took control of Prijedor at the end of April 1992, as war was breaking out across Bosnia. The word "crisis" was a thin gloss to imply some kind of legal justification for the putsch. In reality, these men were the crisis. Their takeover was part of a meticulous plan prepared in Belgrade and reproduced in dozens of towns in Bosnia to assert Serb control of a large horse-shoe of territory, accounting for more than half the country. It was to be called the Republika Srpska and it would be cleansed of non-Serbs by any means necessary. These three men had abso-lutely no administrative experience. They were chosen for their loyalty to the party of Radovan Karadžić, the SDS, and because they had no compunction about the methods used.

Drljača had a degree from a local law school but had spent most of his adult life working as a clerk in the municipal education system. He was made chief of public security with control over the civil and secret police because of his covert party work in the run-up to the war, turning the local SDS into a clandestine armed force. When the signal was given for the seizure of the Prijedor municipality, he had more than 1,700 men with guns at his disposal to deploy in public buildings around the region.[2] But it was also his physical presence — imposing, volatile, aggressive — that set him apart. It was men like this that Karadžić needed to slice Bosnia in half. He thought so highly of Drljača that he later picked him as the Republika Srpska's deputy interior minister.

Kovačević, known to his friends as Mićo, was an anesthetist who claimed to have been born in a Croatian Fascist concentration camp during World War II. Stakić was a doctor. Together they exemplified the medical profession's deep involvement in the ethnic cleansing of the Republika Srpska. Its Red Cross was run by Karadžić's wife, Ljiljana, and the Prijedor branch was complicit in covering up atrocities.[3]

After the SDS seized Prijedor, Stakić was made mayor, with Kovačević as his deputy. They were the middle managers in the ethnic cleansing machine in Prijedor. Drljača, who controlled the men with guns, was its cutting edge.

Together these three men orchestrated the mass deportations of Muslims and Croats from the region, reducing the prewar non-Serb population of fifty thousand to three thousand in a few months. Men and teenage boys were herded into a gulag of improvised internment centers around Prijedor. The worst of these — in an iron ore mine at Omarska, a ceramics factory called Keraterm, and a cinema and a school in Trnopolje — made the town infamous as the place where concentration camps first returned to Europe half a century after the Third Reich. Thousands were executed or tortured to death in the Prijedor camps. In one of the most gruesome mass killings, Drljača organized the execution of two hundred Muslim and Croat men on Mount Vlašić. They were shot at the top of high cliffs and their bodies thrown in the ravine below.

After peace came to Bosnia at the end of 1995, more than sixty thousand foreign soldiers poured into the country as part of IFOR to ensure that the treaty signed in Dayton, Ohio, was upheld. Prijedor and the rest of northwestern Bosnia was run by the British, with Dutch, Czech, and other national contingents serving under them. The patrols were everywhere and they worked. The peace held. Scarcely a shot was fired from the beginning of 1996.

But Drljača, Kovačević, Stakić, and the rest of the wartime crisis staff stayed where they were. Drljača continued to serve as police chief until September 1996. He was forced to step down only after he and his men had an armed standoff in central Prijedor with a Czech patrol, who had tried to confiscate his illegally owned machine gun. Even after that, the Republika Srpska government hired him as a "security adviser" in the Ministry of the Interior, from where he continued to oversee security in Prijedor and much else besides. Human Rights Watch reported in early 1997 that he " 'controls all police issues.' He also carries an illegal weapon and is accompanied by armed body guards at all time."[4]

Kovačević and Stakić also remained in powerful positions: Kovačević as the hospital director and Stakić as the mayor. While IFOR patrolled the streets, these three men continued to dictate the real course of events in the area.

One of IFOR's jobs in implementing the Dayton Accords was to encourage refugees displaced by ethnic cleansing to return to their homes. The troops escorted buses taking them across the front lines to their home villages so as to help them make a decision on whether to move back permanently. But in October 1996, when the UN organized a visit for about a hundred Bosniak refugees to the village of Hambarine, just outside Prijedor, it made the mistake of giving Mayor Stakić an advance list of people who would be on the bus. Their houses were blown up before they even arrived. IFOR strongly suspected that Stakić had passed the list to Drljača, who took care of the rest.[5]

Meanwhile, the reconstruction funds flowing into Prijedor were being channeled to the pockets of the wartime leaders. Kovačević and Stakić were both believed to be skimming off money intended to refurbish the hospital.[6] Drljača was known as Prijedor's "Mister Ten Percent."[7] He ran a protection racket extorting money from small businesses, and in a supreme irony, he was also in charge of the commission on displaced persons and refugees. That gave him control over everyone's fate.

"If you know Simo, you can get a house," an IFOR officer told Human Rights Watch. "If you don't, you can pay him. Everyone in Prijedor knows this."[8]

Prijedor was a particularly vivid example of why the Dayton peace treaty was not working. The strategy of the US military commanders and their NATO allies on entering Bosnia was to keep the peace by a massive show of force, and to do nothing beyond that which could trigger unrest or expose their soldiers to harm, even if it meant cooperating with the warlords. The consequence of the strategy was an outward calm but a hollow peace. Ethnic cleansing was not being reversed, refugees were being prevented from returning home, and people of all ethnicities continued to be cowed by intimidation and criminality.

By the beginning of 1997, the policy began to change. The realization that the strategy was failing filtered up the chain of command from diplomats and officers in Bosnia to the national capitals, where the political scene was evolving. Clinton won reelection in November 1996 and became less constrained by the fear of casualties and more open to the moral and political arguments for pursuing war criminals. Six months later, Tony Blair's

Labour Party won a clear majority in Britain, bringing with it a more proactive view of what British troops could achieve in Bosnia. At the same time, in early 1997 the Hague Tribunal began to issue sealed indictments against war crimes suspects, which were legally controversial but made it easier to catch them unawares.

Drljača and Kovačević were secretly indicted on March 13, 1997, for genocide, while Stakić was charged with crimes against humanity. Four months later, on that sunny Thursday morning of July 10, as Drljača fished, Kovačević sat at his desk, and Stakić drove to work, all three were oblivious to the ground shifting beneath their feet. They would be the first to discover that the age of impunity in Bosnia was coming to an end. On secret memos that had been circulating in London, they were dubbed "the Prijedor Three," the target of Operation Tango, the code name given to NATO's maiden arrest mission in Bosnia.

As Drljača sat in his boat, he was being watched by a group of British soldiers, members of D Squadron of the 22nd Special Air Service regiment, who had staked out the police chief's favorite fishing spot for several days. Fifty yards to Drljača's right and left, in the woods around the reservoir, two pairs of SAS snipers had taken up camouflaged positions ready to block any escape routes. In British military parlance, these were the "cut-offs," part of any ambush. Several other soldiers had crept up behind Drljača's son, Siniša, and brother-in-law, Spiro Milanović, subduing and gagging them in an instant. At 9:30 a.m., just as Drljača was pulling his boat onto the lakeshore, two more soldiers appeared on the path that ringed the lake, walking toward him, waving and shouting, "Hey, Simo!"

The hope had been that a friendly greeting would throw him off guard for a moment. He had seen plenty of British peacekeeping patrols and had been known to play football with the foreign soldiers. But Drljača immediately sensed these were no peace-keepers, and he bolted away from the water and up the slope, his flip-flops falling off as he went. One of the soldiers caught up with him and tackled him, but Drljača pulled a pistol that had been in the waistband at the back of his shorts. He twisted around and shot, wounding the soldier in the leg. The two men wrestled at the lakeside, with the SAS snipers in the cut-offs yelling at the soldier to break free. The moment he was clear, Drljača was hit four times in the back and right side, killing him instantly.

As Drljača lay bleeding on the lakeshore, another group of soldiers from D Squadron arrived at the reception desk at Prijedor hospital, dressed as regular troops, seemingly unarmed and carrying a parcel marked with a red cross. It had to be presented in person to the director, to Milan Kovačević, the soldiers said. They were led to his office but once inside, they pushed past his secretary and pulled out concealed pistols. Kovačević put up no resistance and was marched out of the hospital under the eyes of his staff. Once outside, he was shoved aboard a white Nissan minibus to be taken to the British base for a short helicopter ride to Camp Eagle in Tuzla, to the northeast, and then by American military plane to The Hague.

Stakić, the last member of the Prijedor Three, got lucky. Because he arrived late and his parking spot was taken at the clinic, he had to drive to the other side of the lot, taking him away from the SAS snatch squad that had been poised to leap out of a waiting van and grab him. It was enough of a deviation from the rehearsed plan for his arrest to be aborted.

Stakić fled Prijedor for Serbia as soon as he heard about Drljača's shooting and Kovačević's arrest, and he managed to stay at large for another four years before the Serbian authorities handed him over. He was sentenced at the Hague tribunal to forty years in jail for the murder of more than 1,500 people in the Prijedor municipality.[9] Kovačević would avoid the judgment of a court. He died in his cell of an aortic aneurysm on August 1, 1998.

When the first reports reached The Hague on the morning of July 10, 1997, Operation Tango seemed more a disaster than a triumph. Bob Reid, a former Australian policeman who was head of operations in the prosecutor's office, took the news to the chief prosecutor, Louise Arbour. This was a moment of truth. The tribunal's critics had warned Arbour that arrests would trigger such a powerful nationalist backlash that the Dayton Accords would collapse in chaos.

"If World War Three is going to start, it's about to start now," Reid told Arbour. "One's on his way. They went into Prijedor hospital and got him."

"Oh God! A hospital!" Arbour said in horror.

"Well that's the good news. It gets worse. One's dead."

"Oh God!"

"And the other escaped."[10]

World War Three did not break out. There were sporadic protests in the streets of a few Republika Srpska towns, but the overwhelming response was one of relief. Even for the Serbs, Drljača had been a predatory presence.

Operation Tango brought other headaches, however. When the SAS soldiers arrived at Prijedor hospital with their parcel emblazoned with a red cross, they were technically breaking one of the Geneva Conventions, which forbids soldiers from impersonating Red Cross workers. In the face of vigorous Serb complaints, and concern from the International Committee of the Red Cross, the British government maintained a policy of denial and obfuscation. NATO briefers in Sarajevo were told: "It wasn't a Red Cross parcel, just a parcel with a red cross on it."

Unofficially, the Ministry of Defence in Whitehall was quite aware the rules had been broken. "We have an example of the marking affixed to the package: there is no doubt that it conformed with the legal definition of the red cross emblem," an aide to the defense secretary, George Robertson, wrote in August 1997.[11] The decision was made to admit nothing and hope the storm would pass, which after a week or two, it did.

It soon became apparent that Operation Tango, however messy, had been a watershed. It broke the taboo on NATO's involvement in war crimes arrests, bringing to an end eighteen months of frustration and timidity. It also represented a complete about-face for Britain's role in the former Yugoslavia. For six years, a Conservative Party government had resisted any action that might give the appearance of taking sides in the conflict. It opposed efforts to bring justice to war criminals for fear of derailing a variety of peace initiatives, no matter how tenuous, or of provoking attacks on British soldiers in blue helmets serving as UN peacekeepers. The hands-off policy also reflected a certain amount of pro-Serb sympathy among elements of the British establishment, which took past military alliances in the two world wars as their reference points. To fend off the pressure to intervene, the government of John Major was prepared to be somewhat economical with the truth. The Secret Intelligence Service (more popularly known as MI6) even briefed London-based journalists that the Muslim-led Bosnian army was actually bombing their own people.

*The Guardian*'s Ed Vulliamy was called in by Britain's spooks and told "the Muslim-led government was massacring its own people in Sarajevo to win sympathy and ultimately help from outside."[12] Vulliamy, having spent months under fire in Sarajevo and having seen the UN reports consistently pointing to the role of Serb artillery in the mountains around the city, derisively rejected the MI6 nudge. Others could not resist the "scoop" and the spurious story circulated in the world press for a couple of weeks, leaving a deposit of doubt that is still being mined by conspiracy theorists.

London also sought to hinder an initial UN commission of experts set up to collect evidence on war crimes, and contributed a minimal amount to the fledgling tribunal in The Hague. When Major's government hosted a ministerial conference in December 1996 to oversee implementation of the Dayton peace deal, it pointedly did not invite the ICTY's new chief prosecutor, Louise Arbour. It only relented after the Germans insisted.

"It's not just that they didn't help," said a senior Conservative Party foreign policy official, of her own party. "They actively went out to frustrate efforts to help the tribunal."[13]

The issue divided British officials. Diplomats and soldiers in Bosnia could appreciate firsthand the damage that impunity was doing to Bosnia's fragile state. In late 1996, the British ambassador in Sarajevo, Charles Crawford, fired off angry telegrams to the Foreign and Commonwealth Office (FCO) in London. He recalls telling his bosses: "We have to arrest these people and pull out the poison, because we can't expect the Bosnians to take us seriously if they think these people are still running the show. We are shooting ourselves in the foot."[14]

When the tide began to turn in Washington, and Operation Amber Star was established in the spring of 1997, the United Kingdom sent government officials, army officers, and policeman to the US Special Forces Command in Stuttgart to take part in the feasibility study.[15] The idea was to stay in the loop and not fall out of step with the Americans, but the British maintained a skeptical presence. When the whole venture became bogged down by Franco-American distrust, it came as a relief to London.

The clear tipping point for the UK role came on May 1, 1997, with the landslide election of the Labour Party under the reformist leadership of Blair. It ended eighteen years of Conservative rule and brought Robin Cook to the FCO. Cook was a Scottish left-winger, a former racing tipster, and a sparkling debater. A short, bearded man with a sharp tongue, he had ruled himself out as a potential Labour leader on the grounds he was "insufficiently attractive." In 1997, he came to the FCO's imposing home on King Charles Street with the promise of introducing "an ethical dimension" to British foreign policy.

Bosnia, recovering from a brutal conflict and patrolled by British troops, was the obvious place to start. In opposition, Cook had forged links with the Helsinki Committees for Human Rights, a network of activists across Europe dating back to the Cold War. When conflict came to Yugoslavia and the nationalist fever took a grip among the elites and masses alike, the Helsinki Committees in Belgrade and Zagreb became some of the few bastions of liberal humanism in the face of a collective hysteria. To educate himself on Yugoslavia during his time in opposition, Cook did not rely on the filter of the FCO briefings, as his predecessors had done. He invited the Helsinki activists to London.

Confident of victory weeks before the May vote, Cook had also met with Madeleine Albright in a London hotel and made clear his intent to take a more active role in supporting the Hague Tribunal. Albright was delighted. She had been pushing the US military to carry out arrests since becoming secretary of state in early 1997 but had been confounded by layer on layer of passive resistance from the Pentagon. Now she had an important ally.

If the British were prepared to take risks to capture the war crimes suspects, the Joint Chiefs of Staff would find it much harder to claim it could not be done.

Days after Labour came to power, the Cabinet Office provided the new government with a policy paper, arguing the pros and cons of war crimes arrests:

> *After the atrocities of the Bosnian war, parliamentary, public and media opinion expects action. The continued presence of indictees alongside SFOR troops in Bosnia damages the credibility of the international effort and provides the Bosniacs [sic] with an excuse to hold back on the implementation of the Dayton Agreement. Moreover, the ICTY is the first international tribunal of its kind since the Nuremberg tribunal was established in 1946. It has been followed by a similar tribunal for Rwanda. Failure to make progress on prosecuting Bosnian war criminals would undermine the wider efforts of the international community to make it clear that there will be no refuge for those who commit crimes against humanity.*
>
> *In addition to these general arguments, there are particular reasons for wishing to detain Radovan Karadžić, who exerts a malign influence on the peace process. His removal, though a high-risk operation, could prompt a more constructive Bosnian Serb attitude to peace implementation, and allow the authorities in the Republika Srpska the opportunity to pursue policies consistent with the peace process.*[16]

In the first week of June, Britain's top soldier, the chief of the defence staff (CDS), Sir Charles Guthrie, visited Sarajevo to assess preparations for Operation Tango and came away believing it would be better to do it sooner rather than later. The FCO reported: "Operational planning is in hand. Provided that this is satisfactory, an operation could be conducted within days. CDS is concerned that operational security would be compromised if this were delayed. And there is a training exercise from 16–29 June which would provide a useful diversion."[17]

There was a problem, however. Having agreed in Stuttgart to take part in Operation Amber Star, the United Kingdom could not act unilaterally. If there was to be a joint operation with the Americans and French to catch Karadžić or Mladić, an exclusively British operation to snatch relatively low-level suspects in Prijedor could derail it, causing the fugitive leaders to raise their defenses or flee.

Cook's dilemma was summed up in a Foreign Office reply in early June to a tip-off from the Ministry of Defence that Operation Tango was ready to be put into action. It was written by Kim Darroch, the head of the Eastern Adriatic Department, who played a central role in coordinating British arrest operations. "The Secretary of State was grateful for your warning of a possible UK operation to catch the Prijedor Three. He has noted that he has doubts, if this jeopardises the bigger fish operation. On the other hand, he is aware that we should keep open the prospect of setting this example if the bigger operation is not going ahead anyway."[18]

While a final decision was being weighed in Whitehall, Operation Tango was being rehearsed at the SAS training camp at Pontrilas in rural Herefordshire. Set amid pasture and thick copses about five miles from the Welsh border, it looked from a distance like any other small farm. It was only on closer inspection that it was apparent there was something out of the ordinary about the place, like the full-size mock-up of a commercial airliner looming over the hedgerows, used to practice storming hijacked planes.

For members of the Regiment, the Bosnia mission had a familiar feel. They were accustomed to manhunting from tours of Northern Ireland, where 22 SAS was deployed in pursuit of commanders from the Provisional Irish Republican Army. "For anyone who was in Northern Ireland, this wasn't new for us," said one former member of D Squadron. "Everything was about rehearsal. We formulated the plan and then it was rehearsed again and again at Pontrilas. We would mark out the streets or the landscape on the ground so we'd know our way around."

Once the rehearsals were over, the capture teams from D Squadron were flown to Split, on the Croatian coast, and then taken over the border into Bosnia a few at a time, in the back of regular army trucks, to avoid alerting the local population that a special operation was being prepared.

The headquarters of the British garrison in western Bosnia was a giant metal factory just outside Banja Luka, the biggest town in western Bosnia. MI6 ran a station in a cluster of Porta-kabins inside the compound, consisting of an SAS component, two detachments from the Special Forces Signals Regiment to provide communications, and one detachment from the Intelligence Corps for recruiting mostly low-level local agents useful for spotting threats. They also had a hangar for their small collection of battered local cars used for covert surveillance.

In preparation for Tango and later operations, the SAS snatch teams arriving fresh from rehearsals in Pontrilas were housed in surplus Portakabins kept empty for such occasions. For them, by far the worst part of the mission was the waiting inside these sweltering tin cans, keeping out of sight until the green light was given.

The run-up to Tango was a particular torture. Summer in Bosnia is hot and humid and the operation's initial target window of late June came and went with no action. Uncertainty at

Operation Amber Star, the multinational planning cell in Stuttgart, over whether there would be a large-scale Karadžić operation, put British plans on hold. Darroch explained to his bosses on June 17 that "a decision on the Prijedor Three can only sensibly be taken when the timing of any international action against Karadžić and other high profile indictees is clearer."[19]

In the end, the delay was not fatal for Tango. The army command decided the window could be extended into July with no significant risk of operational secrecy being compromised. Meanwhile the news on June 27 that Slavko Dokmanović had been arrested by Polish GROM troops in Croatia added to the sense of urgency. It increased impatience among the military to show that British special forces were equal to the task and it proved that arrests could be performed without a violent Serb response. Moreover, the news from Croatia raised the concern that the Prijedor Three would be spooked into taking flight before they could be arrested. The trio stayed put, unaware their secret indictments had been delivered to British officers in March. But Tango's planners continued to fret that their luck would not hold and the opportunity would evaporate.

On July 4, the UK defense secretary, George Robertson, sent a letter to Blair and Cook to ask their agreement for Operation Tango to go ahead in the period between July 8 and July 17. They both signed off and on July 8, two days before the SAS went into action, at a NATO summit in Madrid, Blair informed Bill Clinton and the NATO secretary-general, Javier Solana. In a nod to the events about to unfold, the summit communiqué on Bosnia and Herzegovina concluded with the ringing words: "There can be no lasting peace without justice."

The FCO had already made preparations to call British and other international aid workers in the Prijedor area immediately after the arrests were made to warn them against any Serb reprisals. As had been the case in Croatia, there were none.

**THE NEXT SUCCESSFUL ARREST OPERATION** did not come for another five months, and its targets were chosen from across Bosnia's ethnic dividing lines. In 1993, President Franjo Tudjman had launched a bid to expand Croatian territory into areas of central Bosnia which were home to both Croats and Muslims. The techniques used were modeled on Milošević's campaigns, sending Bosnian Croat proxies to terrorize big populations and ethnically cleanse large areas quickly.

In Ahmići, a village along the picturesque green valley of the Lašva River, 103 people were killed, including 33 women and children. Most of the suspects indicted for the massacre had surrendered to The Hague by late 1997 under pressure from Zagreb, which in turn had been leaned on by the United States. But by late 1997, there were still two suspects at large: Anto Furundžija, the leader of a particularly brutal paramilitary unit that called itself "the Jokers," and Vlatko Kupreškić, an officer in the main Bosnian Croat force, the Croatian Defense Council (Hrvatsko Vijeće Obrane, or HVO), whose house in Ahmići was allegedly used as a base for the raid on his Muslim neighbors.

This time it was the turn of the Dutch army to carry out the operation. The Netherlands had taken the lead in pushing Washington to set up Operation Amber Star and was an enthusiastic participant in the coordination meetings in The Hague and Stuttgart. The guilt of Srebrenica, which had been under the protection of Dutch soldiers when it fell, hung heavily on the whole country but especially on its defense minister, Joris Voorhoeve, who was personally haunted by the massacre. He fended off calls for his resignation and instead sought redemption for himself and his country by goading NATO member states into pursuing the war criminals.

When debates over Amber Star in Stuttgart became mired in quarrels between the Americans and French, Voorhoeve opted to pursue an independent mission in tandem with the British, creating a joint intelligence cell in the Banja Luka metal factory.

Under overall British command of the sector, the Dutch had been stationed in central Bosnia, along the Lašva Valley, so it made sense for them to go after the Bosnian Croats. Voorhoeve assembled a mixed force of about a hundred men drawn from the amphibious reconnaissance unit of the Dutch marines and army commandos (Korps Commandotroepen, or KCT) under the command of Marine Lieutenant Colonel Patrick Cammaert.[20]

The joint intelligence cell followed the two suspects' routines. Furundžija spent most of his time in bars while Kupreškić tended to stay at home in Ahmići, on the outskirts of Vitez, where the Dutch had their barracks.

The arrests were carried out by a marine unit in the early hours of December 18.[21] The plan was to capture Furundžija as he returned from one of his epic nights out in Vitez. The commandos looked on from concealed positions around his house as he drove back. He seemed to slow down as he neared home but then—to the surprise and dismay of the Dutch—kept going up the street. It appeared he had been tipped off or suspected the ambush.

However, just as the Dutch were contemplating dumping the mission and returning to their barracks, Furundžija's car came creeping back. He was so drunk he had simply failed to recognize his own house the first time around.[22] Once he got out of his car, he was an easy target. He was seized and driven away within seconds.

The capture of Kupreškić was an altogether tougher challenge. Dutch marines had staked out his garden, using pine branches as camouflage, and waited for him to go to bed with his wife. The telephone lines to the house were cut, and just after midnight, the marines mounted an assault, lobbing grenades onto his bedroom balcony and switching on construction lights around the garden with the intention of blinding him. But as the first of the Dutch commandos came through the door, Kupreškić grabbed a Kalashnikov assault rifle from under his bed and opened fire. One of the bullets ricocheted off the rifle butt of a Dutch soldier who fired back, wounding Kupreškić in the chest, arm, and leg.

Kupreškić survived and in 2000 was sentenced by the Hague Tribunal to six years in prison for his alleged role in the Ahmići massacre. But he was acquitted by the ICTY appeal court the next year after new evidence emerged that he had left the Bosnian Croat police a few months before the attack. Furundžija, the local commander of the Jokers, was sentenced in 1998 to ten years in jail for torture and rape. He was released early from a Finnish jail in 2004.

OVER THE COURSE OF 1997, as the Dutch prepared the Ahmići operation, the British were constructing a covert bureaucracy intended to manage a dozen or so planned arrests on their patch in western Bosnia. It was run from the heart of Whitehall, at the cabinet office, by a committee bringing together MI6, special forces officers, the Ministry of Defence, the Foreign Office, and government lawyers.[23] On the ground, operations were run by the MI6-SAS station inside the Banja Luka metal factory, in coordination with the signals intelligence agency, the Government Communications Headquarters (GCHQ), and the army's Intelligence Corps.

It was the first time all these agencies had been fused together in a task, a brand-new mechanism put together after Operation Tango for finding, tracking, and catching fugitives. But its maiden operation was a complete disaster, a farcical case of mistaken identity.

In the summer of 1998, an SAS unit was hunting a pair of identical twins, Predrag and Nenad Banović, who had been prison guards at the Keraterm prison camp, a defunct ceramics factory on the outskirts of Prijedor. On July 23 the reconnaissance team identified two brothers who appeared to fit the description. The SAS soldiers drove up to them at a street corner in the middle of town, bundled them into a minivan, and sped off. It was only when the plane carrying the suspects landed in Valkenburg Naval Air Base near The Hague that it became clear the SAS had taken the wrong twins.

"The minute they brought them down the back stairs of plane, I thought this isn't the Banović twins," a Hague official who was at the airfield said. "The Banović brothers had earrings all the way along their earlobes. I walked up close to these young guys and they didn't even have scars. They had never had anything in their ears. That's when I thought: Oh shit."

The hapless brothers abducted by the SAS, Miroslav and Milan Vučković, were flown back to Prijedor on the same Royal Air Force plane that had brought them to Holland. They were driven home and paid off with a few thousands deutsche marks but they brought a complaint of abuse against the British troops nevertheless. It was a public relations disaster. The real Banović twins fled to Serbia and a postmortem was launched at the Banja Luka metal factory on how such an embarrassing mistake could have been made. The SAS complained, with some justification, that they had acted as instructed on the basis of faulty intelligence. The intelligence officers blamed bad luck.

"What were the statistics on the likelihood of two sets of twins about the same age living on the same street in the same town? It was one in a million or so, and we thought we'd take that risk," an official involved in the operation said.

After the Banović fiasco, tighter criteria were put in place to minimize the chance of any more incidents of mistaken identity. If the photographs in the target folder were out-of-date, new ones would have to be taken. In the case of Dragoljub Prcać, a former guard at another concentration camp outside Prijedor at Omarska, US intelligence had provided only old grainy pictures of the suspect but had a precise description of his car. The SAS quickly found the vehicle, a white Yugo, and drilled a hole in the tire. When the target saw the damage and looked up and down the street for the vandals, he was photographed from a parked car across the road.

The British soldiers used equally low-tech means of tagging the car so Prcać could be easily followed in heavy traffic. There was no radio device stuck to the chassis, no GPS device hidden under the hood. A British soldier simply smashed one of the wing mirrors so it was instantly identifiable.

Several of the suspects lived in a cluster around the south end of Banja Luka, which the British dubbed "Serbian Knights," after a small road in the heart of the district. The name took on a certain aura. In the eyes of the SAS, Serbian Knights was the Bosnian version of Crossmaglen in South Armagh, Northern Ireland — a tightly knit, totally hostile community. So the men of the regiment operated on Ulster rules.

"We had become pretty good at blending in. Your vehicle had to look like theirs. They could tell if you had a small detail out of place, or if a car was too new or old. If the style of VW Golf badge is not quite right, they would know. They would come up and sniff the air and if some small thing seemed out of place they would go back inside," an SAS veteran of the Bosnian manhunt said. "You can't learn to do that sort of thing overnight. You're hunting a very rare beast that knows its environment much better than you do. Experience is hugely valuable. You've got to be a step ahead."

Rather than venture into the grid of two-story houses around Serbian Knights, the SAS planned their snatch operations on the open road leading into the center of Banja Luka, from where it was easier to make a getaway without being boxed in by enraged neighbors. Radoslav Brdjanin, the first Bosnian Serb politician to be arrested, in Operation Brasen in July 1999, was caught in a classic SAS trap, perfected over the years in Northern Ireland. One unmarked army car pulled out in front of his Volkswagen as he was driving to work, while a second pulled up behind. At a nearby junction, a Land Rover drove out of a side road in front of them, and the trap was sprung. The cars ahead stopped suddenly and the car behind rammed the rear of Brdjanin's Volkswagen, bracketing it and preventing it from moving either forward or backward. The SAS called the maneuver the "T-bone." Soldiers jumped out of the Land Rover and broke the Volkswagen's driver-side window with batons, pulling Brdjanin out of his seat and into the street. His wife was left behind in the shattered glass, screaming.

"They were terrified," said a soldier involved in the arrest, but he insisted: "They were relieved in the end that we were British soldiers and not somebody else. They had a very high expectation of violence. He came along meekly."

The biggest prize of the SAS campaign was General Stanislav Galić, who as the wartime commander of the Bosnian Serb Romanija Corps oversaw the daily sniper fire and the shelling of the people of Sarajevo. In one infamous massacre a mortar bomb targeted the Markale, the city's central marketplace, in February 1994, killing sixty shoppers and injuring more than a hundred. Over the whole course of the siege, an estimated eleven thousand of the city's residents were killed. The Hague Tribunal judgment which eventually jailed Galić for twenty years (increased to life imprisonment three years later after a prosecution appeal) ruled that there was little doubt that his targets had been civilians.

*They were attacked while attending funerals, while in ambulances, trams, and buses, and while cycling. They were attacked while tending gardens, or shopping in markets, or clearing rubbish in the city. Children were targeted while playing or walking in the streets. These attacks were mostly carried out in daylight. They were not in response to any military threat. The attackers could for the most part easily tell that their victims were engaged in everyday civilian activities.*[24]

Such was the air of impunity that set in after the Dayton Accords that even a high-profile suspect like Galić continued to hold office — as a "political adviser" to the Bosnian Serb authorities. After Operation Tango and the other early arrests, however, he went to ground, burrowing into the Serbian Knights and moving around in a variety of cars.

The operation to catch him was code-named Sake, and after months of drawing blanks, it went into high gear when GCHQ scored a hit on Galić's mobile phone on the morning of December 15, 1999. The operational log shows that the SAS team confirmed a sighting of him at 9:13 the same morning on the basis of a photograph SFOR had supplied showing him in shirtsleeves in the Republika Srpska National Assembly. The team followed his Daewoo car back to his apartment.

Compared to the long lead-in to the first arrest operations, the timetable for Operation Sake was radically condensed to minimize the chance that Galić would sense a trap and vanish. The day after the initial sighting, an SAS command post was set up in the Banja Luka metal factory, and the drivers who were to take part in his arrest were dispatched from Hereford. An advance party was deployed on December 18 to stake out the roads around Serbian Knights and watch Galić's movements. The snatch was rehearsed in the metal factory the following night, and the next morning before dawn a team was waiting along the road leading from Serbian Knights into Banja Luka.

At 6:39 a.m. on December 20, five days after his phone call had been intercepted, Galić's car emerged from the district at the junction with the main road and turned right toward town. Within seconds, he was caught in a T-bone by two Land Rovers, then a minivan pulled alongside Galić's trapped car. His window was smashed and he was yanked out and hooded before he could reach his gun. By 7:19 a.m., when the hood was pulled off, he was inside the British base at the metal factory. There, a typically unscientific method was used to check that the SAS had the right man.

"He was put in a container in his evidence suit, and his clothes were taken from him," a former SAS officer involved in the arrest recalled. "He was sitting down on the sleeping bags and hadn't said anything. So one of the guys walked in saying 'Cigarettes for General Galić' and he piped up, 'That's me!'"

By 2000, almost every likely suspect in the British zone in western Bosnia either had been arrested or had fled to Serbia. However, the British team at the Banja Luka metal factory did get

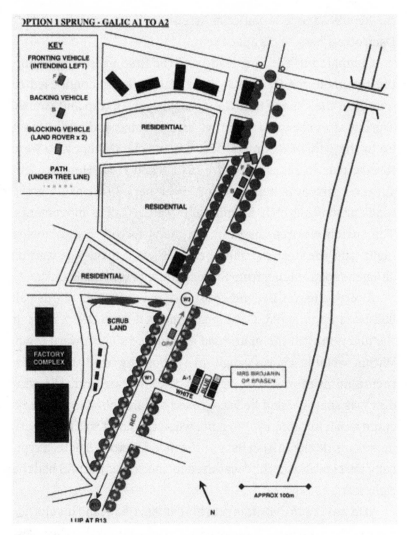

SAS operational plan diagram for the arrest of General Galić.

one last chance to go into action as subcontractors for the American military. For much of the summer of 2001, a US Delta Force detachment based in Sarajevo had been trying to lure one of the suspects on its list out of hiding. The target was Vidoje Blagojević, the former commander of the Bratunac Brigade in the Bosnian Serb army, which had helped in the rounding up of Bosniak men and boys from Srebrenica for execution. He would later be sentenced to fifteen years for complicity to murder.

After the war, Blagojević stayed in the Bosnian Serb army as head of de-mining. Having seen one arrest after another by mid-2001, he became something of a recluse, hardly ever leaving his barracks in Banja Luka. The Delta Force team, however, constructed an elaborate ruse to draw him into the open, involving the creation of a bogus company based in northern Virginia. Through an interpreter, a Delta Force officer telephoned Blagojević to introduce himself as a commercial contractor with access to almost unlimited US aid money, certainly more than his company could use. The "contractor" said he was about to fly to Stuttgart to buy equipment and asked if Blagojević wanted to put anything on his shopping list.

"He bought it hook, line, and sinker," the officer said, but Blagojević was still not willing to travel out of town for a meeting to discuss the purchase in Tuzla, in the American sector. He was prepared, however, to meet closer to home, in Banja Luka. Having spent so much time and money on the sting, the Delta Force team was determined to carry out the arrest even if it meant straying onto British turf.

But the Americans betrayed themselves by the scale of their preparations. So many senior officers flew in from Joint Special Operations Command (JSOC) in Fort Bragg, North Carolina, that the SAS detachment in the Banja Luka metal factory got wind of their presence and guessed what was being planned. The resident SAS colonel called his Delta Force counterpart in Sarajevo and warned him of the high chance of a "blue-on-blue" incident if British forces were not warned. They could easily open fire on the Americans.

JSOC reluctantly agreed to allow the SAS to carry out the arrest, and the senior officers disconsolately flew back home. A meeting was arranged with Blagojević outside Banja Luka's conference center for 10:00 a.m. on August 10, 2001. The American soldiers came with their pickup painted with the livery of the bogus American company and full of the appropriate equipment in case the arrest was aborted and they were forced to maintain their charade. Finally, in the early hours of August 10, the SAS snatch squad flew in from the United Kingdom.

The arrest operation was a reworking of an SAS favorite, the T-bone. As Blagojević drove out of his barracks on the way to the meeting, one car carrying SAS men went ahead of him and a second car fell in behind. As they came to make a left turn into the conference center parking lot, a bread truck emerged in front of them. The car ahead of Blagojević came to a sudden halt and the car behind rammed the back of his car as armed soldiers poured from the bread truck and smashed his window, pulling him out. A Serb police patrol car was parked nearby, and seeing the commotion, the policemen sprang out. But when they spotted the heavily armed soldiers they thought better of it, climbed back in their car, and sat quietly until it was all over.

Like the Americans, the Blair government retained ambitions to capture one of the "big fish," either Karadžić or Ratko Mladić. While these high-value fugitives were in eastern Bosnia, in the French zone, they were out of bounds for the SAS. But with the buildup to the NATO intervention in Kosovo in 1999, it became feasible to carry out raids in Montenegro and even southern Serbia.

In the spring of 1999, MI6 received information that Karadžić was in Montenegro at the same time that the British aircraft carrier HMS *Invincible* was patrolling the Adriatic in support of the Kosovo bombing campaign.

"When we thought we had a bead on Karadžić, Tony Blair signed on to a proposal for running an operation from the aircraft carrier parked offshore," a former senior intelligence official said. "It would have involved a call to the Montenegrin president at the last moment, just to let him know."

However, as often happened in the pursuit of Karadžić, the target failed to materialize on cue, either because he changed plans or because the original tip-off had been bogus.

The British hardly ever contemplated an operation to seize Mladić. The general was believed to be so heavily protected that any such operation would be tantamount to an act of war. Not long after the Kosovo intervention, MI6 got information suggesting that he could be in southern Serbia where British spies had followed a suspected courier to a farmhouse not far from the Kosovo boundary. But the trail went cold. There was no sign of Mladić.

According to a former British intelligence officer, the most frequent method the fugitive general used to transmit messages was to take a mobile phone into a area where there was no signal, put in a SIM card, and enter a text message. A courier would take the SIM card to its intended recipient who would also go to a spot with no mobile signal and put the card into his own phone in order to read the message.

After 2001 and Milošević's fall from power, the focus of MI6's manhunting efforts switched to Belgrade. Working with the Democratic Party camp around Zoran Djindjić, the slim, sharply dressed young liberal leader who helped bring Milošević down in October 2000, British spies were effective in finding some of the war crimes suspects who had earlier eluded the SAS in Bosnia.

However, their efforts to recruit agents inside the support networks around Karadžić and Mladić were a complete failure, and the pursuit of lower-level war crimes fugitives — though initially successful — had unintended, disastrous consequences.

When the SAS snatched the wrong set of twins in Prijedor in 1998, MI6 had taken the blame for the fiasco. Determined to make amends, British spies tracked Predrag and Nenad Banović, the twin guards from the Keraterm concentration camp, into Serbia. In November 2001, they found them selling vegetables at a market in Obrenovac.

The British went to Djindjić and demanded the brothers be arrested. But even though he was the prime minister of Serbia, Djindjić had limited control over the country's security infrastructure, much of which was still loyal to Milošević or to the Yugoslav president, Vojislav Koštunica. Instead, Djindjić called on a paramilitary unit whose defection from the regime at a critical moment in the October 2000 revolution had saved his life and changed the course of the region's history.

Formally known as the police Special Operations Unit, the Red Berets were a lethal amalgam of nationalist militias, elite soldiers, and organized crime. Changing sides at the right time had helped ensure that even after Milošević's fall, they could play both poacher and gamekeeper, running smuggling and prostitution rackets in partnership with the Zemun clan, the most powerful crime organization in the country, while cracking down on their competitors in the name of law enforcement. For them, rounding up a couple of Bosnian Serb hoodlums in Obrenovac as a favor to Djindjić seemed like an everyday errand. The twins were arrested at their vegetable stall on November 8, 2001. But Djindjić had omitted to tell the Red Berets that the Banovićs were war crimes suspects. When the captives were flown to The Hague the next day, the men who had arrested them were apoplectic. Not only were they fiercely opposed to collaboration with a foreign court but many in the ranks had good reason to believe they might one day be indicted for their own wartime acts.

The Red Berets mutinied, blockading one of the main highways into Belgrade. Djindjić negotiated with them, offering one of their officers a top job in the security apparatus. But the prime minister was now aware he could no longer rely on them to keep him in power. He ordered the Serbian Security Information Agency (Bezbednosno-Informativna Agencija, or BIA) to start compiling a dossier on them, collecting evidence of their involvement in war crimes.

"Djindjić told the BIA to make an assessment of the Red Berets' criminal responsibility for wartime acts," said Toma Fila, Milošević's lawyer and a defense counsel for a string of cases in The Hague. "The Red Berets were going to The Hague, so they thought. They felt betrayed. That's why Djindjić was killed."

On March 12, 2002, Djindjić's car drew up outside the main entrance to the Serbian government building in central Belgrade. The previous week he had injured his ankle playing football in a government versus police match, so he mounted the steps uneasily on crutches. He was about to reach the door when shots rang out.

He was hit by a sniper using a Heckler and Koch G3 rifle with a high-caliber bullet that literally blew his heart out his body.[25] The three members of the assassination team had arrived dressed as maintenance men, the gun concealed in a toolbox. One was from the Zemun clan and two were drawn from the Red Berets. The man who pulled the trigger, Zvezdan Jovanović, had been one of the unit's deputy commanders. Boris Tadić, who was Djindjić's deputy in the Democratic Party leadership, believes that the pursuit of war criminals was ultimately the prime minister's death warrant. "I truly believe that was one of the reasons Djindjić, was assassinated," he insisted.[26] They had even called their assassination plot Operation Stop The Hague.[27]

The killers would later tell a special prosecutor that they had done it "because they were patriots and Djindjić was a Hague traitor."[28] But the Red Berets and their accomplices in the Zemun clan had misjudged the national mood. They had previously carried out a string of political assassinations with impunity, and Djindjić, with his sharp suits, his friendliness with Western leaders, and his enthusiasm for reform, was detested by a large section of the Serbian public. But the prime minister proved far more popular in death than he ever was in life. His murder made Serbs realize that they were on the brink of toppling into anarchy. "The bullet that went through Djindjić's heart was aimed directly at the future of democracy in Serbia," Nemanja Mladenovic, a Serbian American political scientist, wrote.[29]

The army and police generals may have distrusted Djindjić and everything he stood for, but they realized that his assassination represented an assault on the state itself. With their assistance, the cabinet launched Operation Sabre, a plan prepared before the prime minister's death, aimed at decapitating the Mafia and eliminating the "deep state," the shadowy security apparatus left over from Milošević's era. More than thirteen thousand people were arrested, including Jovica Stanišić, the former head of Milošević's State Security Service, who had created and run the paramilitary units that had terrorized Croatia, Bosnia, and Kosovo, and his most senior lieutenant, Franko

"Frenki" Simatović. The commander of the Red Berets, Milorad "Legija" Ulemek, was captured along with scores of his men and countless foot soldiers from the allied Zemun clan. Stanišić and Simatović were sent to The Hague. Ulemek was tried in Belgrade. He and Jovanovic were sentenced in 2007 to total of 378 years for Djindjić's assassination.[30]

MI6 played a supportive role in Operation Sabre. British spies had been tracking the movements of many people on the arrest list, and discovered in the wake of the Djindjić assassination that they suddenly had a partner in the shocked Serbian government.

The chief of station in Belgrade was Anthony Monckton, described by a friend as "the classic gentleman spy."[31] He ran Belgrade's cricket club and the UK intelligence operations in Serbia and Montenegro. The son of Gilbert, Viscount Monckton of Brenchley, he was the younger brother of Christopher, a policy adviser to Margaret Thatcher who later aged into an eccentric and outspoken climate change skeptic. Their sister, Rosa, was married to Dominic Lawson, the editor of *The Sunday Telegraph* and a close friend of Princess Diana.

Monckton had made himself an expert on the Red Berets, the Zemun clan, and their tangle of connections inside the government and the security establishment. But his role in helping track down suspects after the Djindjić assassination had made him powerful enemies, particularly in the circle around Koštunica, Djindjić's rival and successor as the Serbian prime minister. The investigation went to the heart of Serbia's deep state and threatened to touch security officials close to Koštunica, who was a nationalist deeply opposed to the involvement of a foreign intelligence service in Serbia's internal affairs. Once Koštunica's policy adviser, Rade Bulatović, was made the chief of the BIA, Monckton was left out in the cold.

On August 11, 2004, the British spy suffered the ultimate indignity for a man of the shadows. His photograph, along with his private contact numbers, were printed on the front page of *Nedeljni Telegraf*, a Sunday newspaper with strong ties to the BIA. The report portrayed him as a master manipulator behind the Djindjić government. He had no choice but to leave.

It was a bitter defeat. MI6 had gambled a substantial share of its resources and manpower on tracking down war crimes suspects, far more than any other Western agency, the CIA included. It had scored some successes, pursuing war crimes suspects who had fled Bosnia and tracking them down in their havens. But the effort came at a heavy price. And in pursuit of the greatest prizes of all, the capture of Karadžić and Mladić, Her Majesty's spies, like so many others, had drawn a blank.

# 4.

# MANHUNTING THE PENTAGON WAY

Everything had to be perfectly lined up like we were
doing the Manhattan Project or something.
It was totally unnecessary to use special forces.
Two fat DC vice cops could have done most of the arrests.
*—former US intelligence officer*

**IN THE SUMMER OF 1997,** the handful of CIA officers who had hitherto been at the core of the American manhunt effort looked on in awe and with a certain unease as military transport planes flew in from Germany, disgorging hundreds of defense intelligence officers and special forces soldiers onto their patch of Bosnia.

Having resisted involvement in the pursuit of war crimes suspects for more than a year, the US Department of Defense had decided that if was going to be done, it was going to be done the Pentagon way, through strength in numbers.

Along with the new arrivals came the military way of doing things, not least the attachment to acronyms and operational code names. The suspects being hunted would henceforward be known as PIFWCs (Persons Indicted for War Crimes, pronounced "pifwicks"). The State Department hated it. David Scheffer, the ambassador at large for war crimes, pronounced it "such a lame term it sounded as if the subject had sprung out of Winnie the Pooh and thus was unworthy of the attention of real soldiers."[1]

The term stuck all the same. Henceforth, the military would be hunting PIFWCs, and that was not the only exercise in rebranding. The CIA station in Tuzla, which was the US headquarters in northern Bosnia, was renamed Razorback for the purposes of the manhunt, and the Sarajevo station became Buckeye. Both were scaled up dramatically in manpower and resources. Each was still run by a CIA head of base, but the deputy post and much of the staffing would come from the Defense Intelligence Agency (DIA) and the special forces.

The surge in the American presence rendered it impossible to maintain a low-key profile. The staff of the CIA station in Sarajevo had been scattered among a variety of anonymous safe houses and had learned to dress and behave like locals, but they now had to accommodate an influx of forty-six DIA personnel, who looked like they all had been shopping in the same store.

"They all had North Face jackets, buzz cuts, and drove Croatian hired cars," complained one former intelligence official in Sarajevo. "They stood out a mile." There was not enough room for all of them, so the overflow were put in Portakabins cordoned off by wire and "keep out" signs at the back of the hotel that served as headquarters for SFOR in the Sarajevo suburb of Ilidža. Told not to ask any questions, their NATO colleagues referred to the new tenants as the GIBs (Guys in Back).

The GIBs came armed with reams of forms to fill in about the mission targets. It was sleuthing by numbers. One of the questions caused the newly arrived intelligence officers a particular headache. They had looked everywhere in Pale, the capital of the Republika Srpska, and could not find the Apostolic Nunciature, the diplomatic mission of the Vatican. The inquiry drew a stunned silence from the CIA case officers in Sarajevo. Pale was not even a one-horse town. Before the war, it had been an alpine village. It did not have a proper town hall, let alone a Nunciature! The Bosnian Serb leader Radovan Karadžić and his officials used a hotel and a car-parts factory for their meetings.

The DIA officers were insistent. On their files, they had Pale down as a capital city. There should be an Apostolic Nunciature somewhere.

"The Serbs are Orthodox, they think the pope is the goddamn antichrist! They have since 1054!" a US intelligence officer finally yelled at them in frustration.

The origins of this preoccupation eventually became clear. It dated to the Panama invasion of 1989 and the capture of the country's dictator, General Manuel Noriega, a former CIA asset whose repression and drug trafficking eventually became so brazen, Washington could no longer turn a blind eye. The operation to capture him was code-named Nifty Package. SEALs blew up Noriega's plane and his personal gunboat, cutting off his routes of escape, but the dictator fled to the Apostolic Nunciature in Panama City, which led to a ten-day siege. To try to flush him out, the US Special Forces Fourth Psychological Operations Group blasted rock music at the papal building at top volume from giant loudspeakers night and day. They made a special point of playing Guns N' Roses songs.

The papal nuncio, Monsignor Jose Sebastian Laboa, told Noriega he could endure the aural assault no longer and threatened to move out and establish an embassy elsewhere, which would leave his unsolicited guest without diplomatic immunity. Noriega had nowhere else to run. He finally gave himself up on January 3, 1990, and was flown by Drug Enforcement

Administration agents to Miami where he stood trial for drug trafficking, racketeering, and money laundering. Operation Nifty Package had left its mark. Ever since then, DIA officers had been required to locate the papal mission in any capital where they operated, lest history repeat itself.

One of the special forces officers involved in the capture of Noriega was given command of the US manhunting effort in Bosnia seven years later. Brigadier General William G. "Jerry" Boykin was an unusual character. He was a fervent evangelical Christian who saw his military career literally as a crusade. He would later get himself into hot water in Washington by declaring he had defeated a Muslim adversary because "I knew that my God was bigger than his. I knew that my God was a real God and his was an idol." In 1997, however, he was only just emerging from a crisis of faith.

After taking part in Nifty Package in Panama, Boykin and an eight-man Delta Force unit were sent on the hunt for the Colombian drug lord Pablo Escobar in July 1992.[2] His next mission would change both his life and US military doctrine. In the operation to arrest two Somali warlords in Mogadishu in October 1993, sixteen Delta Force soldiers under Boykin's command had been killed and Boykin himself was badly wounded. The experience had led him to question his belief in God. To make matters worse, his long-suffering wife, after too many unexplained absences on secret missions, had left him.[3] Boykin was a man trying to climb out of a deep well of despair, but he had all the right credentials for the Bosnia job.

In Bosnia, the theory and practice of manhunting would become a central part of what special forces did for a living, and the lessons learned in the Balkans would be taken on to Afghanistan and Iraq. Before Bosnia, however, the missions in Panama,

Colombia, and Mogadishu represented the sum total of their manhunting operations to date, and Boykin had been involved in all of them.

Starting in mid-1997, Boykin ran the American manhunt in Bosnia from Patch Barracks, the headquarters of US Special Operations Command Europe near Stuttgart, Germany. This was also the headquarters for Operation Amber Star, the five-nation mission to hunt war criminals, which was by then hobbled by the breakdown in the US-French relationship in Bosnia. Instead, Boykin was ordered to focus on a purely American hunt for Karadžić, code-named Green Light. He would also be responsible for tracking down the indicted suspects living in the northern sector of Bosnia under US control, an area that included Han Pijesak, the stronghold of the Bosnian Serb general Ratko Mladić.

To fulfill his mission, Boykin had the pick of America's covert, or "black," special operations units, Delta Force and SEAL Team Six (ST6), many of whom already had Bosnian experience. They had been involved in a covert operation run out of Zagreb to drop arms to the beleaguered Muslim-led Bosnian army in 1995, and later that year, small teams were sent into the Republika Srpska to identify sites of mass graves after the Srebrenica massacre. A special forces soldier who took part in several arrests recalled that his first visit to Bosnia had been at night to explore these sites. Walking through a field he stumbled across "a femur, then a skull, and then a whole body with clothes on, decomposing in the bushes."

The special forces and intelligence teams assigned to Buckeye in Sarajevo were ordered to work solely on the hunt for Karadžić and Mladić, but daunting obstacles were put in their path from the very beginning. First, although the United States and France were no longer chasing the Bosnian Serb leader together, Karadžić was in the French zone. Any serious mission to go after him would require informing the French to avoid a potentially disastrous friendly-fire incident. But in the eyes of the US special forces officers, doing so would immediately compromise the mission.

Second, Operation Green Light was paralyzed by self-imposed constraints and conflicting agendas, which put Boykin in a near-impossible position. He was taking direct orders from General Wesley Clark, the NATO commander in Europe, who had come to the job with a commitment to the aggressive pursuit of the war criminals. But Boykin also had to consult the top US commander in Bosnia, the head of SFOR, General Eric Shinseki, who was far less enthusiastic, fearful that any capture operations would trigger a backlash against his troops.

Meanwhile, at the top of the chain of command, General John Shalikashvili, the chairman of the Joint Chiefs of Staff, still felt he had been bounced into the manhunt mission by an alliance of General Clark and Secretary of State Madeleine Albright, and he remained highly skeptical.

The outcome of this tangle of overlapping authorities and interests was a lead-foot compromise. The United States would enter the pursuit but only with overwhelming force and rigid rules. The shadow of Mogadishu still loomed large. Risk control and strength in numbers were the Pentagon's answers to all problems.

"The ROE [rules of engagement] were bizarre," said a special forces soldier involved in the early operations. "It was not an administration to do anything risky. If you look at Somalia, that was the catalyst for the whole administration mind-set."

The CIA shared the army's cautious worldview. George Tenet told one of his top Balkan hands that the mission had three priorities: "Force protection, force protection, and force protection."

Yet any operation targeting Karadžić or Mladić was inherently risky because both were known to travel everywhere with a protection team.

But there was an even more basic problem. The large-scale deployment of the Pentagon's manhunters in July 1997 coincided with the first NATO arrest operation, Britain's Operation Tango, to capture three mid-level war criminals in Prijedor, and the shooting of one of them, Simo Drljača. The lethal operation, combined with the conspicuous arrival of large numbers of American special forces soldiers, unsurprisingly unnerved the Bosnian Serb leadership in Pale. From that moment on, both Karadžić and Mladić vanished.

The CIA officers in Sarajevo had strenuously opposed the "low-hanging fruit" strategy. They argued it was pointless targeting junior figures in the hope of gathering intelligence that led higher up the chain, if the early arrests led Karadžić and Mladić to change their habits, abandon their usual haunts, and ditch their phones.

Beginning in July 1997, the CIA officers in Sarajevo would be patched through to a 7:30 a.m. daily videoconference with Boykin in Stuttgart, and each morning they would have no sightings to report.

Every phone number either man had ever used was being monitored. Mladić's hideout in the Tito-era nuclear bunker in Han Pijesak was subjected to twenty-four-hour surveillance. Covert television monitors were also set up around the Famos automotive-parts factory where Karadžić had an office, around his family home in Pale, and even at the Montenegrin cemetery where his ancestors were buried. But all the gadgetry was to no avail.

At about this time, Lieutenant Colonel Rick Francona, an Arabic-speaking Middle East expert at the DIA, was told to abandon his Washington-based work on Iran and al-Qaida and to pack his bags for Bosnia. Francona was reluctant. He was not sure he could even find Bosnia on a map and his career had hitherto revolved around the Middle East. But his preferences were irrelevant. Pressure was building in the chain of command, especially from General Clark, for the Americans to get at least one arrest in the bag by the end of the year.[4]

Francona was one of two DIA lieutenant colonels being sent to take up deputy chief positions at Buckeye in Sarajevo and Razorback in Tuzla, the two centers of the US manhunt effort. His first instinct was to go for Sarajevo, the bigger city with the higher-value targets: Karadžić and Mladić. However, having a beer with a DIA friend with experience in Bosnia changed his mind.

According to Francona's friend, Buckeye was a "political nightmare" micromanaged by the embassy, the Sarajevo chief of station, and Clark's staff at NATO headquarters. Most important, there was "little chance of capturing Karadžić and Mladić because of their extensive support networks in the country."[5]

In Tuzla, on the other hand, the Razorback task force could operate as freely as any US soldiers anywhere. They were part of a CIA structure, therefore not subject to military regulations that — in the post-Mogadishu, zero-casualty era — were absurdly stifling and risk-averse. The military officers attached to Razorback were spread around five different safe houses, operating under the cover of an international firm of pollsters and election observers. They were allowed to roam freely across northern Bosnia in civilian clothes, concealing their own choice of weapons. Francona opted for a Beretta pistol rather than the standard-issue Browning because it had a shorter barrel and was easier to hide.[6]

At Razorback, unlike at Buckeye in Sarajevo, there was at least a fighting chance of capturing the five ICTY suspects on the target list. They were not senior enough to have rings of security around them (only one of them had a bodyguard), and they had not yet fled across the border to Serbia.

In the pecking order of Balkan war criminals, they were a mixed bunch. Only one of them could be considered a mass murderer on a Bosnian scale. That was Goran Jelisić, a gangly youth who had been only twenty-three at the time of his crimes in May 1992. He was a prime example of how the war in the former Yugoslavia had put power in the hands of psychopaths by giving them a gun and complete licence to express their most violent instincts.

Before the killing began, Jelisić had been a mechanic and petty criminal, in trouble with the police over drink and drugs, but his Muslim neighbors insisted he came from a "fine family" and was friendly and compassionate toward them before the war and after. Yet over the course of the eighteen days he was posted as a guard at detention camps in the northern town of Brčko, he went on an unrestrained killing spree.

He would introduce himself to new inmates as "the second Adolf" and would select his victims at random, marching them into a courtyard and ordering them to put their head over a grate. Then he would execute them with two bullets in the skull from a Scorpion pistol equipped with a distinctive long silencer. He was ultimately convicted of thirteen murders, but it is likely he killed many more. He boasted to one man in mid-May that he had reached his "eighty-third affair."

It was not just the combination of his clean-shaven youthful appearance and the gruesome nature of his killing spree that would later draw gasps in the Hague courtroom. The "Serb

Adolf" also stood out because he was just half of a sadistic couple. His girlfriend and future wife, Monika Karan-Ilić, played an enthusiastic part in the torture of inmates at a disused warehouse known as Luka camp, when she was just seventeen. In May 2013, she became only the third woman to be convicted of war crimes in the former Yugoslavia when she was sentenced in a Brčko court to four years in prison.[7]

By these macabre standards, the crimes of the other four suspects on Razorback's list were almost banal. Stevan Todorović was the most brutal of the bunch. He had been the police chief in Bosanski Šamac, on the Sava River, which forms Bosnia's northern border with Croatia. He and his three co-accused* ran the crisis staff of Serb activists that seized control of the town at the beginning of the war in April 1992 and arranged for the non-Serbs to be rounded up, detained, and deported. The task was performed with ruthless efficiency. There were more than seventeen thousand Croats and Muslims living in the municipality before the war — over half the population — and by 1995, there were just three hundred left.

One of Todorović's victims was Anto Brandić, a fifty-two-year-old Croat who was kicked and assaulted with truncheons until he died on July 29, 1992. His widow is still looking for his remains. Several other prisoners were beaten savagely under the children's artwork on the walls of the primary school and left with partial paralysis or other injuries. Todorović's preferred form of torture was to humiliate his prisoners by forcing them to perform oral sex on other men in front of a crowd. His victims knew him simply as Monstrum (Monster). He was indicted for war crimes by the ICTY in July 1995, one of the first on its list.

* The mayor of Bosanski Šamac, Blagoje Simić, and Miroslav Tadić and Simo Zarić.

The Razorback plan was to pick up Jelisić, Todorović, and the other three Bosanski Šamac suspects simultaneously before Christmas 1998, with an eye to the New Year deadline laid down by General Clark. To do the job, the joint task force could draw on a mix of seven CIA and DIA case officers, about half of whom spoke Serbo-Croatian, as well as using surveillance specialists, some drawn from a highly secretive army unit known as Torn Victor.*

The US Air Force contributed a handful of intelligence case officers to recruit informants or to approach the targets themselves. Three of them spoke good Serbo-Croatian, and one of them, who was Ukrainian-born, could pass as a Serb.[8] From the US Marine Corps came a technical support team able to fashion hidden video and audio recorders at short notice. The navy contributed intelligence analysts from its black covert unit, ST6, and a couple of other Navy SEALs who helped with intelligence gathering and provided liaison with the ST6 crews tasked with carrying out the arrests.

The first phase was surveillance. The primary safe house in Tuzla sprouted a copse of radio antennae, loosely disguised by a constant array of laundry hanging from the aerials. Francona judged Jelisić to be so unhinged and dangerous that he blocked any close surveillance by his team, relying instead on long-range cameras mounted on Blackhawk helicopters to follow him from a distance.

Luckily for Razorback, Jelisić made it easy, appearing on German television brandishing a pistol and warning that he had thirteen rounds for his would-be NATO captors and one last one for himself. The backdrop to the interview showed he was in the

*At other times it has been called the Intelligence Support Agency, the Activity, or just the Unit.

northern town of Bijeljina, where it was soon discovered he ran a café.

"In the end, it was Jelisić's own arrogance that led us to him," Francona concluded.[9]

When it came to Todorović and the other three suspects in Bosanski Šamac, more old-fashioned intelligence methods sufficed. In their guise as civil contractors, the air force case officers made the rounds of the bars and seedy clubs of postwar northern Bosnia, sipping beer and waiting for an opportunity to bump into their marks.

Todorović was so easy to approach it became a problem all of its own. His idea of hospitality was to invite foreigners he met in bars to visit the town's brothels, necessitating some angst-ridden administrative exchanges between the Razorback base and Patch Barracks in Stuttgart. Guidelines were issued allowing the base's funds to be spent at the brothels on drinks but not on sex.[10]

The plan was simple enough. On a designated day, three eight-man ST6 boat crews* would swoop in and arrest all five suspects at the same time. None of them would have a chance to warn the others. In the German countryside near Stuttgart, the SEALs bought an old Mercedes 190 sedan of the same vintage as Jelisić's and rehearsed stopping it and dragging him out of the car. Meanwhile, other members of the Razorback team repeatedly drove around Bosanski Šamac in locally registered vehicles, watching Todorović and his three accomplices, and compiling dossiers on their targets.

These carefully laid plans, however, were upset by the Pentagon penchant for doing things on a large scale and by the book.

---

* The SEALs' basic unit.

Not content with using the three ST6 boat crews, a total of a hundred special forces operatives were dispatched from Fort Bragg and Stuttgart, arriving in Tuzla at night in early December in a C-17 transport plane.

The giant aircraft taxied to the end of the Tuzla runway and emptied its cargo, hidden inside transport containers like so many Trojan horses. The idea was to stay as concealed as possible so as not to raise the alarm. It was taken as a fact that the Serbs watched the airstrip carefully for early warnings of upcoming NATO operations. But the arrival of such a large contingent of troops was impossible to hide altogether.[11]

The situation got worse. Unable to stay away from the scent of glory, a general and no less than six colonels flew in from US Special Operations Command in Tampa.

"There was a lot of posturing by headquarters units. They flew at least another fifty extra people along with a staff of about thirty to put their signature on the operation that was actually being done by a small group," said a former special forces officer who was in Bosnia at the time.

General Shinseki, the SFOR commander in Sarajevo, insisted on second-guessing the whole operation. Pointing out that the SEALs were on his turf and it was his troops that would bear the brunt of reprisals if anything went wrong, Shinseki interrogated the planners in Patch Barracks by videoconference on every single detail of the plan, down to the number of steps there were inside the door of a suspect's apartment. One of the intelligence officials taking part thought Shinseki was being so nitpicking that he walked out of the videoconference in protest.[12]

Unsurprisingly, all this activity and the abrupt arrival of so much top brass did not escape the notice of the Bosnian Serbs. Francona heard from one of Razorback's informants that the local SDS activists were aware an operation was imminent. The Serbs even knew the date it would take place but not the targets. Francona dispatched teams to see if the five suspects on the Razorback list had fled. They had not, but Shinseki canceled the operation anyway. The hundred SEALs and other special forces flew home, along with the general and six colonels, and the recriminations began.

The Special Forces Command back in Florida reflexively blamed the French. Francona pointed his finger at the generals for sending in a hundred men to detain a handful of suspects. The SEALs blamed the intelligence officers and the CIA blamed the military in general.

"In four months we pretty much located everyone. Razorback did its job, and then we watched special forces fuck it up," a former agency official told me, still furious seventeen years later. "Everything had to be perfectly lined up like we were doing the Manhattan Project or something. It was totally unnecessary to use special forces. Two fat DC vice cops could have done most of the arrests."

Feeling the pressure of General Clark's deadline for the first American arrest before the end of the calendar year, the Razorback team even considered arresting Miroslav Tadić, an obscure suspect. Tadić was on the bottom of the list in terms of prominence and the gravity of his crimes, but at least he could always be found and easily arrested, because he was a paraplegic confined to a wheelchair. Francona concluded that it would be too pathetic. "General Clark's desire to have a 'perp walk' at The Hague in time for the holidays did not make my cut as a good reason," he wrote.[13]

The team decided instead that if they had to choose one target, it should be the worst of the bunch: the Serb Adolf, Goran Jelisić. It would be a pared-down operation compared to the expensive fiasco in December, with a single target and a single ST6 boat crew to carry out the capture.

**ON JANUARY 22, 1998,** Jelisić was walking out of his apartment block in Bjiljena when SEALs jumped out of two vans parked outside the building and bundled him in the back of one of them, speeding off in the direction of Tuzla. Once there, Jelisić sat at a little desk in the Socialist-era ammunition bunker at the end of the Tuzla runway, which for captured war crimes suspects had become an anteroom to The Hague. An FBI officer came in to read him his rights, and then General Shinseki appeared, staring hard at the captive as he informed him he was under SFOR's control, while Jelisić eyed the American's 9mm pistol nervously.[14] Shinseki turned on his heel and walked out leaving the Serb Adolf to be put aboard a C-130 military transport plane to the Netherlands.

But at least the deed had finally been done. After a year of agonizing, and then another year of false starts and gaffes, the United States had arrested its first Balkan war criminal, a young but shockingly sadistic prison-camp guard, who had styled himself as the reincarnation of the Führer.

Reducing the number of targets to one cut down the red tape surrounding the mission. But it permitted Todorović, the Monster of Bosanski Šamac, to flee.[15] It would take another eight months, a great deal of ingenuity, and an operation that crossed both national and legal borders to catch up with him.

Todorović's route as a fugitive led him into the Serbian underworld where the roots of ultranationalism and organized crime met and intertwined. Karadžić took charge of the operation to extract him from Bosnia and sent him to the Lotus strip bar in Belgrade with an introduction to its owner, Boško Radonjić.

Radonjić was the country's most celebrated hoodlum. He was a returned émigré whose life story embodied Yugoslavia's violent past. His father had been a Chetnik who had been executed by Tito's Partisans, bequeathing to the young Boško a pride in all things Serb and an enduring hatred of Communism. As soon as he could, Radonjić fled postwar Yugoslavia and spent most of his adult life in Hell's Kitchen in New York City, where he added an h at the end of his name to make it easier for his new neighbors to pronounce.

In his adopted home, he remained a fervent Serb nationalist but did not let ethnic identity become a barrier to his career, as he climbed the ranks in New York organized crime. Despite his Balkan origins, he rose to become head of the local Irish American mob the Westies, enforcers for the Gambino crime family under John Gotti. The Dapper Don became a friend and mentor.

In Hell's Kitchen, Radonjić played the part of mafioso with self-conscious relish. He wore pinstripe suits over black crewnecks and usually had a huge cigar clenched between his fingers. In his heyday, he owned a $5 million East Side town house and drove a Rolls-Royce Corniche. But the Balkan don always dressed with a distinct Serb twist, a gold eagle ever present on his lapel. He was known as the Yugo — a somewhat inevitable moniker and one that Radonjić hated. Not only was it a particularly unreliable brand of car back home; it was also the abbreviation for the multiethnic Socialist state he had fled. He was a Serb long before he was a Yugoslav.

To the FBI, Radonjić was first of all a criminal. By 1990 they were closing in, taking a particular interest in his role some years earlier in paying off a jury in one of Gotti's murder trials. The increased attention from law enforcement coincided with the long-awaited collapse of Communism in Yugoslavia. So Radonjić returned to Belgrade where he set himself up in the casino business and soon found in the shambling figure of Karadžić a hero, a cause, and a free-spending customer.

Theirs was a symbiotic relationship. Karadžić, a heavy gambler, would take time off from the conflict in Bosnia to patronize Radonjić's casinos in Belgrade and Zlatibor. In return, Radonjić funded the SDS out of his take and served as a cheerleader, once describing the Bosnian Serb leader as "My angel, my saint."[16] Even when Karadžić was deep in hiding, he would almost always take a call from Radonjić. And in return, Radonjić would look after Karadžić's party lieutenants if they needed somewhere to hide.

So when Karadžić sent Todorović to see Radonjić in early 1998, preparations were already in hand. The mobster sent Todorović to work in his casino, called Club Boss, in Zlatibor, an alpine ski resort in the southern Serbian mountains. Accommodation was not a problem. Todorović asked an old friend, an air force colonel, if he could use his holiday cabin just out of town, where he had often stayed before the war.

It would have been the perfect place to hide had Todorović not left a trail of clues, most of them spilling from his mouth when he was drunk. Before leaving Bosanski Šamac, he had waxed lyrical to his newfound American drinking buddies about his prewar vacations in his friend's mountain cabin. When he fled, the Americans set about interrogating his friends to discover its location, which led them to Zlatibor.

A Delta Force team was sent across the border into Yugoslavia. Driving around Zlatibor in locally registered cars, it did not take the team long to spot Todorović. He was a bear of a man, with a high-domed bald crown and a drooping brown mustache. They followed his Volkswagen Golf back to his cabin and set up an observation post in the wooded mountain slopes above him.

The pursuit of Todorović had taken the Delta Force team out of NATO's jurisdiction in Bosnia. In wartime, that was exactly what the unit was trained to do, operate behind enemy lines. But this was peacetime, and that was as far as the US military's lawyers would allow them to stray.

They could look but not touch.

"We had some strange rules. We did very many crossings for recon purposes, but we were not allowed to go do arrests," said a former US serviceman involved in the Todorović operation.

Instead, the CIA in Sarajevo hired a snatch team locally. It was made up initially of four Serbs who had stayed behind in the Bosnian capital when war broke out. Ignoring Karadžić's calls for Serb solidarity, they fought alongside their Muslim and Croat neighbors in the name of a multiethnic state.[17] Now they were asked to resume their service to that cause, but this time for good money.

They were given a straightforward task. Find the fugitive, grab him, and bring him back to Bosnia where he could be arrested legally by peacekeepers from SFOR. As one former US official put it pithily: "We got contractors in, and they did exactly what they were contracted to do."

The job was indeed done with a minimum of fuss on September 27, 1998. The contractors drove up to the cabin and knocked on Todorović's door. When he opened it, they charged in and beat him to the floor with a wooden bat. The fugitive was bound and gagged and dumped in the trunk of a car, a beat-up old red Mercedes. It was driven to the Drina, put on a small barge, and floated across the river into Bosnia, where the captive was arrested by SFOR soldiers.

The Serbs had been asked to deliver Todorović unbound so US soldiers under the SFOR banner could claim to have performed a "proper" arrest. But the snatch team vehemently refused, arguing there was too great a risk their prize would slip away if left untied. They were allowed to do it their way. The car was abandoned on a country road in eastern Bosnia, with Todorović still trussed in the trunk. The Serb mercenaries called their US army contact, telling him: "You will find your packaged ham in the trunk of a red Mercedes near the Drina."[18]

American soldiers pulled Todorović from the car and took him by helicopter to Tuzla, the US garrison in northern Bosnia. He was flown the same day in a military transport plane to The Hague. Officially, he had been arrested by SFOR in the course of their duties, but Todorović's lawyer, Deyan Brashich, a Serb American, filed a motion calling for an evidentiary hearing on the manner of his seizure, on the grounds he had been kidnapped from outside NATO's jurisdiction.

Brashich demanded that Shinseki attend the tribunal in person to testify, claiming to have evidence of NATO money being paid to his client's abductors. To avoid embarrassment, a plea deal was arranged.

"They begged me to do a deal," Brashich claims. "I was torn between getting the best deal for Todorović and wanting to fuck over NATO for their abuse."

In the end, he chose the first option. Todorović pleaded guilty to the first count on the charge sheet, persecution as a crime against humanity, and the defense stopped its calls for a hearing on Todorović's abduction. For its side of the bargain, the prosecution dropped twenty-six other counts against the defendant for deportation, murder, sexual assault, and beatings.

As part of the deal, Todorović made a rather hedged confession in which he claimed to have been taken by surprise by the Serb plan of ethnic cleansing. He insisted it had been carried out by paramilitaries from Serbia, and he was only sorry not to have been able to prevent it.

"[D]uring that year, the year of 1992, I became aware that Croats and Muslims had suffered a great deal, to my great regret," he told the judges. "That is why I feel very profound repentance and remorse. I pray to God every day for forgiveness for my sins."

He was sentenced to ten years and, with time served and early release, got out in June 2005. He went back to Bosanski Šamac where, on September 3, 2006, he was found at home with a bullet in his head and a pistol in his hand.

Eight years later, Brashich remained mystified by his client's sudden death. He had been in touch with Todorović twice a week and says, "Not once did I have any inkling of depression that would point to suicide."

Their last conversation had been about the European Court of Human Rights, where Todorović thought he could get some compensation for his abduction. Brashich told him he was out of his mind. The other issue gnawing at Todorović was his impending appearance as a prosecution witness in the trial of Franko Simatović, a powerful man at the heart of the Yugoslav security apparatus in Belgrade. He had command of the Red Berets paramilitary unit that had been accused of war crimes in Bosnia. In the spring of 1992, according to his lawyer, Todorović had gone to see Simatović in Belgrade, to persuade him to send the Red Berets to Bosanski Šamac.

Could Todorović have been killed to prevent him from revealing what he knew about Belgrade's role? He was not the only witness to the regime's direct participation in Bosnia's ethnic cleansing to die before testifying at the Hague Tribunal. Another was one of Todorović's accomplices in Bosanski Šamac, Slobodan Miljković, known as "Lugar," the Gamekeeper. Miljković was a member of the Serbian Red Berets militia who slaughtered fifteen Croat and Muslim prisoners in Bosanski Šamac, cutting the throat of one old man with a piece of a broken chair. Miljković was indicted by the tribunal but was shot dead in murky circumstances by a Serbian policeman in August 1998 before he could be arrested. He left behind documents with his lawyer to release in the event of his death, which demonstrated how tightly the Yugoslav security apparatus under Milošević controlled the paramilitaries.[19]

Despite the near debacle in court over Todorović's abduction, the CIA used the Serb bounty-hunters once more in April 2000. For all its legal and political risks it was the only way of making arrests inside Serbia, where most of the worst war criminals had sought shelter.

The target this time was Dragan "Jenki" Nikolić, who was living in Smederevo, thirty miles east of Belgrade. Nikolić had a fearsome reputation and a gruesome charge sheet. He had been the commander of the Sušica concentration camp in the northeastern Bosnian town of Vlasenica in 1992. He personally killed nine of the Muslim and Croat detainees. The oldest of his victims was a sixty-year-old man whom he beat and tortured for seven days before the man finally died.

For his beatings, Nikolić used a full toolbox of instruments: wooden bats, iron bars, rubber tubing with lead inside. He separated the female from the male inmates, knowing they would be raped. As he later admitted, many of his victims were "people who used to be friends of mine, whom I used to see over the years in cafés, on sports fields, and playgrounds, with whom I spent summer vacations."[20]

He fled to Smederevo after the war, and lived under a false name a short walk from the Danube. However, the fugitive had been careless about talking on his cell phone. On April 21, 2000, two men appeared at Nikolić's house, identifying themselves as local police, but as soon as he opened the door he was wrestled to the ground, tied up, bundled into the trunk of a waiting car, and driven to the Drina. It was an almost exact copy of the Todorović operation. There were flashlight signals sent across the water and the package was once more put on a boat to be floated to the American soldiers waiting on the Bosnian bank.

Nikolić ended up in The Hague as intended, but not everything went according to plan. Some of the mercenaries who conducted the Nikolić operation were caught and put on trial in Serbia.[21] As details of the abduction surfaced in the Serbian court, Nikolić's lawyers in The Hague argued that such a blatant kidnapping on Serbian territory invalidated the tribunal's jurisdiction over the case. This time, however, the prosecution refused to make a deal, opting to fight the case in court.

Ultimately, in October 2002, the judges sided with the prosecution. They ruled that as the kidnapping was carried out by persons unknown, there was no clear violation of sovereignty. Nikolić had been knocked about somewhat in his journey to Bosnia, which "raised some concerns," but his treatment had not been of an "egregious nature."[22]

The overall sense of the decision, in which the judges drew comparisons with the abduction of Adolf Eichmann by the Israelis from Argentina in May 1960, was that the crimes committed by Nikolić had been of such gravity that the law could allow a certain degree of flexibility when it came to the means used to bring him to justice.

Furthermore, the tribunal noted the arrest took place within an extensive legal framework, including UN Security Council Resolution 827, which first established the court and gave its arrest warrants precedence over local laws. By the time this decision was handed down, however, the war against terror was in full flow and the rendition techniques learned in the Balkans were being employed far and wide in the quest to hunt down al-Qaida members. But although the same skills were required, the terror renditions had little if any of the legal underpinning so delicately sewn together for The Hague operations. Rendition was an unintended legacy. The road that began with the best of motives in the Balkans, ended up in Guantánamo Bay.

# 5.
# THE HUNT IN CROATIA

There will be no Muslim areas except as
a small part of a Croatian state.
—*President Franjo Tudjman*

What was most important to me was that guilt was
individualized, not collective, and that we shouldn't be
constantly held collectively responsible.
—*President Stjepan Mesić*

FOR FRANJO TUDJMAN, the very idea of Croatian war criminals was an oxymoron. As far as he was concerned, the forging of a modern nation-state, free and independent for the first time since the twelfth century, was a self-sanctifying crusade. Blood spilled and excesses committed were justified by the greater good. "Croatian men, who were liberating the country from evil, cannot be held accountable," Croatia's first president declared.[1]

Peter Galbraith, the US ambassador in Zagreb for five years, found it hard even to engage Tudjman on the matter: "I don't think he ever grasped the issue. It didn't fit the narrative of Croatia being the victim. He considered war crimes to be something that the Serbs did. They weren't something that Western, civilized Croats did."[2]

Tudjman was not alone in seeing his people as victims. Most Croats and many in the international community felt the same way, and not without cause. In 1991, Slobodan Milošević had used the Yugoslav National Army (Jugoslavenska Narodna Armija, or JNA) to partition Croatia by force after it declared independence, and oversaw the killing and removal of Croats from areas he claimed to be inherently Serb. Cities were shelled indiscriminately, and mass atrocities were committed in towns like Vukovar.

But Croat forces had also been responsible for significant war crimes in Croatia and in Bosnia, and the ICTY set about investigating three campaigns in particular. The first was the ethnic cleansing of Muslims from Bosnia's Lašva Valley, carried out in the first half of 1993 by local Croat militiamen with Zagreb's backing. The second occurred in September of the same year, when more than a hundred Serb civilians were killed in an offensive on the Medak Pocket, an area near the Croatian town of Gospić, which had also been the site of atrocities. In the third, more than four hundred Serbs were murdered in the immediate aftermath of Operation Storm, the final offensive in 1995 to recapture the Croatian Krajina region from Serb separatists. Most of the victims were elderly villagers unable or unwilling to flee.

Tudjman viewed the tribunal investigation of these atrocities as a personal affront, and for good reason. He had had a hand in all of them.

Tudjman had been a teenage Partisan during the Second World War and a committed Communist after it, rising rapidly to become the youngest general in the JNA. The parallels with Milošević, his Serbian equivalent and nemesis, are striking.

Tudjman's father and stepmother were found dead from gun-shot wounds soon after the war, presumed to have committed suicide, like Milošević's parents. And like Milošević, Tudjman underwent the same ideological transformation from Commu-nist to nationalist, though he had made the journey nearly thirty years earlier and with a great deal more conviction.

He retired from the army in 1961 so he could dedicate him-self to writing history and in the process was caught up in the nationalist revival of the sixties known as the Croatian Spring. He argued that the crimes of the country's Nazi-backed Usta-sha regime during the war had been exaggerated by the Commu-nists as part of their plot to suppress Croatian national identity. His beliefs cost him two spells in jail, and by the time Yugoslavia reached the point of collapse, his seniority, scholarly image, and the patina of time spent behind bars as a political prisoner made him an obvious national leader.

Tudjman was sixty-nine by the time Croatia seized its chance for independence. With his swept-back gray hair, beaked nose, and perpetually vexed expression, he had the general demeanor of a particularly angry owl. He grew ever more imperious in the role of president, outfitting his guards in pseudo-historic liver-ies. And the infatuation with flamboyant uniforms was only one of the ways in which he came to resemble Tito. Like his former Partisan commander, Tudjman saw himself as father, embodi-ment, and architect of the nation, but in his case it was a nation defined by blood and culture, not by ideology.

Determined to forge a state of a size he felt was befitting of Croatia's history and destiny, Tudjman personally orches-trated the ethnic cleansing of Muslims and Serbs in Croat-held areas of Bosnia, a territory he thought undeserving of national status.

In January 1991, sweaty but triumphant in a tennis-club locker room after winning a doubles match, he described his vision of a transformed Yugoslavia to *The Guardian*'s correspondent Ian Traynor:

> *The country, he laughed, would be reorganised along the lines last tried in 1939, when the Serbs and Croats reached a deal to turn Yugoslavia into a Greater Croatia and a Greater Serbia. That, of course, meant wiping Bosnia off the map, with Zagreb and Belgrade slicing it up between them. Bosnia's Muslims might be less than keen on the idea, but Tudjman had nothing but contempt for them, convinced they were just apostate Catholics and cowardly Croats, who would come to thank him eventually.*[3]

Two months after that tennis match, the Croatian leader evidently sought to turn his dream into reality, meeting Milošević in March 1991 at one of Tito's old hunting lodges in northwest Serbia, where the two were reported to have discussed the carving up of Bosnia.[4]

Both leaders later denied there had been an agreement on partition, but there is little doubt it remained Tudjman's cherished goal at least until 1995. At a London banquet in May of that year to mark half a century since the end of the Second World War in Europe, he took out a pen and sketched the division and annihilation of Bosnia on the back of a menu for the benefit of the British Liberal Democrat politician Paddy Ashdown. Ashdown recalled in 1998: "I asked him what about the Muslim areas. He said: 'There will be no Muslim areas except as a small part of a Croatian state.'"[5]

In August 1995, Tudjman took charge of Operation Storm, the offensive against the Serb enclaves in Croatia, as transcripts of planning meetings at his residence in the Brijuni islands would later illustrate.[6] And when mass crimes were committed, the Croatian president did nothing to punish those responsible.* There was no shortage of material to pack Tudjman's burgeoning dossier in The Hague.

It was to nobody's surprise that investigators made little headway when they came to the Croatian capital, Zagreb, seeking help in gathering evidence and finding suspects. Tudjman prohibited Croatian army officers from meeting ICTY investigators.[7] When the Bosnian Croat military commander Tihomir Blaškić was indicted in 1995 for the wartime killing of Bosniak civilians, Tudjman responded by making him inspector general of the Croatian army.

And Tudjman's resistance went beyond such passive-aggressive gestures. Under direction from the president's office, Croatian military intelligence, the Security Information Service (Sigurnosno-Informativna Služba, or SIS), ran an extensive and sophisticated counterintelligence campaign, code-named Operation Hague, to protect indictees and subvert the tribunal's investigations.

As part of the operation, ICTY prosecutors were placed under surveillance and SIS planted a female agent inside the tribunal as an interpreter. Her true status only became apparent after she left The Hague, when she resurfaced as a senior diplomat in a Croatian mission abroad, an extraordinary career progression for a translator who had supposedly been a private citizen. An ICTY investigator also had her hotel room broken into while she was visiting Zagreb and ten disks of evidence collected on the

---

*Prior to 2001, the Croatian legal system prosecuted only one war crimes case against a Croat.

Medak Pocket killings were stolen. And from the outset, potential Croatian witnesses were threatened with reprisals if they cooperated with the tribunal. Those who tried to give evidence in secret often had their identities leaked and found themselves denounced as traitors in the nationalist press.

In 1997, SIS hid an entire archive detailing the wartime operations of the main Croat militia in Bosnia, the Croatian Defense Council (Hrvatsko Vijeće Obrane, or HVO). The box files filled with orders and memos vividly illustrated the direct control exercised by Croatian army headquarters over the ethnic cleansing campaigns.[8] For Tudjman's government it represented a dangerous smoking gun, and orders were given to smuggle it across the Bosnian border into Croatia. There the documents were stuffed into filing cabinets in various defense ministry facilities[9] and eventually transferred to the Zagreb headquarters of the civilian intelligence agency, the Croatian Information Service (Hrvatska Izvještajna Služba, or HIS), which was run by Tudjman's son, Miroslav.

When Carla Del Ponte became the chief prosecutor in 1999, she spent much of her time with Croatian politicians trying in vain to get access to this critical documentary evidence and found the experience vividly reminiscent of her past encounters with the Italian Mafia. She would confront the same *muro di gomma*, the rubber wall.

*They would smile at me. They would shake my hand, make promises, construct a magnificent* muro di gomma, *and then resort to stealth and deception and attack from behind... Instead of attempting to uncover the crimes and bring the perpetrators to justice, as they had promised to do, Tudjman and other Croatian leaders had, for more than three years...*

*mounted an organized, covert effort to obstruct the tribu-*
*nal's work.*[10]

But Tudjman had a weakness. He could ignore Del Ponte and
the ICTY, but he could not ignore the Americans. Military Professional Resources Inc., a US contractor run by ex-generals,
helped train the Croatian army that drove the Serbs out of Croatia and halfway across Bosnia in 1995.[11] But it went deeper than
that. The president conceived his fight for nationhood as a clash
of civilizations with Catholic Croatia as the defender of Western values in a region menaced by the twin shadows of Eastern
Orthodoxy and Islam.[12] Strategically, he believed the new Croatia must look to the West.

"Croatians were always more vulnerable to US pressure
because they wanted to be part of NATO, they wanted to be part
of the EU, they saw themselves as part of the West. And they
were dependent on us for winning the war," Galbraith recalled.[13]

Tudjman eventually bowed to Washington's pressure to
relinquish his dreams of a Greater Croatia and, to the fury of
many in his own party, he unceremoniously disowned the Croatian Republic of Herzeg-Bosnia, the ethnic statelet he had propa-
gated in Bosnia. Then in March 1994, the Croatian government
signed an agreement in Washington by which Bosnia's Muslims
and Croats would unite in a federation to fight the Serbs.

"Tudjman, for all his grumpy nature and parochial thinking,
was obsessed with being part of Euro-Atlanticism," said a Croatian diplomat who worked closely with the president. "It made
him easier to manipulate. But in the end his weakness actually
saved him from all this [Greater Croatia] madness."

Tudjman belatedly realized that awarding Blaškić a top army
job just days after his indictment had been a snub too far. The

gesture had demonstrated contempt for the court and angered Washington. When the US defense secretary, William Perry, arrived in Zagreb in the spring of 1996 threatening to cut military aid, Tudjman quickly got the message. He performed an abrupt about-face. Blaškić was put under house arrest and then, on April 1, was ushered aboard a plane to The Hague.[14]

Blaškić was not alone in being sacrificed. Under American pressure, Tudjman's government also arranged the surrender of a group of ten Croats indicted for mass atrocities in the Lašva Valley. Almost the entire Muslim population of the fertile region had been either slaughtered or driven from their homes. Fourteen Bosniak settlements were pillaged and burned. The worst single massacre was in Ahmići, where more than a hundred Muslim civilians were killed, including thirty-two women and eleven children. Some were burned alive in their homes. Ćazim Ahmić, one of the few survivors, lost fifty members of his extended family in a single day. Compounding the shock was the apparent involvement of some of his Croat neighbors. These were people with whom he had spent a life in intimate contact, celebrating births in each other's homes with brandy and coffee.

"I see no cause, no reason at all for them to attack me, to kill my wife, to kill my mother, to shoot at me. What was the cause? I am not a politician, so I do not know why or how this happened, or what was the reason for all of this," a bewildered, grief-stricken Ahmić told the tribunal.[15]

Like most of the victims in Yugoslavia's violent collapse, the Ahmić family had no idea why they had been chosen for slaughter. How could they possibly know that their existence had become an anomaly on a map drawn up elsewhere? Ethnic cleansing was murder from the top down.

Dario Kordić, the head of the Bosnia and Herzegovina branch of Tudjman's party, the Croatian Democratic Union (Hrvatska Demokratska Zajednica, or HDZ), was the middle man who ensured the leader's ambitions were turned into actions in the heart of Bosnia. The slight, bespectacled former journalist over-saw the Lašva Valley campaign and presided at meetings where the destruction of Ahmići was planned. All the while he was act-ing as a proxy from the Tudjman regime, which looked after him in return. For years after his indictment, he was sheltered in a state-owned Zagreb apartment.[16]

"Kordić was clearly under Croatian state control. They could not pretend they did not know where he was," Galbraith said.[17] The Americans stepped up the cost of defiance. The military training contract was suspended, and US diplomats approached the Council of Europe, a club for European democracies, to block Croatian membership until the Lašva Valley suspects were sur-rendered. They sought to starve Tudjman of the tokens of West-ern approval he craved.

The strategy worked, delivering a large batch of indictees to The Hague at minimal diplomatic cost. Kordić and his nine co-defendants, drawn from the HVO — and in particular from its most brutal unit, the military police counterterrorist platoon known as the Jokers — were handed over in the fall of 1997. Prod-ded by Zagreb's mix of blandishments and threats, they turned up at the Split airport on October 6 in dark business suits, look-ing like a somewhat surly trade delegation, to board a Dutch military flight to The Hague.[18] A crowd of supporters gathered, many of them weeping, to hear Kordić deliver a short valedic-tory speech promising to "return with our heads up high."[19] Several of his codefendants did indeed come back soon, after it became apparent that some of the prosecution cases were hastily assembled and flimsy. But in February 2001, Kordić was sentenced to twenty-five years in prison for crimes against humanity.*

Tudjman sidestepped his own long-delayed appointment in The Hague, dying from stomach cancer in December 1999. In fact, he could have safely lingered a lot longer. It took a full fourteen years before ICTY prosecutors followed the paper trail to the wartime president and his immediate circle. It was not until 2013 that Tudjman was formally judged to have led a "joint criminal enterprise" to persecute, abuse, rape, and kill Muslims and Serbs in the Croatian Republic of Herzeg-Bosnia.[20]

TUDJMAN'S SUCCESSOR AS PRESIDENT, Stjepan "Stipe" Mesić, had been a senior HDZ member and Tudjman's tennis partner. But he had broken with his former master over the war in Bosnia and had even appeared as a confidential prosecution witness in the Blaškić case. "They thought to be a good Croatian, you also had to lie," Mesić said. He argued there was a another, higher form of patriotism: to tell uncomfortable truths about one's country. "What was most important to me was that guilt was individualized, not collective, and that we shouldn't be constantly held collectively responsible."[21]

The political realities in Croatia were less straightforward. The reach of Tudjman's "deep state" — the elaborate, entrenched security apparatus he left behind — gradually became evident after the old autocrat's death. Mesić learned the secrets

---

* As for the rest of the Lašva Valley Ten, two had their charges dropped before going to trial, four were eventually acquitted, and the remaining three — Mario Čerkez, Drago Josipović, and Vladimir Šantić — received sentences ranging from six to eighteen years.

of Operation Hague and stopped it, ordering Croatia's spy network home from the Netherlands. "I saw they weren't there to cooperate with the tribunal but were there to obstruct its work," he said.

The Croatian deep state even reached into the president's own office. There was a phone on Mesić's desk which he was told was a hot line established between Tudjman and Milošević at the beginning of 1991. Nine years later, Tudjman was dead but Milošević was still at the other end of the line, clinging to power in Belgrade. But Mesić did not know how to call him. "I was told the telephone was operated by a certain code which was secret and the secretaries didn't know it. Only Tudjman knew the code."

The father of modern Croatia had taken the secret to his grave. But he had left behind a room filled with eight hundred cassettes and fourteen thousand pages of transcripts of his secretly recorded conversations. Like Richard Nixon, the old man had taped everything. On assuming office, Mesić ordered the recording to cease except for some official meetings, but he could never be sure the intelligence agencies had removed all the bugs. The first time Del Ponte came to visit the new president, on April 4, 2000, Mesić warned her that whatever they said was probably being listened to by his intelligence services, over which the new president exercised only partial control.[22]

Mesić swiftly handed the Tudjman tapes over to the ICTY,[23] but the HVO archive that was so critical in telling the story of the war in central and southern Bosnia remained in the hands of the intelligence agencies. To get hold of it, Del Ponte needed to enlist the support of the new prime minister, Ivica Račan.

Račan, a former Communist turned social democrat, was in a more complex position than the president. He was trying to juggle a coalition of six parties, not all of which were in favor of working with the ICTY. It did not help that the intelligence agencies themselves were divided. Professor Ozren Žunec, the new HIS chief, was prepared to let ICTY investigators view the HVO archive, but there were plenty of intelligence officers still loyal to Franjo and Miroslav Tudjman who were determined to stop them.

The ensuing battle over the HVO papers was ultimately a struggle for control over the new Croatia's founding myth. Tudjman loyalists sought to suppress any suggestion that the Homeland War had been tainted by atrocities. For their part, Mesić and Račan naturally had every interest in exposing Tudjman's hubris and excesses.

The tribunal investigators found themselves caught in the cross fire. On May 2, 2000, they were escorted by HIS agents to a nondescript house in Samobor, a small picturesque town west of Zagreb. There, over the course of the next few days, documents from the elusive HVO trove were discreetly delivered, a few boxes at a time. The ICTY analysts were allowed to pore over them and ask for photocopies of designated pages. But they were not allowed to take them away or step outside the Samobor safe house, even for a sandwich or a breath of air, for fear they would be spotted by pro-Tudjman intelligence agents.[24]

For all this discretion, the secret document trawl in Samobor was discovered and leaked by the Tudjmanite faction inside HIS, three weeks after it began. A photograph of the safe house was splashed across the front page of a Zagreb newspaper along with an article describing the smuggling operation in detail. The covert spy-versus-spy battle had broken into the open. The Račan government surrounded the HIS headquarters in Zagreb with heavily armed special police to prevent the archive being destroyed by renegade intelligence officials, and for some hours the struggle over the nation's collective memory became a stand-off in the streets of the capital. Ultimately, the show of force worked. The hardliners backed down and were purged from the intelligence agencies, which were reformed and restructured. The HVO archive was transferred to the state archives and made permanently accessible to the tribunal.[25]

In its relations with the ICTY, Croatia faced the same para-dox as Serbia. The tribunal put far more pressure on the elected liberal governments in Zagreb and Belgrade than on the authoritarian regimes that had preceded them and had led their nations into war. It was unfair but understandable. As democratic governments handed over more documentary evidence, the tribunal issued more indictments and the governments were asked to catch or surrender more defendants, incurring greater wrath from the nationalists. In Serbia, the backlash led to the assassination of the reformist prime minister Zoran Djindjić. In Croatia, it came close to toppling the first post-Tudjman government.

As rumors spread in early 2001 that Mirko Norac, Croatia's youngest general, would be sent to The Hague for his involvement in the killing of civilians in Gospić, war veterans took to the streets in protest. More than one hundred thousand people gathered in Split on February 11 under the slogan "We are all Mirko Norac." The governing coalition split over the crisis and would almost certainly have fallen had Del Ponte not granted Prime Minister Račan an eleventh-hour reprieve, allowing Norac to stay in Croatia and face homegrown justice. The trial, in the port city of Rijeka, marked the first time Croatian soldiers were convicted of war crimes in their own country. In March 2003, Norac was sentenced to twelve years in prison.

The government in Zagreb argued the Norac trial demonstrated Croatia was quite capable of holding its own generals to account. The Americans, British, and Del Ponte were unconvinced. They saw the trial in Rijeka as an exception, in which a particularly brave judge, a woman named Ika Sarić, had shrugged off death threats and abuse. There were few if any other judges like her.[26]

Del Ponte was insistent that every other senior Croat on her list would face justice in The Hague, and in September 2002, she presented an indictment for Janko Bobetko, Croatia's highest-ranking wartime commander. Bobetko had been Tudjman's favorite general and was the army's chief of staff during the Medak Pocket killings, for which Del Ponte deemed he had full command responsibility. Although the elderly warhorse, who was in his eighties, had largely been a figurehead, he had presented himself in his memoirs as a hands-on commander, with control of his troops and their operations. He had incriminated himself.

On hearing the news of an impending indictment, Račan put his head in his hands in despair. "If I cooperate in this, my government will fall. Do you want Croatia's government to fall?" he pleaded with the ICTY prosecutor. Del Ponte was unmoved. "If I start taking into account your political situation, I will never complete my work," she told the prime minister.[27]

Like Tudjman, Bobetko was an old Partisan, a whale of a man who had acquired the aura of nationalist icon. Even as his health began to fail, he vowed to make a last stand at home, sprawled on his favorite armchair, his gun at his feet and guarded by Croatian special forces soldiers. The only way his enemies would get him, Bobetko told reporters, was if "they carry me out of my house dead."[28]

The blazing last stand never happened because the government never dared arrest him. But on April 29, 2003, Bobetko spared the country's rulers from their dilemma. He died at home at the age of eighty-four, his lungs filling with fluid and his heart failing, defiant to the end.

Bobetko's death, however, did not get the Račan government off the hook. Far from it. The failure to arrest him made Del Ponte all the more determined to round up the remaining Croats on her list, and she made it clear that Croatia's access to international capital and its progress toward membership in the European Union hung in the balance.

Račan was in a crushing bind. More than three years after Tudjman's death, the prime minister was still unsure whether he could trust Croatia's intelligence agencies in the hunt for fugitives, yet he had to show the electorate he was making progress along the road to EU membership. He had to take action.

First, he invited MI6 to send its own team to track the fugitives. The prime minister met two senior officials from the spy agency at the beginning of 2003 and, according to a Croatian diplomat present at the meeting, "Račan's argument was: If you think you can do better, come in and help us."[29] The British were chosen in part to convince them that the government was trying its best. Moreover, MI6 had a recent history of cooperation with the Croatian police—a joint effort to stop the diehards of the self-styled Real Irish Republican Army from buying weapons from Croatian and Bosnian Croat gangs. A rocket fired at the MI6 headquarters on the Thames at Vauxhall in a brazen 2000 attack had found its way to London from Croatia.

The second part of the Račan plan was to create a team of Croatian untouchables, highly motivated and insulated from the rest of the police force, whose sole duty would be to track down war criminals. It was placed under the personal command of the chief of police, Ranko Ostojić, who had worked with the British on the

IRA arms dossier. He took the best young officers from the organized crime department and swore them to secrecy about their task. They approached the hunt the same way they had battled the Croatian mob, relying heavily on a network of informants in the underworld where gangsters and war criminals overlapped. By March 2003, the unit had found its first suspect.

His name was Ivica Rajić, a former HVO commander from central Bosnia who was wanted by The Hague for a string of war crimes, including the liquidation of Stupni Do, a Bosniak village in the highlands some twenty miles north of Sarajevo. In reprisal for a Bosnian army attack, Rajić's men went into the village on October 23, 1993, and killed everyone they could find: thirty-seven Muslim men, women, and children. Only six of them were later deemed to have been combatants. When they were finished, the HVO unit destroyed the village. The remains of seven members of the same family — two men, three women, and two children, aged two and three — were found burned to death inside a shed.

Ten years after Stupni Do, and eight years after he was indicted for his crimes, Rajić was still at large. He was living near Split under a succession of assumed names, first Viktor Andrić and then Jakov Kovač, with matching identity documents provided by Croatian military intelligence. But one day in March, he was spotted on the street by someone from his hometown in Bosnia, and the message rattled along the grapevine of Split's crooks and informers until it reached Ostojić's war crimes unit.

Rajić's presence on the Croatian coast should not have come as a surprise. His wife worked for the Croatian Defense Ministry, which had taken good care of her, providing her with an apartment in Split, a job managing an army-owned hotel, and two businesses: a café and a shoe shop. The police team staked out all these locations, watching everyone going in or out. For the first few days there was no sign of their quarry, but then one of the watchers noticed a man delivering cylinders of cooking gas to the café. He shuffled along pushing his trolley of cylinders and carried them in through the back door. He looked every inch a humble tradesman and the policeman would have thought no more about him had he not spotted the same man a couple of days later outside Mrs. Rajić's apartment block.

The man was older and grayer, but he bore a distinct resemblance to wartime photographs of Rajić. Yet the police team could not be certain. Rajić's Croatian military records, including his fingerprints, had unaccountably disappeared from the Zagreb archives, along with any other official record he had ever existed.[30] The problem was solved with the help of two investigators working closely with Ostojić: Christopher Looms, a former British intelligence officer, and Oscar Vera, a US State Department official serving as an adviser to the SFOR commander in Bosnia. They recalled that Rajić had been a JNA officer before leaving to join the HVO. There was a copy of that database in Belgrade, and the Hague investigators arranged for Rajić's prints to be shared with Ostojić's team in Zagreb.

After a couple of weeks of surveillance, Ostojić's special unit had realized that Rajić's life had its own routine. He lived outside Split during the week in a little seaside town across the bay called Kaštela but would pay weekend visits to his wife and daughter in Split. His wife would give him a lift back home but the family took elaborate precautions to avoid him being spotted along the way. Before leaving, his daughter would mount a motor scooter and ride around the block a few times to satisfy herself there was no police presence. The suspect's wife would then walk out of the front door of the apartment and get her car while he would leave by the back and amble to a traffic light at a nearby street corner. When his wife's car stopped at the light, he would jump in and duck down until they reached Kaštela.

Once the team had worked all this out, grabbing the suspect was relatively straightforward. It was done with the brutally simple methods perfected by the SAS in Bosnia. When he was being driven back to Kaštela in his wife's car on the afternoon of April 5, an unmarked police car drove in front of them at the same instant a minibus full of members of Ostojić's unit pulled alongside. He was yanked out and driven away.

The more complicated part of operation involved what came next. Ostojić could not count on anyone but his own handpicked team. After all, Rajić had been successfully hidden for six years, furnished with false papers, and had all his records removed from the archives. He clearly had protection in high places in military and intelligence circles.

"We didn't know if Rajić had support standing by," Ostojić said. "We didn't know if someone would try to take revenge on us."[31] The police chief could never be sure his men had not been watched while they were observing Rajić. All he could do was take precautions. He had six teams of five men deployed that day, and no one team knew about the others. Two of these teams were posted along the road out of Split to Bosnia in case Rajić's former HVO comrades should try to rescue him. Two other teams were on the roads running northwest and southeast along the coast to block an escape by sea. A fifth was on standby near the arrest point lest the snatch squad in the minibus come under attack.

Once the suspect had been seized, the minibus did not go to Split airport as that was where Rajić's protectors would look first. Nor did it drive all the way back to Zagreb. That would have taken many hours, more than enough time to arrange an ambush along the road. Instead, the policemen drove thirty miles up the coast to the town of Benkovac where a helicopter picked up Rajić and his captors and flew them to the Zagreb airport. He was transferred on June 24, 2003, to The Hague, where he eventually pleaded guilty to "grave breaches of the Geneva Conventions" and became a cooperative witness for the tribunal. In May 2006, he was sentenced to twelve years in prison.

The Rajić arrest had come as a shock to Croatia's intelligence agencies, who had no inkling an operation had been under way to catch him. Determined not to be blindsided again, Franjo Turek, the head of Protuobavještajna Agencija, Croatia's counterintelligence agency, ordered Ostojić to be put under surveillance. And Turek soon discovered that the police officer was in close contact with MI6 officials in the British embassy in Zagreb. In Turek's eyes, it had all the hallmarks of a plot against Croatia.

At the end of 2003, Ostojić lost his political backing and Turek seized his chance. The Račan coalition finally collapsed. Ivo Sanader, the leader of HDZ, Tudjman's old party, became prime minister after campaigning on a promise not to surrender any more of Croatia's generals to The Hague. On Turek's prompting, Sanader promptly fired Ostojić along with all the members of the special war crimes unit. Mesić was still president, but even he sided with Turek, who had strong connections with key members of the presidential staff.

The abrupt firing was a brutal betrayal of Ostojić, whose sin was to have been too effective in his implementation of official government policy to cooperate with The Hague. It also marked a reversion to the war crimes policy of the Tudjman era. Sanader would not condone any special police effort to catch the men on the Hague list, but he would facilitate the surrender of suspects willing to accept financial incentives from the state. In fact, for all his patriotic posturing during the election, Sanader was soon handing over suspects at a faster rate than his Social Democrat predecessor. The cooperation did not go unrewarded. In June 2004, Croatia was formally recognized as a candidate for EU accession.

However, one significant Croatian suspect was still at large, and the longer he eluded his pursuers, the more popular he became. His name was General Ante Gotovina, and he was fast becoming the government's biggest headache, the longest shadow over its European aspirations.

Born on the Adriatic island of Pašman, Gotovina had run away to sea at sixteen and jumped ship in Marseille to join the French Foreign Legion in 1973. He served under the nom de guerre Ivan Grabovac before retiring in 1978 with the rank of master corporal. His five years in the legion had earned him French citizenship and he stayed in France, trading on his military contacts. Along with some of his former comrades, he provided the security at rallies and marches staged by the French far right.

An arrest warrant was issued in 1981 against him and a fellow legionnaire for robbing a wealthy French safe manufacturer Henri Salomon, but he would later claim to have been framed by the security apparatus around the Socialist president François Mitterrand, who was obsessed with the threat of a right-wing coup. Gotovina fled France for Africa and then Latin America where he took a variety of security jobs, training right-wing paramilitaries in Argentina, Guatemala, and Colombia. After a few years, Gotovina returned to France under a pseudonym but was arrested and sentenced in 1986 to five years for the Salomon robbery. The newspaper *Le Monde Diplomatique* reported he was released after just a year, "in circumstances that remain obscure."[32] In 1991, Gotovina went home for the first time in two decades to a newly independent homeland where his past transgressions would be forgotten.

He was ideally suited to his destiny as national idol. He was young, fit, and — despite a prominent beak of a nose — photogenic in a uniform. He was revered for the same reason he was later indicted in The Hague: for his command of the southern front during Croatia's triumphant Operation Storm to recapture the Krajina in 1995. That made him a hero of the Homeland War in the eyes of most of the Croatian public. For Del Ponte that made him ultimately responsible for the killing of Serb civilians in his sector.

Tribunal investigators had asked to interview him in 1998 about the deaths of civilians who had been captured by his soldiers in areas of the Krajina, but Tudjman had forbidden any contact with the court. Finally, in June 2001, prosecutors delivered a sealed indictment to Zagreb naming the general. Yet the Račan government — still shaken by the Norac experience — waited a month before issuing an arrest warrant, and in that time Gotovina had been tipped off and vanished.[33] His lawyers would later argue that his experience of being set up in France for political reasons convinced him that he would not be given a fair trial in The Hague.

Del Ponte was determined to block Croatia's EU membership until Gotovina was caught, and she was given unwavering support from London. For MI6, catching Gotovina became something of an obsession. The agency had little involvement in the Rajić operation, having decided to focus on the fugitive general, and the longer Gotovina evaded Britain's spies, the more determined they were to catch him. The pursuit was code-named Operation Cash, a pun on their suspect's name: *Gotovina* means "cash" in Croatian.[34]

Operation Cash focused its efforts on the port city of Zadar, near Gotovina's Adriatic birthplace on the island of Pašman. British intelligence tapped the phones of ultranationalist leaders and mob bosses in the area, two groups with a great deal of overlap. In particular, the British spies kept tabs on Hrvoje Petrač, a prominent mobster who reportedly helped finance Gotovina's early years in hiding. But Operation Cash did not lead to the prize. The British agents felt that every time they were making progress, they ran into obstruction from Turek. MI6 had seen Turek as its primary adversary ever since he had helped engineer Ostojić's dismissal at the beginning of the year. On top of that, he was refusing to maintain his agency's close relationship with British intelligence. To MI6 he was at best a nuisance and at worst complicit in sabotaging the hunt for Gotovina. He had to be unseated.

After a concerted diplomatic campaign, the British succeeded in persuading Sanader to fire Turek in the summer of 2004. But it proved an empty victory, and a costly one. On August 26, the Croatian weekly *Nacional* published an exposé of MI6 operations, portraying them as a violation of national sovereignty. The headline read "British Spies at Large in Croatia," and the article claimed MI6 had "for months been unhindered in its activities across the country, wiretapping and monitoring Croatian citizens it considers of interest for security reasons."[35]

Turek denied responsibility for the leak, but the magazine had clearly gotten hold of the Gotovina file somehow. *Nacional* published pictures of Looms and Vera, and surreptitious photographs of their meetings with Gordan Malić, one of Croatia's best-known investigative journalists. Malić had published a series of articles in a rival magazine, *Globus*, about organized crime and war criminal networks, and the two Western investigators had sought to draw on his expertise. But *Nacional* spun these encounters to look like a British-run spy ring. For the next three years, Malić was obliged to live under police protection.

*Nacional* also printed a photograph of one of the blue mobile interception vans it claimed MI6 had imported to conduct surveillance. The leak, coming less than two weeks after Anthony Monckton, the head MI6 officer in Serbia, had been outed by a Belgrade newspaper, completed a woeful month for British intelligence.* Operation Cash was definitely over and MI6 withdrew its regional operations to Hungary to lick its wounds.

"In the end, they believed they had been set up. They were pretty grumpy and never forgave us" said a Croatian official who had been involved in liaison with the British spy agency.

MI6 were even grumpier when a proposal it sent to its Croatian counterparts in February 2005 designed to help get relations back on track was immediately leaked to *Nacional*. It included a list of senior Croatian officials the British wanted prosecuted for allegedly protecting Gotovina. It was a major embarrassment for the British, but it was a disaster for the Sanader government. The EU membership talks slated to start in mid-March 2005 were abruptly canceled by Brussels, and Del Ponte heaped contempt on Zagreb's efforts in her report to the UN Security Council in June 2005.[36]

Gotovina's downfall finally came in a manner that had become familiar to the tribunal's manhunters—a close relation using the wrong phone. In Gotovina's case, it was his wife, Dunja, the first female colonel in the Croatian army. At the end of September 2005, she had forgotten to change SIM cards

*See chapter 3.

before phoning her husband. The Croatian authorities were able to track the call to the Canary Islands and listen to the voice at the other end of the line. It undoubtedly belonged to the fugitive general. Sanader excitedly summoned Del Ponte to Zagreb and played her a recording. "She will never get me," the general was heard boasting to his wife.[37]

Yet as soon as the tribunal began to celebrate the prospect of the capture of one of its most wanted fugitives, the trail suddenly went cold. There were no more calls from Gotovina's Canary Islands number, and when approached for help by the ICTY, Spanish intelligence was uncooperative. Del Ponte began to fear that the general may have been tipped off and fled to sea.

The despair was lifted by a simple piece of background reading. Florence Hartmann, Del Ponte's spokeswoman, picked up a Croatian biography of Gotovina which described an interlude spent on the island of Tenerife during his time as a French legionnaire. He had fished, sailed, and had a romance with a local schoolteacher who taught him Spanish.

This time the prosecutors did not go to Spain's intelligence service but to the police, who took the simple, shoe-leather approach. Officers went from one hotel to another on Tenerife, looking through registration cards. At the Hotel Bitacora, on the south end of the island, they came across the name of Kristian Horvat. Gotovina had used the same alias before and its existence had even been in the press, but he had run out of passports and aliases. For him, Tenerife was the end of the trail.[38]

Gotovina was arrested on December 7, 2005, in a near-empty hotel restaurant where he was sharing a bottle of red wine with an unidentified woman companion. The fifty-year-old fugitive was wearing a crisp white shirt and a tailored charcoal jacket for the occasion. The scene led Del Ponte to wonder whether his wife's use of the wrong SIM card really had been a mistake, musing "perhaps after so many years with her husband on the run, she had done it purposely."[39] Gotovina's lawyers insisted the woman was a family friend and that they were accompanied at the hotel by a male acquaintance, an Australian Croat named Jozo Grgić.

In Gotovina's room, the Spanish police found a laptop, €15,000 in cash, and two passports, a Croatian one under the name of Kristian Horvat and a French document in his own name. Del Ponte had been convinced that the fugitive was being sheltered in Franciscan monasteries in Croatia and had taken her suspicions as far as the Vatican.* But the well-thumbed travel documents suggested monasteries were not Gotovina's style. The passports were filled with recent stamps from Tahiti, Argentina, China, Chile, Russia, and the Czech Republic. He had spent his four years at liberty touring the globe, becoming, according to one Croatian official, a sophisticated man of the world who "read the *Financial Times*, *Le Monde*, as well as being a talented painter with a solid knowledge of art history."

He had also acquired even more powerful friends than the Franciscans. The French security establishment believed in protecting its own. Gotovina's French passport, earned by his five years in the legion, was renewed in 2001, weeks before he was indicted.

The extent of Gotovina's enduring French links became clear with the publication in 2009 of notebooks kept by France's most senior spymaster, Philippe Rondot, who detailed a history of contacts between the former legionnaire and French intelligence agents involved in secretly supplying weapons to the

---

* For Del Ponte's dealings with the Vatican, see chapter 7.

Croatian war effort. In March 2005, Rondot recorded that the general had "let me know that he will never reveal any ties that may have existed between him and us during the war." The following month, after a meeting with France's defense minister, Michèle Alliot-Marie (known by her initials, MAM), Rondot noted his "refusal to capture General Gotovina by deception: MAM agrees."[40]

The Hague investigators came to believe Gotovina's jet--setting lifestyle on the run reflected the cosmopolitan nature of the legionnaire network hiding and supporting him with the tacit consent of the French government.

The pursuit and capture of Gotovina was a demonstration of the tribunal's tenacity in tracking down fugitives, no matter where in the world they sought refuge. His eventual trial, however, descended into farce. In 2011, he was sentenced to twenty-four years in prison for his command role during Operation Storm. Nineteen months later, largely on the same evidence, he was acquitted by the tribunal's appeal court, which had changed its standards for assessing command responsibility. The majority decision on appeal was one of most dramatic about-faces in the tribunal's history, and it triggered a public fight among the judges. Whether it had been Gotovina's acquittal or the seven years he spent in jail, both sides could at least agree there had been a miscarriage. The unique achievement of the Hague manhunt was to ensure that every fugitive on the indicted list faced the tribunal. But once they got there, there was no guarantee of justice.

# 6.
# GORILLAS AND SPIKES

We had the tradecraft, we had the equipment and training,
but we didn't have an understanding of the terrain.
—*US Special Operations Forces senior officer*

**BY THE SIDE OF A BOSNIAN MOUNTAIN ROAD** not far from the Serbian border, on a miserably wet night in early 1998, two dozen American special operations soldiers lay in wait for Radovan Karadžić with what promised to be one of the stranger ambush plans in military history. It involved a ten-foot length of rubber tire, titanium spikes, an improvised concussion grenade, and a gorilla suit.

The suit had not come cheap. It was a full-body costume with lifelike fur and it had been shipped by a combination of commercial and military flights from the United States to Bosnia within twenty-four hours of being ordered. The 1st Special Forces Operational Detachment Delta—generally called Delta Force—pride themselves not only on their fitness, resilience, and skills but also on their ability to think outside the box. The gorilla suit was their out-of-the-box solution to the vexing problem of how to catch Karadžić.[1]

The Delta Force team leader on the ground, Pete Blaber, was tipped off by a Bosnian Serb source that Karadžić would be crossing the Serbian border near the town of Loznica for meetings in and around Pale. According to the source, there was a forty-eight-hour window in which this trip would take place, and Blaber only had thirty-six hours to prepare before the window opened.

The tip was considered firm enough for Blaber to travel the same day from the Delta base at Fort Bragg, North Carolina, to the US garrison at Tuzla in northern Bosnia. He touched down at night with ten other Delta Force soldiers and they drove straight to a safe house, a stone cottage overlooking the town, where twenty members of his unit had already set up camp. He recalls relishing the moment of arrival at two o'clock in the morning: "As I drove up to the darkened cottage with headlights turned off and night vision goggles turned on, I took a second to appreciate the moment. *This is why I joined Delta — disguises, deception, and diversions*, I thought, smiling with self-actualized satisfaction."[2]

The promising aspect of the plan was that Karadžić was expected to follow a mostly deserted mountain route on his way to Pale, offering plenty of opportunities for ambush. The more worrying element was that the Bosnian Serb leader would be accompanied by four well-trained, experienced bodyguards, and possibly his daughter, Sonja. A shootout in which there was a chance Karadžić, his daughter, and American soldiers could get killed was unacceptable to Washington.

The challenge was to minimize the risks while maximizing the chances of success. Part of the solution was an ingenious new weapon developed in Austria for blowing the doors off buildings from a distance. It was a sausage-shaped charge on the end of a twelve-inch stick that could be shoved down the barrel of a rifle and fired. It produced no shrapnel, just a wave of pressure. So with a bit of improvisation, it could be used to concuss the occupants of a car without killing them. A member of Blaber's team who went by the nickname "Predator" had taken the liberty of testing the grenade on some of the unit's cars, driven by a handful of fresh recruits keen or gullible enough to volunteer. It worked. The rookies were concussed but survived.

However, this stun grenade would only work if it hit the target car's side door panel directly, and to be sure of that, the car had to be moving no faster than twenty miles per hour. How to achieve that? A hairpin bend would help but some other distraction was needed to gain a few vital extra seconds to fire the round. Against veteran bodyguards, the usual tricks of the trade, the broken-down car or the bogus police checkpoint, would only heighten their sense of danger. It had to be something that thoroughly confused them. During an all-night brainstorming session, one of the Delta team remembered a 1980 spoof horror movie called *Motel Hell*, in which a pair of killers use cardboard cows to stop victims on the road. From there, it was but a small leap of imagination to arrive at a gorilla suit.

Blade, the soldier who had the idea, put it this way: "The shock of seeing a freaking gorilla walking down the road, along with their uncontrollable curiosity to understand what the hell it's doing in the middle of Bosnia, may just make them pause a couple of more seconds, which ought to create the perfect conditions for us to fire the rounds and conduct the capture."[3]

It was cognitive dissonance, deployed as a weapon. And just in case it failed to work, the Delta Force team in Tuzla improvised another piece of military engineering. They cut the tread off a truck tire, flattened it into a ten by two foot strip, and drove hundreds of razor-sharp titanium spikes through it. This spiky rubber mat could be pulled across a road using a thin nylon line and used to blow out the toughest of car tires.

On the first night of Karadžić's supposed travel window, the Delta team made their way to the ambush site in civilian clothes and five locally registered cars to hunker down with their custom-made equipment and the gorilla suit. Everything was lined up for a performance destined to go down in Delta history but for one thing: the appearance of its unwitting star, Karadžić.

He failed to show up either night in the forty-eight-hour period predicted by Delta's informant. Blaber thought the trap should be held open longer and wanted to stay in position. He was overruled. Special Operations Command was perpetually nervous of the team's cover being blown. So, despondent, they drove back to the stone cottage in Tuzla. Blaber eventually returned to Fort Bragg, where his next assignment a few months later involved thinking up ways to track a new target — someone he had never heard of: Osama bin Laden.[4] He took the gorilla suit with him to Afghanistan in case a similar opportunity might arise there, but it never did.

The spike mat had a fuller career ahead of it, becoming standard issue in police departments around the world. It also got another outing in Bosnia, where it worked perfectly. It was used to seize Major General Radislav Krstić, the one-legged commander of the Drina Corps of the Republika Srpska army, whose troops had overrun the supposedly UN-protected Muslim enclave of Srebrenica in July 1995.

Krstić was a tall, thin, vain man, a stickler for discipline and the bitter guardian of a deeply personal grudge, having stepped on a land mine in 1994 that blew off his right leg below the knee. The next year, when Bosniak men and boys attempted to escape execution by scrambling across the wooded hills above

Srebrenica, this is what Krstić told Colonel Dragan Obrenović, one of his junior officers at the scene:

> *Obrenović: We've managed to catch a few more, either with guns or mines.*
> *Krstić: Kill them all. God damn it.*
> *Obrenović: Everything, everything is going according to plan. Yes.*
> *Krstić: [Not a] single one must be left alive.*
> *Obrenović: Everything is going according to plan. Everything.*
> *Krstić: Way to go, Chief. The Turks are probably listening to us. Let them listen, the motherfuckers.*
> *Obrenović: Yeah, let them.*[5]

By the end of 1998, Krstić was made a lieutenant general and became the commander of the Bosnian Serb Fifth Corps. On December 2 of that year, he was driving from his headquarters on the way north for a meeting in the town of Brčko on the Croatian border. The trip involved crossing from French-run eastern Bosnia to the American-run northern zone. That created a risk for Krstić because US troops had already carried out war crimes arrests, but as far as the general was aware he was not on the Hague list. He did not know a sealed ICTY indictment charging him with genocide and crimes against humanity had been delivered a month earlier to the US command in Tuzla.

As he entered the American zone, Krstić found himself driving behind two civilian vehicles. Then two more cars appeared behind him which were drawing up close to his rear fender when the two vehicles ahead suddenly turned sideways, blocking the road. At the same moment Krstić's tires blew out and the air outside the car seemed to explode.

The spike mat had been pulled out in front of him and an Austrian stun grenade had been fired at the car, disorienting his bodyguards. The vehicles behind swiftly drew alongside and American soldiers leaped out, breaking his window with steel hammers. Within a few seconds of the blast Krstić was being dragged out through the window so forcibly his prosthesis became detached. "Shit! His leg just fell off," one of the soldiers was heard to say into his radio.

The general's stump was bleeding by the time he was flown to The Hague, and the leg would bother him throughout his trial. He was eventually sentenced to thirty-five years for aiding and abetting genocide, but the proceedings also provided a second measure of justice. They forced him to sit through the testimonies of survivors and families of the dead. One widow pleaded with him to identify a burial site where she might recover the bones of her husband. Another witness had lost her husband and two sons. The younger of the two was just fourteen when he was dragged away by Serb soldiers. Ever since, she'd had an obsession with hands.

> I keep remembering the hands of my little boy holding mine, and of my husband holding me... How is it possible that a human being could do something like this, could destroy everything, could kill so many people? Just imagine this youngest boy I had, those little hands of his, how could they be dead? I imagine those hands picking strawberries, reading books, going to school, going on excursions. Every morning I wake up, I cover my eyes not to look at other children going to school, and husbands going to work, holding hands. [6]

During some of this testimony, the normally impassive Krstić was occasionally seen to wince, but it was never clear whether a shard of guilt had pierced his thick armor of indifference and denial, or whether it was just his leg acting up.

His arrest was a significant milestone in the long hunt. To date, he was the highest-ranking indictee to come before the Hague Tribunal, which had been under fire for trying only camp guards and junior officers. On August 2, 2001, he became the first person the ICTY convicted for genocide.

After Krstić, the American forces in Bosnia made it their business to track down the rest of the Srebrenica suspects on the Hague list. They came with abundant manpower, formidable technical assets, and lots of money. They paid out significant sums in return for information. In one case, a reward of $250,000 was shared by a whole village, where it helped fund a new school.

In April 2001, the Delta unit came for Dragan Obrenović, the colonel who had been at the other end of the chilling conversation with Krstić about the Srebrenica executions. At the time, Obrenović was thirty-two years old, a career soldier, and the deputy commander of the Zvornik Brigade of Drina Corps. The brigade's military police had guarded the thousands of captured men and boys from Srebrenica. Members of its 4th Battalion had mowed down a thousand of them in a field. Its engineering company had dug the mass graves.

Like most of the key participants in the Srebrenica massacre, he was promoted after the war, made commander of a motorized brigade. But his career had been clouded by a feud with a fellow officer, and he had been temporarily relieved of his duties. On Sunday April 15, Obrenović was in the garden of his parents' house in Kozluk, on the west bank of the Drina where it formed Bosnia's eastern border with Serbia. He was smoking a cigarette and reading a book in the spring sunshine. It appeared a perfect moment of serenity, not more than a stone's throw from the village landfill where hundreds of victims from Srebrenica had been lined up and executed, the bodies falling among the splintered glass from Kozluk's bottling plant.

Obrenović had been watched for some time by a US special forces observation post on a hill on the western end of Kozluk. On this Sunday morning, three teams of Delta Force soldiers, including (in a new departure for the unit) a woman, were driving slowly through the village waiting for authorization to seize him. The reconnaissance sergeant on the hill gave the go-ahead as soon as he saw Obrenović was alone, but by the time the cars reached the house, the target's mother had come out into the garden to join him. The snatch plan went ahead anyway. One of the cars parked at the end of the road to stop traffic while the other two converged on the Obrenović home. Four soldiers, all in civilian clothes, came through the garden gate while another team leaped over the fence and walked up behind him. Obrenović dropped the cigarette and the book, and was hustled into one of the cars, which sped away. His mother was left behind, hysterical. According to one of the soldiers involved in the capture: "She ran into the driveway and lay down, screaming. That helped us because the Bosnian Serb police thought she was injured and called in an ambulance. In all the confusion we just drove out past the house while the Serb police held up the traffic to let the ambulance it. She was the best diversion we could have hoped for. We all had weapons under our clothes and were ready to shoot our way out if necessary."[7]

At The Hague, Obrenović struck a plea deal with the prosecution, admitting his guilt and agreeing to testify in other trials. On December 10, 2003, he was sentenced to seventeen years in prison. After serving seven years in a Norwegian jail, he was granted early release in September 2011.

# Up To $5 Million Reward

## Wanted

### For crimes against humanity

**Slobodan Milosevic**
President of the Federal
Republic of Yugoslavia

### For genocide and crimes against humanity

**Radovan Karadzic**     **Ratko Mladic**

**Milosevic**, **Karadzic**, and **Mladic** have been indicted by the United Nations International Criminal Tribunal for the Former Yugoslavia for crimes against humanity, including murders and rapes of thousands of innocent civilians, torture, hostage-taking of peacekeepers, wanton destruction of private property, and the destruction of sacred places. **Mladic** and **Karadzic** also have been indicted for genocide.

To bring **Milosevic**, **Karadzic**, and **Mladic** to justice, the United States Government is offering a reward of up to $5 million for information leading to the transfer to, or conviction by, the International Criminal Tribunal for the Former Yugoslavia of any of these individuals or any other person indicted by the International Tribunal.

If you believe you have information, please contact the nearest U.S. embassy or consulate, or write the U.S. Department of State, Diplomatic Security Service at:

## REWARDS FOR JUSTICE

Post Office Box 96781 • Washington, D.C. 20090-6781 U.S.A.
email: mail@dssrewards.net • www.dssrewards.net
1-800-437-6371 (U.S.A. Only)

US State Department wanted poster for Milošević, Karadzić, and Mladić.

The Srebrenica arrests were critical in bringing some justice for the massacre, but the leaders who had overseen the mass murders were still at large. Back in Washington, the success in arresting the Srebrenica killers had also served to highlight the sense of frustration overhanging the pursuit of Radovan Karadžić and Ratko Mladić.

The more elusive they became, the more earlier missed opportunities rankled. Some in the Clinton administration believed there had been a genuine chance to negotiate Karadžić's surrender in 1999, and it had slipped through their fingers. Over the summer of that year, Karadžić had held a series of meetings with retired US colonel Paul Nell, who was working as an intermediary for Louise Arbour, the ICTY chief prosecutor at the time. The meetings took place in a restaurant in Pale, in villages along the Montenegrin border, and finally in Montenegro on Mount Žabljak.[8] Each time, Karadžić's guards took elaborate security precautions. Nell was blindfolded and taken along a circuitous route to the rendezvous, changing cars along the way.

Karadžić had first floated a surrender deal not long after the war,* and he did so again at his last meeting with Nell in Montenegro in September 1999. Once more, his public image was a key consideration in the bargain. He was willing to give himself up but it had to look like a capture. He did not want to be seen as surrendering. Nor did he want to await trial in Scheveningen prison at The Hague with the other war crimes suspects. In Karadžić's proposed scenario, he would turn up to hear the charges in a moment of televised drama but would then return to the outskirts of Sarajevo, under some kind of house arrest, where he would write his memoirs and settle family business

---

* See chapter 1.

while waiting for the trial to begin. He would hand over $2 million in bail money, as a guarantee he would turn up in court. But he wanted all charges connected to the Srebrenica massacre dropped.

Nell insisted he could engineer a compromise that would be acceptable to Washington and the ICTY. Soon after the September meeting with Karadžić, the retired colonel went to see Jacques Klein, the American diplomat who had engineered the first arrest of a suspect by international troops two years earlier.* By now he was the international community's deputy high representative in postwar Bosnia. The two men met in Klein's house in Sarajevo and planned the logistics for Karadžić's handover, which was to take place on the boundary of the Muslim-Croat Federation and the Republika Srpska.

"I was going to drive out in my car to the zone of separation, on the road to Pale, and Karadžić was going to get in it and they were going drive the car to the airport and straight on to a plane, a C-123 transport, which would fly it to The Hague," Klein recalls.

Klein's armored white Volvo would then drive out of the plane in Holland and take Karadžić, the most wanted man in Europe, to the ICTY headquarters in The Hague. It would have been a breathtaking coup, but it turned out to be too good to be true.

Some of the fugitive's conditions were nonstarters, particularly the idea of simply dropping the Srebrenica indictments. But Nell seemed confident that Karadžić would ultimately accept that this was nonnegotiable. In return, he hoped the tribunal would be flexible on the conditions of pretrial detention. For some of those in Washington who had been driving the American

---

* See chapter 2.

campaign to track the war criminals for years, it seemed a tantalizing opportunity.

Nell had called the State Department and given the impression that Karadžić was ready to get into a car and drive to Sarajevo airport with him within hours if Washington agreed to the terms. After more than two years of failure to snare this elusive quarry, the instinct of some officials was to play along at least until he was in custody and then seek to renegotiate the terms.

However, several other senior figures disagreed. General Wesley Clark, the commander of NATO and US forces in Europe, would not contemplate a house arrest, arguing that NATO would have no legal basis for such an extended detention. Clark called James Steinberg, the deputy national security adviser in the White House, and James Dobbins, the president's special adviser on the Balkans. They agreed with Clark that the house arrest was problematic, both legally and politically. How would the people of Sarajevo react to the presence of Karadžić living in NATO-provided comfort while he penned his version of history and dabbled in the Pale real estate market?

The State Department official who received Nell's call was ordered to write a cable rejecting the deal. He felt so strongly that the United States was making a historic mistake that he flatly refused and Steinberg drafted it instead. "We have only ourselves to blame he was at liberty for another nine years," the official said, still ruing the decision fifteen years later.[9]

In fact, it was never really clear how close Nell had come to bringing Karadžić in from the cold. It is hard to imagine Carla Del Ponte beginning her term in office bestowing such special treatment on a man charged with genocide, and there was certainly no way she would agree to dropping the Srebrenica charges.

On the other side of the negotiation, the Karadžić family itself was divided. Radovan's wheeler-dealer brother, Luka, had served as an intermediary in the early stages of the talks, but the fugitive's wife, Ljiljana, and daughter, Sonja, were said to be determinedly opposed to his surrender. By October 1999, the Nell-Karadžić talks had collapsed.

Nearly a year later, both Mladić and Karadžić were still very much at large. It was clear that Mladić had found permanent haven in Serbia under the sheltering wing of the Yugoslav National Army. However there were still persistent rumors that he made occasional forays into Bosnia to see relatives in the eastern highlands. Meanwhile Karadžić was widely believed to be hiding out somewhere in the mountain villages along the Bosnian border with Montenegro.

From The Hague, Del Ponte was taunting the US military for its impotence. "The Americans want zero risk, which is impossible if you want to arrest a criminal," she told the *Financial Times* in August 2000.[10]

The Clinton administration did not need reminding that time was running out. Clinton had five months of his term left, and a central foreign policy goal, the arrest of the top war criminals, remained a conspicuous hole in the presidential legacy. In the summer of 2000, the national security adviser, Sandy Berger, set up a new task force in the White House to mastermind a last-ditch effort to make high-profile arrests.

Lawrence Rossin, a former director of South Central European Affairs at the State Department, was asked to run the revamped campaign. Gregory Schulte, a former Defense Department official who had been the director of NATO's Bosnia Task Force from 1992 to 1998, and then special assistant to the president for implementing Dayton the following year, was lured back from the Pentagon to help. Michael Hurley, a former CIA officer who had also served as the Balkans director in the National Security Council, was brought in to provide a solid link to the intelligence agencies.

"It was an attempt to revitalize the effort, because it just wasn't getting the job done. There was no vibrancy to it," one of the officials on the team said.

The team's brief was to shake every possible tree to see if some overlooked clue might come loose. The $5 million bounties for Karadžić and Mladić would be given greater publicity and there would be a propaganda campaign in the regional press warning the fugitives they had not been forgotten and their days of impunity were numbered. There was a new secret presidential intelligence finding, directing the NSA to devote more of its resources to the electronic hunt for the suspects. The CIA's veteran assistant director for intelligence collection, Charles Allen, held a weekly secure videoconference in which all the intelligence agencies and the White House would swap progress reports, and the Pentagon promised to streamline its cumbersome and risk-averse procedures for approving arrest operations.

In reality, this rebooted effort was aimed at just one of the fugitives. Mladić was considered too rooted in Serbia, too well protected by the regime and the army, to be considered a feasible target. The hunt was almost solely about Karadžić, and in the fall of 2000, out of the blue and with perfect timing, a new opportunity to trap him appeared to present itself.

In October, both the CIA and MI6 were reporting a spike in intelligence chatter that Karadžić was about to bolt across the Drina into Serbia. Informants for both spy agencies claimed he would make the crossing on a small boat at a point on the river north of Zvornik. The intelligence was detailed. There was even a date and a three-day itinerary for the would-be escape: a rehearsal on day one, a day of observation to see if there was any reaction to the dry run, and then on the third day, Karadžić would cross.

Here, it seemed, was the possibility of redemption for the special forces after so many near misses and failures. An extensive surveillance operation was mounted around the Drina. Observation posts dotted the woods above the expected crossing point and reconnaissance specialists drifted through the zone disguised as locals on farm vehicles and bicycles.

Sure enough, on the predicted day, a motorboat chugged from the Serbian side to a jetty on the Bosnian bank. No one got on or off and the boat returned. For the next twenty-four hours nothing seemed to happen, but that was as predicted, so SEAL Team Six snatch squads were put in position along the river in preparation for the third climactic day.

They waited but the boat did not move and no one came.[11] Another hope withered. The question was whether it had ever represented a genuine opportunity or was just a carefully staged piece of theater. It was quite possible that such a heavy US military presence in the forests and along the riverbanks had been spotted. There was another possibility that the trackers at the ICTY thought even more likely: American and British intelligence was simply being gamed by Karadžić's entourage.

"The agencies would come to us with all sorts of tips based on these informants, who were often paid informants, and they were almost always worthless. This was no doubt just the same," said a member of the Hague tracking team.

The stakeout on the Drina turned out to be the Clinton White House's bitterly disappointing last chance at glory for capturing Karadžić. But the manhunt in Bosnia did not end when Clinton left office in January 2001. It carried through into the early months of the George W. Bush administration. The new national security adviser, Condoleezza Rice, and her deputy, Stephen Hadley, pledged to keep up the pressure. In fact, in those last months of the decade between the Cold War and 9/11, the Bosnian manhunt was the US military's biggest deployment of a special mission unit anywhere in the world.

"We were pleasantly surprised how much Hadley was up for it. There was no letup," said a former senior administration official.

In May 2001, the leadership of the task force was given to a Delta Force aviator, Lieutenant Colonel Andy Milani, who was told he could draw on the best "high-end" soldiers and equipment the US military had to offer. There was no longer resistance from the regular "green" army chain of command running SFOR. In fact, SFOR's newly arrived assistant chief of staff for operations was clearly fascinated by the manhunt and was soon spending much of his time hanging around Milani's operations center at Camp Butmir, at Sarajevo airport. His name was Brigadier General David Petraeus.[12]

Petraeus, who had met Milani in Fort Bragg prior to their Bosnia postings, would turn up to Milani's briefings taking notes and asking probing questions. He was not, strictly speaking, in the special operations chain of command. His excuse for being there was that he was responsible for SFOR support for the task force. The real reason he spent so much time on the manhunt was that he was deeply impressed by the special forces world, its night helicopter flights and sudden raids. Later he would make such warfare a central pillar of his counterinsurgency strategy in Iraq and Afghanistan.

"One day I put him on a helicopter and dressed him up [in civilian attire] and a ball cap" Milani said. After a trip across eastern Bosnia's vertiginous highlands, the helicopter was met by Milani's Delta Force soldiers. "We jumped in a van with blacked-out windows and you could tell he was like kid in a candy store."[13]

The future CIA director was taken along to meet the task force's intelligence collectors and sources. He visited safe houses and even went on night raids. As a senior officer he would wait in a vehicle while a house was surrounded and secured before emerging to knock on the door to deliver a letter from the SFOR commander to a shocked householder, usually someone suspected of being part of Karadžić's support network.

On at least one occasion he turned up in the middle of the night in Pale, at the famous pink house owned by Karadžić's wife, Ljiljana, inviting himself in. It was called the "Eddie Murphy Routine," inspired by the 1982 hit movie 48 Hrs. In the film, Murphy played convict Reggie Hammond, a poacher-turned-gamekeeper helping Nick Nolte's rugged cop find a band of murderous criminals by rattling their friends and lovers. Petraeus was supposedly playing a Balkan version of the Murphy role.

What worked in the movies did not work on Ljiljana Karadžić. She never let slip any detail about her husband's whereabouts and never led the Americans to him. On one occasion in 2001 it appeared that for once Petraeus's visit had at least rattled her a little. The Bosnian manhunt was the first special forces operation to use surveillance drones systematically and one of their first targets was Ljiljana. They relayed video of her packing suitcases in the back of her Audi A8 and driving off. She was followed on land and in the air but drove into a garage, from which several similar cars emerged later, throwing her pursuers off the scent.

The evasive tactics were the work of the Preventiva, as the group of bodyguards around Karadžić were known. They had used similar methods to bring husband and wife together the year before.

"I jumped from car to car, led by some people I did not know," Ljiljana later recalled. "Everything was so fast. Our meeting was brief, two hours altogether, but poignant."[14]

A further American attempt to get to Karadžić through his inner circle failed spectacularly when the task force decided to make an approach to his longtime driver. A letter offering immunity, protection, and money in return for betraying his boss was delivered to the driver's house in the middle of the night. The plan backfired. The driver was terrified, fearing Karadžić himself had written the letter to test his loyalty. He went straight to the Bosnian Serb authorities who took the matter to the US embassy in Sarajevo. From there it went to George Tenet, the CIA director, who went ballistic — so angry in fact that the CIA station chief denied having agreed to the plan in the first place. The affair escalated into a fierce fight over who was telling the truth, and in the end Milani was persuaded to say, through gritted teeth, that the CIA had not been consulted after all. That way everyone concerned could keep their job, but it left the task force bitter and Karadžić at liberty.

The task force did all it could to shake out the bureaucratic kinks that had held back the manhunt for so long. The NSA had hitherto refused to allow raw intercepts of conversations to leave its headquarters in Fort Meade, Maryland, but that meant that the analysts in the best position to understand their significance, those based in Bosnia, could never get to hear them. The NSA director, Michael Hayden, was persuaded to make an exception for the Karadžić hunt.

Meanwhile, Petraeus and Milani flew to Paris, with the blessing of Lieutenant General John Sylvester, the SFOR commander, to make a deal with French intelligence. The American argument was that the French did not have a fraction of the US intelligence-gathering capacity, so why not let the Americans do the job. Somewhat to Petraeus and Milani's surprise, the French readily agreed.

The Americans refused to give up the hunt. Like a sheriff's posse unwilling to admit defeat, they were ready to try anything. Every single possible clue was scrutinized. The task force looked for satellite dishes on houses in remote locations and found out who was subscribing to Belgrade newspapers in out-of-the-way villages, on the grounds that a top war crimes fugitive and former political leader would have a greater appetite for news of the outside world than his rustic neighbors. Based on intelligence reports about their target's nocturnal habits, they scanned for late-night log-ins from remote corners of Bosnia on pro-Serb news websites. All the while, helicopters buzzed day and night over Ljiljana's pink house.

Some years later, a thorough search of the Karadžićs' house did uncover a trove of personal letters from the Serb Pimpernel. But the find in 2005 failed to lead to the fugitive, and ultimately deepened the humiliation of his frustrated pursuers. The letters illustrated how the Karadžićs, this apparently frumpy and provincial couple, had run rings around the formidable multibillion-dollar intelligence operation focused on them.

"Thank you for the gifts. The clothes are small and the T-shirts might be two sizes too small, so don't send any more. The coloured shirts are OK, although as XXL they could be a little big, but that's a compliment to me. I think they make me look very elegant," Karadžić wrote to Ljiljana in 2002. "I also have sufficient socks for now."

Not only do the letters make clear that she was able to send him care parcels but they also proved that she had been able to elude her minders and visit him.

"I believe that you want to come as much as I want that. But I cannot decide and R is working through some things...to try to make that happen," Karadžić writes. It was never clear who R was. "[T]hey saw you before and nobody made a connection."[15]

You did not have to read between the lines to see Karadžić's supreme confidence that he was miles ahead of his pursuers. He spelled it out. It would "take a battalion" to find him, he boasted to Ljiljana. In fact, it was worse than even Karadžić knew. Many battalions had tried to catch him and failed.

Years later, on the basis of interviews with Karadžić's inner circle, the Hague tracking team at the ICTY came to the conclusion that he had crossed the Drina by boat with a couple of bodyguards on his way to his new life in Serbia on the night of December 24, 1999,* a full ten months before the big US special forces stakeout on the river and nearly eighteen months before Milani and Petraeus arrived in Bosnia.

It is not clear whether he continued to make trips into Bosnia to see his wife or whether the many and varied reported sightings were counterintelligence chaff, intended to distract and confuse. It does appear Ljiljana continued to see him, but those meetings could well have been in Serbia where he felt more secure. Overall, it is hard to escape the conclusion that by the time Washington decided to devote significant resources to the hunt in Bosnia, it was already too late.

ON SEPTEMBER 11, 2001, when the airliners hit the Twin Towers in New York, the cream of America's special forces, 150 men from Delta Force and SEAL Team Six, were in a huge C5 Galaxy

* Christmas eve in the Western Christian calendar but not for the Serbian Orthodox church.

transport plane flying to Bosnia. It so happened that on that particular day, the whole Joint Special Operations Command national force was on its way to take part in quarterly exercises. The idea was to stage a war game in a foreign location with a bit of an edge to it, somewhere there had recently been fighting and where potentially hostile individuals abounded.

Milani had been waiting for the inbound troops in the operations room at the air force base at Tuzla when the shocking images from New York appeared on the television screens. The C5 landed shortly after the second plane hit the South Tower, and it was abundantly clear what was happening. Milani went onto the runway to meet the senior officer as he was getting off the plane and suggested he might just as well get back on and fly home. It was likely his men were going to be needed elsewhere very soon.

After watching the television news for a few minutes at the base, the stunned colonel agreed. By the time the C5 had flown back home, it was the only aircraft being allowed into US airspace. The soldiers returned to a country that had changed forever. Just over a month later, on October 19, many of the men who had been in that C5 took part in a helicopter-borne assault on Kandahar in the first US action of the Afghan war.

In the space of a few moments, the Bosnian manhunt had gone from being the number one priority for US special forces and intelligence agencies to a mere afterthought. The operation was rapidly asset-stripped. All the manpower, skills, and equipment from the search for Karadžić and Mladić were diverted to Afghanistan, leaving the mission unaccomplished.

US forces in Bosnia tracked down war criminals with terrible atrocities to their name, Srebrenica in particular. But they failed to achieve their stated objective, to find the leaders. Looking back ruefully on the episode, a top US Special Operations Forces officer said, "We had the tradecraft, we had the equipment and training, but we didn't have an understanding of the terrain."

That was one of the lessons learned in Bosnia and taken to Afghanistan and Iraq. The Balkans had been a laboratory for new manhunting techniques, not just gorilla suits and titanium spikes. It was the first place the special forces used drones and deployed mixed teams of men and women. They became far more integrated with the CIA. It was where the military learned that when it comes to tracking individuals, less is more.

"Everything we learned about manhunting in Bosnia, we used again and again in Afghanistan and Iraq," Blaber said. "It was transformational."[16]

Bosnia was also the place where the CIA and US special forces became adept at renditions, though the military resisted using that word. Veterans of the Bosnian operations are adamant about the distinction between transfers to The Hague and midnight flights to torture chambers in undisclosed locations.

"What we did there was underpinned totally in terms of legality," a senior special forces officer said. "It had nothing to do with what came later."[17]

In fact, the first renditions of the post-9/11 era took place in Sarajevo. A few days after al-Qaida attacks on New York and Washington, a joint interagency counterterrorism task force was formed in Sarajevo under the command of General Sylvester, with Petraeus as his deputy.[18] On September 25, Milani led a raid on the Hotel Hollywood, on the western end of the Sarajevo airport. Soldiers from the Tenth Special Forces Group,* wearing civilian clothes and carrying empty suitcases, checked into the hotel and then broke into rooms being rented by two al-Qaida

---

* Milani could not use Delta Force because of a bureaucratic glitch. The unit's deployment order specified it could only hunt war criminals.

suspects, believed to be planning attacks on the US and UK embassies in Sarajevo.

One was an Egyptian, Abd al-Halim Kafgia, and the other was a Jordanian, Jihad Ahmed Jamalah.* Interrogations and analysis of their computers led to a wider ring involving three more Egyptians, another Jordanian, and five Pakistanis, and disclosed links between an Islamic charity and terrorist groups using Bosnia as a hub.

Kafgia and Jamalah had been roughed up in the course of their arrest. Kafgia in particular was hit hard on the head. They were covered in blood, and Kafgia was unconscious when they were brought to Petraeus, who according to a witness to the scene "freaked out" at their condition. They were held and questioned for three days by US interrogators before being handed over to the Bosnian authorities who organized their rendition to Egypt and Jordan.[19]

The hunt for war criminals had switched in the space of a few days to a search for terrorists. Milani went on to command the 160th Special Operations Aviation Regiment, known as the Night Stalkers, which flew helicopter night raids in Afghanistan and Iraq. Petraeus left the Balkans in July 2002 to take command of the 101st Airborne, which was already training at its base in Fort Campbell, Kentucky, for the Iraq invasion. He would go on to run the US military's Central Command, and the NATO force in Afghanistan, before heading the CIA. In each job, he relied heavily on counterinsurgency tactics led by special forces using night raids to kill or capture enemy commanders, tactics he had watched being used in the confounding hunt for Karadžić.[20]

---

* These were the names, as released by SFOR. It is unclear what happened to either of them once they were sent back to their home countries.

# 7.
# THE TRACKING TEAM

They were screaming that they don't have the bodies.
Well, I will deliver the bodies.
—*Louise Arbour, Chief Prosecutor, ICTY*

CRIMES AGAINST HUMANITY, like a lot else in the Balkans, was a male-dominated field. Only one of the 161 names on the Hague Tribunal's wanted list of indictees was female.* On the other hand, the two people who did more than any other individuals to ensure the suspects were all tracked down happened to be women.

Louise Arbour and Carla Del Ponte, chief prosecutors at crucial periods for the ICTY,[1] shared some other traits: a diminutive stature, minority status in their home countries, and a tenacity borne of careers fighting male condescension, browbeating, and worse. From the prosecutor's office in The Hague, they took on reluctant generals, apathetic diplomats, hostile governments, blackmail threats, and abuse. In so doing, they ensured the manhunt was never abandoned or forgotten.

---

*Biljana Plavšić, the former biology professor and Karadžić deputy who became his rival as postwar president of the Republika Srpska.

Other than that, they had little outwardly in common. While Del Ponte was Swiss Italian, a chain-smoking and hard-nosed prosecutor with few social graces, having been tempered by years of combat with the Mafia, Arbour came from academia, a French-speaking Quebecois, who taught criminal and human rights law, and whose iron determination was well sheathed beneath a genteel and scholarly exterior.

The two women also arrived at two very different phases in the tribunal's history, requiring each to develop contrasting strategies and prosecutorial styles. During Arbour's three years at the helm, starting in October 1996, NATO was dominant in Bosnia, where most of the fugitives were living. Her strategy was to impose maximum pressure on Western governments and their generals in Bosnia to carry out arrests, and to start using sealed indictments so the suspects would have no warning NATO was on their trail.

By the time Del Ponte took up the post, in September 1999, Arbour's dual strategy had run its course. Almost all the remaining suspects had fled Bosnia and were hiding under the skirts of sympathetic nationalist governments in Serbia or Croatia. Del Ponte's approach had to be different. She traveled constantly to Washington and European capitals to remind governments, as forcefully as necessary, of the moral imperative to tie financial aid and progress toward European Union membership for both countries to the delivery of fugitives to The Hague. The role fit the abrasive side of her personality perfectly.[2] At the same time, she built up the tribunal's own investigative and analytical arm so she would not have to accept at face value what she was told by the Serbian and Croatian governments. She came to negotiations armed with dossiers compiled by her own tiny intelligence agency, which made officials across the table fear her all the more.

The Chief Prosecutors of the International Criminal Tribunal for the former Yugoslavia (ICTY). Top row: Richard Goldstone (1994–96), Louise Arbour (1996–99); bottom row: Carla Del Ponte (1999–2007), Serge Brammertz (2007– ).

Her successor, Serge Brammertz, a Belgian prosecutor, continued her policy of zero tolerance for noncompliance, albeit in a more low-key, less confrontational manner. He shrugged off pressure from some European countries to tone down his reports on cooperation to the UN Security Council, and he was ultimately rewarded for his quiet but unyielding persistence. The last, most significant arrests took place during his term in office. But the tribunal's strategic direction was first set by Arbour and Del Ponte, whose obstinacy helped save the tribunal when it was in danger of sinking into irrelevance.

The quality of some of the indictments the two prosecutors issued has since come under critical scrutiny. But there is no real debate about their commitment to tracking down the suspects and bringing them to trial.

The ICTY's ultimate success in accounting for all 161 names on its list has made it easy to forget that when Arbour first arrived in The Hague, the tribunal was facing impotence and even collapse. Of the seventy-six suspects indicted by the ICTY by that time, only seven were sitting in the cells set aside for them at Scheveningen prison. In the absence of detainees, Arbour's predecessor in the prosecutor's office, Richard Goldstone, had issued scores of indictments based on the available evidence. But most of those cases were against small fry — camp guards and foot soldiers of ethnic cleansing rather than the true instigators of the horrendous policy. And only one trial had been launched with a defendant in the dock.

That single defendant was Duško Tadić, a Bosnian Serb police officer who had taken part in the killings and torture in the infamous Omarska prison camp, and who had been fortuitously spotted by survivors in a government office in Munich.[3] After lengthy negotiations with the German courts, Tadić became the first resident of Scheveningen in April 1995, nearly two years after the tribunal was established.

The Hague had also played temporary host to General Djordje Djukić and Colonel Aleksa Krsmanović, two Bosnian Serb officers who had taken a wrong turn in the snow near Sarajevo airport and run into a Bosnian government checkpoint on January 30, 1996. In view of the lack of defendants in Scheveningen and fears of what might happen to the two Serb officers in a Sarajevo jail, Goldstone hastily arranged for them to be flown to The Hague for questioning. Krsmanović was quickly released for lack of evidence but an indictment was put together against Djukić on the grounds that, as a logistics officer, he had abetted Ratko Mladić in laying siege to Sarajevo and shelling civilians. But the general was released two months later because he was in the advanced stages of pancreatic cancer, from which he died within a few weeks. The whole debacle served chiefly to sour relations between the ICTY and the NATO peacekeeping force, whose task, in the eyes of its commanders, had been unnecessarily complicated and politicized by the decision to ship the two officers to The Hague. As a result of the experience, new "rules of the road" were agreed on between the court and NATO, stipulating that indictments had to precede arrests rather than the other way around.

Of the few inmates who trickled in, the majority were Bosniaks. Bosnian Muslims had been the principal victims of the slaughter, but the Bosnian army had committed atrocities, albeit on a much smaller scale. In May 1992, when the central Bosnian town of Konjic came under heavy fire from the Yugoslav army and allied Serb militias, its Muslim and Croat defenders took reprisals against the local Serb civilians. They were rounded up and taken to a Socialist-era barracks called Čelebići, along with

Serb prisoners of war. Civilians and soldiers were brutally tortured by the guards, and at least a dozen died.

Four Bosnian army soldiers were indicted and three were ultimately convicted, including Esad Landžo, a particularly sadistic guard who had nailed a Serb badge to the forehead of an elderly prisoner, killing him, and forced a pair of heated pincers into the mouth of another inmate, cutting out his tongue.[4] These were among the ICTY's first prisoners because the government in Sarajevo was eager to show its cooperative spirit, in the expectation it would spur on arrests of the principal architects of the country's ethnic cleansing in Belgrade and Zagreb. But in the first eighteen months after the war, that was clearly not happening.

"When I first came in 1996, there were about seventy-five people indicted publicly. They had these big [wanted] posters. When you traveled in Bosnia you would see them. The posters were everywhere, which led to a very convenient mutual avoidance: The indictees avoided NATO; NATO avoided the indictees," Arbour said. "There was no real hope or any strategy at that time to go and capture those who were basically sheltered by their own governments. I thought: This is ridiculous."[5]

She pointed out to anyone who would listen that the tribunal had been established in 1993 under Chapter VII of the UN Charter. That meant members of the Security Council who had voted it into existence had theoretically committed themselves to ensuring it was allowed to do its job by any means necessary, including force. Arbour's challenge was to align the practice with the principle.

"I said, Look at the statutory powers we have. We are a Chapter VII organ of the Security Council of the United Nations. How much more legal and political clout do you want? Let's just do it. We have a mandate to apprehend these people and if someone objects, we'll deal with it when the time comes."

Arbour took her Chapter VII powers to NATO command-ers, along with a sheaf of other UN Security Council resolutions empowering their troops to make arrests. But before she did so, she made two critical changes to the way the tribunal went about its work. First, she winnowed out the weakest indictments against the most marginal suspects, so as not to spread the tri-bunal's resources too thin. She wanted to tell Washington and other Western governments that the war criminals she was after were truly guilty of the worst offenses and would have a good chance of being convicted if caught.

Her second innovation was to persuade the judges at The Hague to issue sealed indictments, to give NATO the advan-tage of surprise. "Operationally, it gave a tremendous advan-tage to NATO," Arbour said. "If you try to apprehend someone who knows he is under indictment, it's very hard. But these guys [under sealed indictment] were unsuspecting and they had reg-ular meetings with NATO so it was like a dream scenario oper-ationally. Secondly, it sent a signal to those who were publicly indicted that it might be a good idea to surrender because now NATO was in the arrest business."

Arbour continued: "The other side effect of these secret indictments, which was really good for the heart of the pros-ecutor...is that all the bad guys were afraid. To some modest degree they experienced what they inflicted on others, which is fear...Even with those to whom nothing ever happened, to have lived under this climate of uncertainty and fear was some kind of sweet revenge. The whole operation started looking real."

The Hague operation may have started to *look* real, but it could only *be* real if nation-states with real armies cooperated. As Arbour toured Western capitals in early 1997, she found little enthusiasm to help her catch suspects. In Washington, the State

Department, under the new management of Madeleine Albright, made sympathetic noises, but it had no troops. The Pentagon ignored Arbour. In London, the Foreign and Commonwealth Office (FCO) was looking in vain to Washington for a clear lead, and the British army was deeply skeptical of the whole enterprise, questioning the legal basis for NATO arrests. In France, both the diplomats and soldiers were determinedly hostile. Arbour seemed to be getting nowhere.

By February 1997, she was sufficiently despairing of NATO cooperation that she floated a daring and original idea: She would assemble her own multinational posse to send in pursuit of the fugitives. And she persuaded her hosts in The Hague, the Dutch government, to help her organize this personal SWAT team.

"I got the judges to once more amend the rules in a way that I'm not sure even the judges understood... that would allow me to initiate an arrest," she said. "I went to the Dutch... and asked them if they were interested in exploring [the use of force] outside NATO and SFOR... if like-minded states would do it under my authority to arrest."

An extraordinary meeting with special forces, intelligence officers, and legal experts from the United States, Britain, and the Netherlands was organized for her by the US embassy in Paris on February 5, 1997. The officials listened carefully and agreed to consult their capitals, while reminding Arbour that she would be risking her career and the future of the tribunal if things went wrong.

Arbour was all too aware of the dangers. If she prosecuted defendants who had been dragged into court by her team of "guns for hire," the arrests would be challenged by the defense. All she could hope for was to win the argument in front of the bench at the tribunal. It was entirely a leap of faith.

"Having been a judge myself, I was quite happy to push that issue to the judges. I figured they were screaming that this tribunal was going nowhere and that they may have to have trials in absentia. They were screaming that they don't have the bodies. Well, I will deliver the bodies. If they want to set them free, be my guest. I was prepared to go to court and say: Listen, we are operating in a hostile environment with no support, you tell me what I should do... This one I'm going to push back to you. You're nicely paid and not doing all that much at this stage."

If the arrests were botched and people were hurt or killed, however, Arbour would indeed take all the blame. The Americans, British, and Dutch said they would consider lending special forces soldiers to a snatch team but rejected outright her proposal that detentions would be dual-key operations, which both she and the military commander could cancel at the last moment. She would have little control and almost all the responsibility.

"I wanted to have the capacity to put the brakes on it, and they said, No—if it's a go from the beginning, then we decide what to do. So I had pretty cold feet on this. I would have done it if there was no choice, but it was my neck on the line, with people potentially being killed, and I would have no control. So this really was desperation."

Much to her relief, Arbour never had to resort to the extreme gamble of assembling her own snatch squad. In the summer of 1997, NATO finally got involved in the Balkan manhunt on its own, a decision triggered by a cluster of converging factors: Tony Blair's election in Britain in May; a successful UN-led arrest operation against Slavko Dokmanović in eastern Croatia; and the arrival of the forward-leaning General Wesley Clark at NATO's European command.

As a result, NATO in effect became the ICTY prosecution's enforcement wing in Bosnia, but a somewhat independent one. Once Arbour's office delivered an indictment to NATO, she could not call off an arrest operation or dictate how it should proceed. In the end, given the legal gray area involved and the rough edges of the detention methods used by NATO troops, Arbour's hands-off role worked to her advantage. "There was something called 'Orange.' When an operation was launched, I would be told the Orange code is on. On both sides, I was happy not to know too much, so I could stand up in court and the prosecutor's office could have some distance from the operations."

NATO involvement and the sealed indictments gave the tribunal teeth and turned Arbour into a powerful figure. In his history of the Hague tribunal, John Hagan, a Canadian American professor of law and sociology, depicts Arbour as the sort of "charismatic leader" who proved that individuals can alter the course of history. "Starting with a tribunal whose credibility was in grave doubt, Arbour became the leader of a prosecutorial team that brought meaningful international criminal law enforcement to the Balkans, nearly tripling the size of the tribunal in the process."[6]

Arbour consequently became a target for nationalist networks in both Serbia and Croatia, who tried blackmail and on at least two occasions even assassination as a means of getting rid of her.

After a meeting with one diplomatic delegation from the region, an ambassador* whispered to her that there were rumors circulating that she had "a gambling problem." Arbour was shocked and angry: "I thought what the hell is he talking about.

---

* Either Serbian or Croatian but Arbour would not say which.

I assumed it was some opening for [blackmail]. I said I used to play a lot of poker when I was in law school but I have outgrown that. I don't have a gambling problem, or a drinking problem or an adultery problem. I don't have any kind of problem. But thank you for your concern."

In late 1997, the Dutch security service informed her that there was a credible threat against her life and advised her to stop driving her own car around The Hague. She was assigned a driver and a bodyguard for the rest of her term. One particular threat, emanating from Croatian extremists, followed her even after she left the prosecutor's office to take a seat on the Canadian Supreme Court in Ottawa.

"When I went back to Canada, I thought I was finished with surveillance, so I bought myself a Cabriolet, with the top down and the heater up. It lasted about three or four months and one day I came out of court and the RCMP* were there waiting for me and they said, 'We have a threat which we take very seriously and we have to put you in close protection.' And it lasted for five or six months. They said, 'We have a lot of details and we have information that they will use an operative that is known to our intelligence services, and until we have located him you will be under protection.'"

The threat persisted into 2000, after Arbour became a member of the board of directors at the International Crisis Group, a think tank and advocacy organization. When she went to a board meeting in Jakarta, the Mounties went with her.

By the time Carla Del Ponte succeeded Arbour at the Office of the Prosecutor in September 1999,† she was already accustomed

---

* Royal Canadian Mounted Police, also called the Mounties.

† Del Ponte also took on the chief prosecutor's role in the International Criminal Tribunal for Rwanda, where she served until 2003.

to assassination threats. As Switzerland's attorney general she had gone after the Russian Mafia, the Colombian drug cartels, and the Cosa Nostra where it hurt them most, their Swiss bank accounts. The Sicilian Mafia tried to blow her up in 1988 along with her friend and colleague, the Italian anti-Mafia prosecutor Giovanni Falcone. The Italian Carabinieri found a hundred pounds of the plastic explosive Semtex packed into the foundations of Falcone's house in Sicily one day while Del Ponte was his guest. Four years later the Mafia killed Falcone by detonating a half-ton bomb hidden in a culvert under a highway as his car went by.

Having failed to kill her, the Mafia branded Del Ponte "La Puttana" ("the whore") and the nationalists in Serbia and Croatia followed their example. When she arrived in Belgrade, billboards on the road in from the airport were emblazoned with the words "Carla the Whore." The Yugoslav minister of justice, Petar Jojić, sent a letter on May 24, 2000, to The Hague addressed to "The whore Del Ponte." Similarly, in the Croatian press she was frequently called "the whore of The Hague," depicted in cartoons as an evil dominatrix.[7] With Del Ponte as a target, rampant nationalism mutated easily into vicious misogyny.

Undeterred, she conducted a relentless campaign to persuade Western leaders to support the Balkan manhunt, paying little heed to protocol. She took Condoleezza Rice entirely by surprise when she jumped into the US national security adviser's car to make the case. She confronted the Catholic church in 2005 over allegations that Franciscan monks were harboring the Croatian general Ante Gotovina. Monsignor Giovanni Lajolo, who as the Vatican secretary for relations with states was in effect the Holy See's foreign minister, tried to fob her off, remarking acidly that if she wished to see the pope, she could always come to St. Peter's

Square on Sunday. Del Ponte matched his contempt and raised it a notch or two: "Grazie. I am not here as a pilgrim, I'm a prosecutor. I have heard that our fugitive is hiding in a Roman Catholic monastery. I have heard that the Vatican has the best intelligence service in the world. So I would think it would be easy for you to find out whether he really is in one of those monasteries in Croatia."[8]

At this, the monsignor tossed a set of Vatican commemorative coins across his desk and stormed out of the chamber.

Arbour's and Del Ponte's legacy was to make the Hague Tribunal a gatekeeper. Access to financial aid and entry into the European Union became institutionally dependent on a positive report from the ICTY chief prosecutor to the UN and to the EU, boosting the power of the role exponentially. In the endgame of the manhunt, when it boiled down to the last handful of names on the list, this extraordinary and unprecedented authority made all the difference.

The pair left a second important concrete legacy — the ICTY's own tracking unit. In early 1997, as a low-cost alternative to Arbour's suggested armed posse, the British government offered to organize the funding and staffing for "a unit to keep track of indictees." The FCO noted in January 1997 that the response had "so far been fairly encouraging."[9]

"The Tribunal say[s] that a team of seven will be needed if they are to carry out this function effectively," the memo stated, adding that the United Kingdom would contribute one member of the unit, seconded from the British security services, on top of £200,000 in voluntary assistance. Three other countries had also offered staff or money. A year later the unit was established as the Fugitive Intelligence Support Team, presumably so it could enjoy the fearsome acronym of FIST. But the reality was somewhat less formidable.

The first team member did not report for duty until 1998, and for the initial two years, FIST amounted to no more than a couple of investigators and an administrative assistant at any one time. Among the first of the gumshoes was a former British military intelligence officer who had served in Bosnia. A second Briton arrived from the UK domestic security service, MI5, but he left after a few months to be replaced by an American special forces colonel.* In 1999, Peter Nicholson, another UK military intelligence veteran, was brought in to run the embryonic team.

FIST had an office with a combination lock on the door but no identifying nameplate, adding to a general air of mystery surrounding its activities. Even within such a small team there was distrust and personality clashes. The US special forces colonel had formerly run the embryonic US interagency task force in Bosnia established at the beginning of 1997 to chase war crimes suspects, and as far as his new colleagues at The Hague could tell, he was still working for US intelligence. He certainly kept to his own timetable, sometimes disappearing for weeks on end without explanation. And he told stories of high derring-do in the Balkans that his fellow British and Australian investigators found hard to believe. The trust deficit came to a head one night when, in an effort to build an esprit de corps, the team went out for a drink in The Hague and things went disastrously wrong. At some point, the American colonel intimated, in a characteristically conspiratorial whisper, that he was carrying a gun. The British military intelligence officer challenged him to produce the weapon, which the American refused to do, indicating it was in his briefcase, which he flashed open and closed. There was a moment of silence before the Englishman made a lunge toward the case as

---

* Most of the tracking team's members asked for their names not to be made public.

the American struggled to lock it, producing an unseemly bar scuffle among members of what was optimistically imagined to be the secret spearhead of the Hague Tribunal's endeavors.

The tracking unit was considerably expanded by Del Ponte and in 2002 was renamed the Tracking, Intelligence, and Fugitives Unit (TIFU), with seven to eight investigators, supported by intelligence analysts and linguists, who began to build up a searchable database and mapped the networks surrounding each fugitive on extensive spreadsheets and organization charts. For the first time, a slush fund was established to pay informants.

TIFU was better resourced than FIST, but it still suffered from constant internal friction: between investigators with police and intelligence backgrounds, and between the Anglo investigators — the Americans, British, and Australians — and their French counterparts.

The friction was not just personal but institutional. When Del Ponte appointed Patrick Lopez-Terres, a French magistrate, as the chief of investigations in March 2001, she went against the direct advice of George Tenet, the CIA director, who warned he would cut off the flow of US intelligence to the tribunal. Del Ponte reasoned that the CIA had always been fairly miserly when it came to useful information anyway, so there was not much to lose. Appointing Lopez-Terres was also a key part of her strategy to reorganize the prosecutor's office, eliminating the divide between lawyers and investigators imported from English common law traditions. He had been a French *juge d'instruction*, an investigating magistrate, a role that straddled the divide.

Tenet delivered on his threat. When Lopez-Terres took up his post, he found the doors to US intelligence slammed shut on him. There was even a telephone on his desk he could not use. It had been a hot line between Lopez-Terres's predecessor and the CIA station chief in The Hague. Because France was not a member of Five Eyes — the exclusive Anglo-Saxon club that shared electronic intelligence comprising the United States, the United Kingdom, Canada, Australia, and New Zealand — there was a whole class of potentially useful intelligence he could not be privy to.

When Nicholson left the tracking team in 2003 to concentrate exclusively on his original ICTY role, running the tribunal's military analysis unit, he was replaced by the colorful but divisive figure of Raymond Carter. Carter was a French National Gendarmerie colonel, proposed by the ministry of defense in Paris, although his special skill was underwater knife combat. Personal tensions bubbled up soon after his arrival.

The CIA and MI6 would not deal with Carter by dint of his nationality, and even France's DGSE kept him at arm's length, as he was not one of their own but a policeman. He began to see the lack of cooperation as deliberate obstruction motivated by a covert desire to protect the war criminals.

"I came to the conclusion that the pursuit of international justice ends where politics begins," Carter said.[10] On at least one occasion in March 2004, he believed he had solid intelligence on Karadžić's impending arrival in Zaovine, on the Bosnian-Serbian border, but NATO commanders on the ground took days to respond. As Carter became more distrustful of the intelligence agencies and more secretive, his colleagues in the tracking team faulted him for not sharing information, and grew restive.

The team established a de facto division of labor, in which Carter dealt with the Karadžić portfolio and the rest of the TIFU team followed other fugitives, with surprising success.

Small, underfunded, and scrappy as it was, the tracking unit proved itself a far better value for money than the leviathan Western intelligence agencies involved in the pursuit. That was in part because the commitment of the CIA, MI6, or DGSE waxed and waned depending on their other priorities. They kept a lot of information to themselves. It went against the grain in all three agencies to share intelligence with outsiders, especially a motley group of investigators like the tracking team. There were complex issues of national security and source protection to consider. The end result was that potentially useful intelligence on the location of the remaining fugitives never got to the people who would ultimately have to go out and arrest them.

By contrast, everything the tracking unit learned went exclusively and immediately toward locating fugitives. Furthermore, it had inherent advantages when it came to gathering intelligence. Would-be informants were generally more willing to pass on tips to investigators from a UN-sponsored tribunal than to spies from a foreign government. The flow of information gave Del Ponte, and later Brammertz, ammunition when they confronted the recalcitrant governments in Belgrade or Zagreb. Having an in-house intelligence agency allowed the prosecutors to judge whether they were being taken for a ride by top officials and the security services. It helped them distinguish between truth and obfuscation, genuine effort and pantomime.

"We were able to construct a perception that we were tenacious and we were not going to let go," said Christian Axboe Nielsen, a Danish analyst for the tracking team. "It was tenacity backed by analysis. When we delivered something to them, they had to take it seriously. It was about obstinate, cajoling oversight that forced other international and domestic agencies to do their job. We made it difficult for them to maintain a consistent lie. They would need a continuity person, like in Hollywood, to keep track of holes and contradictions in the narratives they were trying to spin, but they didn't have this. They were sloppy.

But conditionality was the absolute key. If it had not been for EU conditionality, hardly anyone would have been caught."[11]

In more than a handful of cases, the ICTY team ran the suspects to ground themselves, all but forcing local authorities to step in and make the arrest.

In August 1999, the tracking unit discovered that General Momir Talić, the Bosnian Serb army chief of staff, would be flying to Vienna to take part in a regional seminar run by the Austrian National Defense Academy. Neither Talić nor the Austrian government were aware that he was under sealed indictment for genocide as a result of his role as a military commander in northwestern Bosnia during the war. Arbour opted not to tell Vienna before he arrived.

"We had someone in Belgrade with binoculars to say he's got on the plane, and then we had someone in Vienna to say when he got off the plane and went through customs," Arbour said. Only when Talić arrived at the Defense Academy did ICTY officials deliver the arrest warrant to the Austrian Foreign Ministry. The police politely but firmly arrested the general during a coffee break in the seminar. The Austrians duly transferred Talić to The Hague on August 25, but they were furious with Arbour. "They said, You should have told us ahead of time, but we said, Well in that case, you would have refused to allow him to come, because you don't want an indicted war criminal on your territory. So we would have been left empty-handed."[12]

After the assassination of the reformist prime minister Zoran Djindjić in March 2003,* there was a brief flowering of cooperation between the tracking team and the Serbian security services, who arrested everyone on their watch lists — more than thirteen

* See chapter 3.

thousand people, including a handful of war crimes suspects.

One of those caught up in the tail end of Operation Sabre* was Veselin Šljivančanin, a Montenegrin army officer who had played a role in the Ovčara farm massacre in November 1991. Šljivančanin had been a major in the Yugoslav army at the time, commanding a motorized brigade in the area that included a contingent of military police. They and the rest of Šljivančanin's soldiers withdrew from the scene on the night of November 20, leaving the captives at the mercy of Serb paramilitaries, who executed 264 of them.

Šljivančanin denied any prior knowledge of the killings, but the prosecutors at The Hague argued he must have been aware and had at the very least failed in his duty to protect his prisoners. He was indicted by the ICTY in November 1995, but until the fall of the Milošević regime he had little to worry about. The Yugoslav courts cleared him and he was promoted to lieutenant colonel with a command near his home in Montenegro.

With the end of the old order, however, more and more of his fellow indictees had given themselves up, been arrested, or simply were grabbed by unknown assailants and delivered into the hands of NATO troops in Bosnia. Šljivančanin vowed not to be taken alive: "I was always armed and always on the move. From the beginning of 2003, I was never at home. I went around Serbia and Montenegro, never staying with people who knew me. And I never stayed in the same place more than one night...I had a mobile phone, but I turned it off where I was staying. When there was something important to say, I would go to a monastery and turn it on, say what had to be said, and turn it off before moving on. I'm not religious but I thought that would confuse them and

---

* See chapter 3.

make them think I was going between monasteries. I had plastic explosive which I had wrapped in a belt around me. I had a gun and grenades, and I had three loyal friends. I tried to convince them that if the police came, I must not be taken alive. But none of them wanted to be the one to shoot me. They talked among themselves to decide who would have to do it. I had sleepless nights over it. If they got killed and I survived, how could I live with that? In February 2003, I told them to go. Just one of them would be in touch. We had a code and a table of numbers to say what each code meant, but I carried on moving between Belgrade, Zlatibor, and Montenegro, all the time with a detonator and explosives. People were afraid when they saw me. A friend said to me afterward he couldn't wait to see me and then couldn't wait for me to go again."[13]

On June 13, 2003, his fiftieth birthday, Šljivančanin visited his Belgrade apartment to spend some time with his daughter. He arrived with his suicide belt and personal arsenal, but she convinced him to disarm and hang the belt up on a coat hook. Šljivančanin took the day off and relaxed. But he had been too predictable by far. From their years of manhunting, the ICTY tracking team had come to realize that even war crimes suspects are sentimental about their own birthdays, and they persuaded the Serbian authorities to watch the Belgrade flat.

The special police came for him at two in the afternoon. When they were unable to knock down the reinforced steel door, they punched a hole in the wall with hammers. Šljivančanin's daughter put herself between him and his explosive belt.

"She lay on the weapons, and said, 'Father please don't use it…' She took my weapons and said, 'Be dignified. You will win through. Be strong.' And when your daughter tells you that, what else can you do?"

Šljivančanin gave himself up and was transferred just over a fortnight later to The Hague, still wearing the same yellow T-shirt, shorts, and slippers he was captured in. When the Belgrade security establishment turned against you, it did not spare your dignity.

Within a few months, the doors that had suddenly opened for the ICTY after Djindjić's murder swung shut again. The shock wore off, the nationalist camp regrouped, and its leader, Vojislav Koštunica, was elected Serbian prime minister in March 2004. Joint manhunt operations between the ICTY and Serbian security services began to leak once more. When the tracking team found the Croatian Serb warlord Goran Hadžić in the northern Serbian town of Novi Sad, it took the precaution of asking the French intelligence agency to rig up cameras outside the house where he was staying, before delivering the sealed indictment and arrest warrant to the Foreign Ministry in Belgrade on the morning of July 13. Within a few hours, a car belonging to the Serbian intelligence agency, BIA, pulled up at Hadžić's hideout, and the fugitive emerged with a suitcase. He was whisked away—hard proof if any were needed that the Serbian security apparatus was playing a double game. Hadžić had seven more years of liberty before becoming the last man on the list to be ensnared.*

"They sent a BIA courier to pick him up and we never saw him again until 2011. It was a disgrace, it really was," a senior ICTY official said.

It was not the first time this had happened under the Koštunica government. Four months earlier, the tracking team had found Colonel Ljubiša Beara, Mladić's chief of security in the Bosnian Serb army, who had personally handled the complicated

* See Introduction.

logistics involved in the execution and burial of the victims at Srebrenica. He had organized the buses that transported them to the execution sites and told the firing squads where to be and when. He even arranged for construction equipment to be on hand to dig the mass graves.*

In March 2004, Beara was thinner, balder, and grayer than the chubby red-faced colonel who orchestrated the Srebrenica massacre, but an ICTY investigator staked out his hiding place and satisfied himself that Beara was indeed there. He passed on the address through Serb officials to BIA, and Beara disappeared soon after.

The investigators of the Hague tracking unit were furious, but they got even. They went back to the same informants and got a new address, in a village near the Serbian town of Užice.

"This time we put investigators at either end of the street with video cameras. So we warned the Serbian government don't embarrass yourselves a second time," an ICTY official said.

The house was surrounded and Beara gave himself up on October 9, 2004. Koštunica's government declared it to be a "voluntary surrender," which provoked some dry mirth at The Hague. "Sure he surrendered. He surrendered when he was surrounded," said a senior tribunal official.

Almost all the transfers on Koštunica's watch were officially deemed "voluntary surrenders" to protect the prime minister's nationalist credentials. Fugitives who came forward were offered a package that included legal and financial aid for their families. Even so, very few surrenders were truly voluntary in any real sense. Police General Sreten Lukić, wanted for taking part in the ethnic cleansing of Kosovo, was taken in April 2005

---

* Beara would ultimately be convicted of genocide and sentenced to life in prison.

from a hospital bed where he was recovering from heart surgery and arrived in The Hague in his pajamas. His appearance was still called "voluntary."

The Bosnian Serb army's intelligence chief, Zdravko Tolimir, the thin gray eminence at General Mladić's shoulder during the mass killings at Srebrenica, was abducted by BIA agents inside Serbia, interrogated, bound, hooded, and shoved in the back of a car on May 31, 2007. He was smuggled over the Drina into Bosnia near Bijeljina, and then told to walk along a forest lane. A hundred yards down the track he was met by Bosnian Serb police, who handed him over to NATO.

The ICTY tracking team believed that there was only one truly voluntary surrender in the Koštunica era, and that was the one performed by the ultra-nationalist rabble-rouser Vojislav Šešelj. The bespectacled, perpetually snarling warlord was accused of recruiting brutal paramilitary groups to help carry out ethnic cleansing in Croatia and Bosnia. He appeared one day in February 2003 at the ICTY's Belgrade outpost with his suitcase, demanding to know who was going to pay for his ticket to The Hague.*

Under Koštunica, Serbia was prepared to sacrifice pawns and political rivals but not the top fugitives. In 2008, however, the balance of power between the pursued and their pursuers shifted in the latter's favor. The ICTY's allies in Serbia grew stronger. The country's pro-European president, Boris Tadić, won reelection in January and set about tightening his grip on the deep state intelligence and security services. And as Tadić grew stronger, his nationalist rival, Koštunica, grew weaker, until his coalition collapsed and he resigned in March.

---

* In November 2014, Šešelj was released from The Hague for cancer treatment in Serbia, with the verdict on charges of murder and torture still pending.

At the same time, Tadić's office and Serbia's own war crimes prosecutor, Vladimir Vukčević, found ways of working around the BIA, which was still controlled by a Koštunica loyalist, Rade Bulatović.

The new alliances, brokered by the ICTY tracking team, came into play in the pursuit of Stojan Župljanin.

Župljanin was the wartime security chief in Banja Luka, where he had run a special police unit responsible for atrocities against Muslims and Croats across western Bosnia. He had gone into hiding in 1997, leaving Bosnia and traveling abroad on a false passport to Nigeria, Hungary, and Russia, where he worked on construction sites.

Early in 2008, lonely and exhausted, Župljanin turned up in Serbia using the name Branislav Vukadin. Within days, the tracking unit received a tip from a contact in the Bosnian Serb police that Župljanin was living with a mistress in Niš. The unit worked with Tadić's office, which tried playing one Serbian intelligence agency against another.

The Military Security Agency was asked to stake out Župljanin's apartment before its civilian counterpart, the BIA, was informed. The message was duly passed on to the BIA, but Bulatović's men seemed to hesitate. When BIA agents turned up a day later, on March 26, Župljanin was gone.

However, in his hurry to leave, he left behind letters, photographs, and notebooks, more than a thousand pages filled mostly with self-pitying reflections on his plight, but also a few leads for his pursuers, including code names for his web of supporters. One code name led to another woman friend in Pančevo, just outside Belgrade. This time BIA agents carried out the surveillance without telling Bulatović. With his patron, Koštunica, gone, they knew the spy chief would soon be gone too, and they looked to their future. "Don't share your destiny with Rade," a Tadić aide had told them.

For the first few days that the Pančevo woman's phone was tapped, there was no sign anyone was with her. But as she was chatting with a friend on Wednesday, June 11, a demanding male voice could be heard clearly in the background. "The pie is ready in the oven. Take it out before it burns," Župljanin said. They were some of his last words as a free man. A few minutes later, the police were at the door. After a four-year trial in The Hague, he was sentenced in March 2013 to twenty-two years in prison for extermination, murder, torture, and persecution.

When there was a reward involved, the ICTY tracking team often helped organize the payment. Tribunal rewards were relatively modest, but the unit also arranged payments for the US State Department, whose Rewards for Justice scheme often paid out hundreds of thousands of dollars. The top bounties of $5 million for Karadžić and Mladić were never disbursed, but a tracking team member once accompanied an informant who had helped in finding one of the Srebrenica killers to a US embassy to collect $250,000. "He was shaking. It was eighty-one years' salary for him. I took him back to the tribunal office to count the money. I gave him $10,000 in cash and we put the rest in a diplomatic bag to The Hague, and then put it in a Swiss bank account for the informant."[14]

The ICTY tracking team also served as the connective tissue between the world's intelligence agencies in a way that allowed it to pursue suspects around the globe, although those pursuits were not always successful. In the case of Željko Ražnatović, known and feared universally as Arkan, the chase took the pursuers on a tour of Europe's football stadiums, but they always seemed to be one step behind. During the war, Arkan had gathered the muscle for his paramilitary unit, the Tigers, from the Red Star Belgrade supporters club. And after the war was over, he plowed a large amount of his war spoils into another Belgrade team, FK Obilić. Within one season he helped take them from relative obscurity to the 1998 Yugoslav championship.

The tracking team received several tip-offs suggesting that Arkan attended away games incognito. With the help of the local police, the unit staked out a Red Star game against Belgium's Germinal Ekeren in Antwerp in September 1997, and then an Obilić match against Atlético Madrid in the Spanish capital a year later.

On both occasions, police officers were stationed at every entrance with copies of Arkan's photograph, and members of the tracking team watched closed-circuit television screens in the security control rooms, each time without success. In the end, Arkan's criminal past caught up with him before the ICTY. He was gunned down by assassins from a rival crime syndicate, believed to be connected to the Milošević family, in the lobby of Belgrade's Intercontinental Hotel on January 15, 2000.

The unit had better luck in the case of Dragan Zelenović, one of the Bosnian Serbs involved in the Foča rape camps. Bosnian intelligence discovered his wife was making calls from her local post office to Sochi on the Russian Black Sea coast where Zelenović had been working on a building site under an assumed name. By conducting a reverse search of the online telephone directory, the tracking team discovered Zelenović's alias and got the Russian security services to arrest him in August 2005.

The same sort of networking helped snare Milan Lukić, one of the more grotesque butchers of the Bosnian war. The former waiter and his cousin Sredoje had formed a family-based death squad in Višegrad at the very beginning of the war and carried out wanton mass killings of the town's Muslims wherever they came across them. The Hague investigators believed he may have personally murdered more people than any other single indictee on the ICTY list.

He had managed to stay on in Višegrad months after his October 1998 indictment for murder and extermination, running a café and driving around town in a distinctive and expensive Nissan sport-utility vehicle under the noses of French peacekeepers. As the pressure grew on the French to take action, however, he crossed the border into Serbia where he became involved in a drug trafficking ring linked to Preventiva, Karadžić's security entourage.

In early 2003, Lukić had a violent falling out with Karadžić's men over profit sharing, culminating in an exchange of fire in which Lukić was reportedly injured. Through intermediaries, he made overtures to The Hague to discuss a possible surrender, raising the prospect that he might provide leads that would point to Karadžić's whereabouts, but he failed to turn up to two meetings arranged with the tracking team.[15]

The wind continued to turn against Lukić. A Serbian court sentenced him in absentia in September 2003 to twenty years in prison for the killing of sixteen Muslims taken off a bus and executed on the Bosnian-Serbian border in 1993, and a month later, he lost yet another layer of protection with the indictment of his uncle Sreten, a police general, for war crimes in Kosovo.*

Lukić ditched the idea of surrendering to the ICTY and took flight again, this time to South America, carrying forged identity papers. He could perhaps have stayed there indefinitely if it had not been for the complicating factor of his own ego. In April

---

* Sredoje and Sreten Lukić are now serving a total of forty-seven years in prison. Milan was given a life term.

2004, two independent journalistic bodies, the Institute for War and Peace Reporting and the Balkan Investigative Reporting Network (BIRN), published a report on his involvement in drug trafficking and his falling out with the Karadžić network. Lukić sent an e-mail to a Belgrade radio station in protest, swearing loyalty to his wartime leaders. He declared: "Mladić has always been and will remain the true hero and idol, and Karadžić is the leader of my people."[16]

Lukić may have been a master butcher of men, but he had little talent for concealment. The e-mail gave away his rough location, having come through a server in Brazil. The tracking team disseminated the details and quickly got help locating him from intelligence agencies in the United Kingdom, France, Croatia, and Serbia.

"This time everyone cooperated, because everyone considered him a bastard," a senior Hague investigator said.

The BIA watched Lukić's wife and tipped off the Croats when she crossed the border in August 2005. The tail was then passed to the Directorate for Territorial Surveillance, the domestic French security service, as she traveled to Paris and boarded a flight at Roissy Airport to Buenos Aires.[17] Meanwhile, MI6 had been following Lukić's trail as he cross the Brazilian border into Argentina. He was arrested on August 8 when he met his wife at the Buenos Aires airport.

Much of the tracking team's work was slow, painstaking, and unglamorous, filtering the flood of tips from informants, checking them against known facts, and scanning press reports while preparing briefs for the prosecutors so they could maintain effective pressure on governments to produce results. It was often a thankless slog, but every so often the arrest of someone like Milan Lukić, a mass murderer responsible for hideous crimes not seen in Europe for more than half a century, gave the team members all the motivation they could possibly want.

"I loved the concept of using what I was taught by my government to get these fuckers," said a former British military intelligence officer. "And the best of the people I worked with felt the same way."

By the end of the manhunt in the summer of 2011, the team could claim principal credit for at least half a dozen arrests and key assists in dozens more. The tracking unit's disproportionate success raised the question of why it remained so small. In a tribunal costing upward of $100 million a year, the outlay for a team of half a dozen investigators and analysts was trivial. They were always overstretched and there is little doubt a bigger, better-resourced team would have brought fugitives to The Hague at a faster pace. As with so much of the manhunt, success had more to do with the persistent efforts of individuals than with the institutions they worked for.

# 8.

# THE STRANGE DEATH OF DRAGAN GAGOVIĆ

Your life can't be cheaper than mine.
—*Dragan Gagović, wartime police chief of Foča*

**IN THE SPRING OF 1992,** it seemed to the people of the bucolic stone towns along the Drina River gorge that a fearsome beast had woken from a half-century slumber and reached out from the bowels of the earth to take them straight to hell.

In a few terrible weeks, bands of Serb police, soldiers, and paramilitary units descended on every town with a significant Muslim population. Many Muslim men were executed where they were found, in their homes and on the street. Women and children were rounded up and locked in makeshift concentration camps, where many of the women were raped. For most of the victims this catastrophe came out of the blue. They had been sentenced in absentia and without their knowledge, so the untidy human kaleidoscope in Bosnia could conform to the neat ethnic boundaries on maps drawn up many miles away in Belgrade.

Foča was one of the more inconvenient spots for the cartographers of Greater Serbia. It is a town built on a sloping shoulder of green land under the tree-covered peaks of the Dinaric Alps. Even the brutalism of 1970s Socialist architecture had failed to spoil the beauty of the location. It was home to twenty-one thousand Muslims and eighteen thousand Serbs. As in most Bosnian towns, the mosques stood close by the churches.

On April 7, 1992, marauders descended from the mountains to grip Foča by the throat. For anyone under forty-five who had known only the peace and coexistence of the postwar years, it came as an overwhelming shock. For the elderly, it was the return of a long-suppressed nightmare. In 1941, Croatian Fascists, the Ustasha, had marked in blood the eastern extremity of their territorial claims for a Greater Croatia by executing many of Foča's Serbs. Two years later, the Chetniks, an extreme Serb militia, swept into town from the opposite direction and unleashed revenge by proxy. Having chosen to collaborate with the Ustasha, the Nazis, and the Italian Fascists, the Chetniks were free to pursue their own agenda, and mercilessly preyed on the town's Muslims, who they saw as little more human vermin.[1]

The terrifying impression of a half-forgotten monstrosity from the past was deepened by the marauders' choice of costume. The Serb irregulars swaggered into Foča in 1992 dressed as 1940s Chetniks, who in turn had affected the fur caps and wild facial hair of nineteenth-century Serb *hajduk* marauders against the Ottoman Empire. They were a historical reenactment society that brought back past atrocities with real bloodshed.

Amid the terror of those first days in April, two policemen made an abortive attempt to protect the last shreds of the social fabric that had held Yugoslavia together, before it was blown away by the nationalist hurricane. One was a Muslim, Himzo Selimović. The other was Dragan Gagović, a Serb. Selimović was a little chubby with a drooping mustache and hangdog eyes that gave him a prematurely aged and melancholy appearance. Gagović was round-headed and fit, a martial-arts devotee. In

April 1992, they were both thirty-one — well-educated, dedicated young professionals.

They had been brought up to believe Yugoslavia would last forever. But the stresses of ethnic division had been building rapidly since the 1990 elections, the first reasonably free poll in nearly seventy years. The Bosnian branch of the League of Communists had imploded while the country was in the throes of political and economic crisis. The certainties of half a century crumbled and the ragged plasterwork of Tito's land of Brotherhood and Unity fell away. In its place, no one seemed to offer anything tangible to believe in, except the nationalists promoting ethnic solidarity. In Foča, as in most towns across Bosnia, the Serbs overwhelmingly voted for Radovan Karadžić's Serb Democratic Party (SDS), the Muslims for Alija Izetbegović's Party of Democratic Action, and the tiny Croat majority of about two hundred mostly for the Croatian Democratic Union.

With the political arena recast as an ethnic battlefield, the sense of dread was fed by television images of real war next door in Croatia, but still very few of Foča's townspeople had any notion of the flash flood of violence hurtling toward them down the Drina gorge. Selimović and Gagović knew more than most. Soon after the 1990 elections, the Foča police came across trucks crammed with weapons belonging to the Serb-dominated Yugoslav National Army (JNA) being driven down the back roads of eastern Bosnia. In the autumn of 1991, Selimović impounded a consignment of mortars and assault rifles, but senior JNA officers intervened and ordered him to release it. The whole country was being seeded with weaponry. This was the RAM plan, put together by top Serb officers in the JNA two years earlier, aimed at establishing a Greater Serbia through the strategic use of terror. Women and children would be targeted deliberately to break the spirit of the Muslim population before it had the chance to think about resisting. The survivors would flee the country and Bosnia would simply cease to exist. The agents and beneficiaries of this disintegration would be Karadžić's SDS. The weapons were destined for its activists, who hid them and waited for the call to arms.

The final signal for the war to begin was the arrival of the full menagerie of Serb and Montenegrin paramilitary groups, including the Tigers, the Panthers, and the White Eagles, who had gorged on blood and loot the previous year in Croatia and were now unleashed on Bosnia by Slobodan Milošević, the Serbian president, orchestrating the mayhem from Belgrade.

It began on April 1 in Bijeljina, close to the Drina in the far northeastern corner of the embryonic state, on the border with Serbia. A group calling itself the Tigers — led by the most rapacious and aggressive of the Serb warlords, Željko Ražnatović, universally known as Arkan — took over Bijeljina's main buildings and main roads, shooting the town's Muslims casually in the street. The American photographer Ron Haviv snapped a picture of one of Arkan's men, wearing sunglasses and with a cigarette nonchalantly held in one hand while kicking an executed woman in the head, which would become an enduring emblem of Bosnia's ethnic cleansing.

Six days later, on April 7, 1992, it was Foča's turn, and the pattern was the same. The Tigers and the other groups arrived and were immediately joined by local Serb extremists who were quickly realizing that open season had been declared on murder, rape, and pillage — as long as the crimes were wrapped in the flag and the victims were Muslim.

Those Muslim men not subjected to summary execution were taken to Foča's huge prison, known as the KP Dom,* where about five hundred are thought to have been shot or bludgeoned to death, their bodies thrown into the nearby Drina. Women and children were interned in sports halls and schools, where hundreds were repeatedly raped and assaulted before being deported to Montenegro.

By April 9, it was clear to Selimović his position was no longer tenable. He was holding on by his fingernails in the police station while mayhem coursed through the town. The SDS had ordered the Serb officers to set up their own unit on the ground floor of the building, just below him. He had only eight Muslim officers left, and the streets were full of Serb gunmen. He ordered his men to slip out one by one. Like a captain of a doomed ship, Selimović was the last to go.

He met his fellow officer, Dragan Gagović, as he was going out of the door. Selimović confronted him over the unfolding disaster outside. "You have always behaved correctly, a true officer of the law, but look where Karadžić is leading us," he said. "We'll have blood coming up to our knees!" Most of Foča's Muslims would stay, Selimović predicted. They would think they would not be harmed if they kept their heads down while the storm passed. But they would be wrong, fatally wrong.

"Please help these people," Selimović pleaded. Gagović broke down and cried. Then he vowed that if Selimović and his Muslim comrades could not stay at their place of work, he would leave too, and he was true to his word, walking out with his fellow Serb officers half an hour later.[2]

Selimović fled to a friend's apartment, but over the ensuing twenty-four hours it was clear he would not be safe there. Serb paramilitaries were going door to door through the

* Kazneno-Popravni Dom (House of Criminal Corrections), widely known and feared as KP Dom.

neighborhood. He could see them out of the window. His last chance for survival was to call the one friend who could save him.

"You have two choices: to help us to escape or to allow us to be killed," he told Gagović. There was silence on the other end of the line for two minutes as the bonds of duty and friendship were tested against Bosnia's violent new realities and Selimović's life hung in the balance. Then Gagović made a decision. He would help.

"Your life can't be cheaper than mine," Gagović said. He told Selimović to be at Foča's town hall within ten minutes and he would try to find someone trustworthy to get him out of town. Failing that, he would come himself. Selimović waited, anxious and exposed outside the building, staking everything on Gagović's good faith. But the uncertainty lasted only a few minutes. Again, his friend kept his promise. A Serb policeman materialized and drove Selimović north toward Goražde, a town still under the control of the three-day-old Bosnian government in Sarajevo.

Selimović and Gagović never saw each other again. On April 19, a little more than a week after Selimović's hasty departure, Gagović led his men back to the Foča police station and resumed work. In Karadžić's newly cleansed Republika Srpska, he became Foča's chief of police.

"This was his great mistake," Selimović said later. "He could have left Foča. He could have resigned."[3]

Selimović survived the conflict in Goražde. What his former friend Gagović did over the same period became a matter for the Hague Tribunal. He was indicted in June 1996 for crimes against humanity.

While Gagović was police chief, 1,500 Muslims were thought to have been murdered in Foča and the surrounding villages.

Similar massacres took place all the way up the Drina valley. What set Foča apart and what propelled the town into the history books was the scale of the crimes committed against Muslim women. The mass rape of women and girls as young as fifteen was so systematic, so widespread, and so depraved, that it changed the laws of war. After Foča, the use of sexual violence as a weapon would be considered a crime against humanity. Rape has been used a tool of terror through the centuries, but at the Nuremberg trials in 1945, it was not specified in the court's charter. Making Foča a test case, the Hague Tribunal corrected the omission.

Gagović was indicted by the ICTY in part because of his position as police chief throughout the war. He was deemed responsible for the gruesome conditions in Foča's municipal sports hall, where more than seventy women, children, and elderly men were held from July to August 1992 in a single room measuring twelve by seven yards. Food was irregular and meager. There were no blankets or towels. Women and girls were repeatedly taken out of the hall by groups of soldiers to barracks or apartments, where they were gang-raped. As a result they often bled heavily, but no medical care was provided. Two of the women died. The hall was easily visible from Gagović's office and there were police guards on the door. According to the indictment, Gagović presided over the whole abomination, deciding which women should be detained, and had visited the hall on several occasions.

He was also accused of committing one rape. A group of detainees from the sports hall came to appeal to him in mid-July to stop the abuse. Not only did he do nothing to protect them but the next day he took two of the women to an apartment where he was alleged to have raped one of them at gunpoint.

Like many of the war crimes suspects, it took a while for Gagović to take the Hague Tribunal seriously. Five months after his indictment it was easy to find him. He was still in Foča, walking around town in uniform and drinking in cafés in the company of the UN police monitors based nearby. When I went to interview him in November 1996,[4] finding his address was easy, but the first time he answered the door he claimed to be someone else. When I returned a few days later, however, he dropped the pretense and became increasingly talkative about the war and the charges against him.

"If they arrest me, too bad," he said nonchalantly. He clearly believed his drinking buddies in the UN police would never challenge him and insisted he was innocent of the charges anyway. When he spoke about his case, he looked me straight in the eye and smiled like a man eager for approval, even friendship.

In his version of events, he was a small-town police chief, overwhelmed by the influx of bloodthirsty paramilitaries. He was a single man against the tornado and could not stop the atrocities, only mitigate them. The guards at the door of the sports hall were paramilitaries in old police uniforms, not his men, he insisted. And the rape charge was "an outright lie" he said, blazing with indignation: "It is rude and disgusting that the Hague Tribunal could accuse me of such an act."

I asked him Selimović's question: Why had he not just resigned and left town with his former comrade? In response, Gagović portrayed himself as a savior of Muslims rather than their scourge.

"I felt responsible to prevent the looting and burning. It was a very strange time and we could not do more than we did. All people who came to the police station got permission to leave. We gave out three thousand permits," Gagović said. "If I had not been there, three thousand Muslims would not be alive today."

There were two things that immediately distinguished Gagović from almost all his fellow war crimes suspects. First, he did not opt for blanket denial of the mass atrocities, the norm in the Republika Srpska then as it is today. He not only acknowledged that the war crimes in Foča had been premeditated as part of an overall plan for the Drina valley; he was also prepared to go further than any other Serb military or police officer in explaining the mechanics of ethnic cleansing, and the key role of a Serb crisis staff in Foča in overseeing the murders and mass expulsions. He even indicated he might testify against his fellow staff members.

The other striking feature of Gagović's account of wartime Foča was that at least some of his exculpatory claims turned out to be true. Selimović confirmed he did indeed owe his life to Gagović. The two men stayed in touch for some time after the war, sending messages through journalists like me who traveled across the new ethnic boundaries. Selimović sent Gagović news of a newborn daughter and Gagović sent back congratulations, along with a bottle of homemade brandy. Mujo Moco, a Foča cobbler who had escaped to Sarajevo, confirmed that the Serb policeman had also rescued his wife and daughter.

Gagović insisted he was prepared to go to The Hague once he had collected the signed testimonies of Muslims he had helped. Selimović was reluctant to put his account on paper, however. He would help Gagović if he was innocent, but would do his own research first. The survivors of Foča were having to face the same painful questions as many hundreds of thousands of their fellow Bosniaks. Had their friends been conspiring against them all along? Or if not, how was it possible for a seemingly benign, apparently ordinary neighbor to mutate overnight into a killer, capable of such inhumanity? Was Gagović an ordinary cop pulled down into the cesspit by the evil that swelled around him? Had he been falsely accused? Or had he fooled them all, plotting the liquidation of Foča's Muslims even as he drank with them and laughed at their jokes?

On Gagović's long list of Muslims he claimed to have saved, there was a subset of women he had sheltered from assault in his own apartment before smuggling them across the lines. Many of them could not be found immediately, having fled abroad, but one woman on the list was still in the Bosnian capital in the winter of 1996. In one of Sarajevo's many smoke-filled and melancholy cafés, she agreed to tell her story on condition of anonymity. Gagović had sheltered her, as well as her sister and mother, in a Foča apartment and had then arranged transportation to Montenegro. His version seemed to be confirmed. But as I was packing away my notebook the woman took a sharp, deep breath and appeared to steel herself. She had omitted something from her narrative, she said. She had left out one particular night, which she had only revealed to her husband and a psychiatric nurse in a refugee camp.

On the eve of her departure from Foča, Gagović turned up unexpectedly at the apartment. He sat down facing her and began talking to her in a way he never had before. He had spotted her before the war, he claimed, and had been overwhelmed by her beauty. He pledged to help her father, who like many of Foča's Muslim men was incarcerated in the town's prison. He even proposed marriage to her.

Frightened, the woman seized on the first excuse that came to mind. She could not get married as she was midway through her studies. The romantic side of Gagović vanished as abruptly as it had appeared. He turned angry and left, slamming the door. Later that night, he returned to the apartment and raped her. It was not a "brutal" assault, she said, but only because she was too terrified of waking her mother and sister to put up much resistance.

"I was afraid he would kill them if they came into the room. I lay there like a corpse. I just remember pleading with him, 'Please don't.' He saved me, but he also destroyed half my life," she said.

There are many different shades of criminal on The Hague list. There are the cold calculators who drew up their maps and then gave the necessary orders to the appropriate people. Some, but by no means all, of this category found a new home in The Hague. Then there are the Stakhanovites of murder with their prodigious appetite for bloodletting. The Bosnian conflict proved these people are around us, submerged like crocodiles, revealing their predatory nature only when the circumstances are decisively in their favor. Foča, it turned out, had more than its fair share drawn from this second group. Gagović's seven co-accused were all indicted on multiple counts of rape and torture. Of the group, Janko Janjić was the most fearsome. He was an occasionally employed mechanic who went by the gang nickname of "Tuta." When the killing started in 1992, he was thirty-four and displayed leadership skills in mass murder that had not been apparent in peacetime. He rose to the rank of a sub-commander of the military police and revelled in his capacity to inflict terror. After the war, he sat outside his café smoking and boasted about his exploits to a CBS television crew. He said if he was paid five thousand German marks, he would explain on camera how he "slit his victims' throats and gouged out their eyes."[5] He was indicted on eight counts of torture and rape as crimes against humanity.

Gagović belonged to a third category. Here was a man clearly capable of acts of honor and kindness before the onset of war. For nine days in April 1992, he even resisted the nationalist drumbeat, withdrawing his men from the Foča police station in solidarity with their banished Muslim comrades. But then he went back and sank into the depravity of wartime Foča. The chaos of Yugoslavia's collapse turned men like Gagović into local demigods with command over life and death. He could dispense mercy to some, appalling cruelty to others. In at least one case, he deigned to free a woman and then raped her. He began with a clumsy attempt at seduction and when that failed, he pulled out his gun and forced himself on her.

In the end, Selimović was forced to face up to the fact his former friend and savior may have mutated into something unrecognizable.

"Gagović saved my life," he told me in late 1996, but he added that, if the charges against him were proved, "I would be ready to kill him. Even if he were my brother, I would do the same." Selimović added: "It doesn't matter how many people he saved."

Gagović was never tried by the ICTY, because he never made it to The Hague. He had set himself up as a karate instructor after leaving the police force and on January 9, 1999, he was driving five young members of his club, all aged eleven and twelve, back home from a martial arts competition at Mount Tara over the border in Serbia. Heading south along the Drina, he turned off on a mountain road to get back to Foča without having to drive through the mainly Bosniak town of Goražde.

It was a vertiginous drive at any time of year, but with snow and ice on the road it was a particularly dicey journey. There was a sheer drop to the Drina on one side and a wall of rock on the other. As he turned a corner, Gagović saw a roadblock manned by French paratroopers. It was intended to look like a regular NATO checkpoint but it had been set up with the sole intention of capturing him. Three years after the Bosnian war, the

French army had chosen Gagović as the target of its first arrest operation.[6]

The Frenchmen from the First Marine Infantry Parachute Regiment had watched Gagović's car cross the Drina and begin the climb. A homing beacon had been put on the white Volkswagen and lookouts posted along the way gave a constant commentary on his progress. They were well aware that he had children in the backseat but pressed on with their mission, regardless.

"Watch out. He's coming but he's not alone!" the paratroopers at the checkpoint were warned.[7] As the car rounded the bend, they waved for Gagović to stop but according to the official account, he sped up instead. He managed to drive around the metal barricade and the soldiers opened fire, spraying the rear of the car with bullets, one of which hit him in the back of the head just below the left ear. The car hit the side of the road, continued up onto the rocks, and flipped over. Amazingly, none of the five children was seriously harmed. One said later that Gagović had told them to duck down, but they were in shock. They had to be pulled out of a car spattered with blood and brain matter.

NATO and the French government quickly claimed Gagović had posed an imminent threat to the lives of French soldiers, driving straight at them, but the hasty explanations left an array of unanswered questions. Most important, why had the French unit persevered with the operation, let alone opened fire, once the paratroopers knew there were children in the car? Just six days before the shooting, the French defense minister had pledged that any operation to carry out arrests of war crimes suspects had to be done in such a way as to ensure that no one was harmed.

"Those people must be apprehended without any bloodletting. We are not staging a Rambo movie there. Real life is not a cartoon!" the minister, Alain Richard, had said in a television discussion with journalists.[8] Yet the French paratroopers did indeed seem to have played Rambo, spraying a car full of children with gunfire to stop a suspect whose everyday whereabouts and routines were no secret. In principle, Gagović could have been picked up almost any day in Foča.

Gagović's own behavior was just as peculiar. At home, he strolled around town with no apparent precautions against arrest. So why did he risk his life and the lives of the five children in his care in a desperate effort to avoid being stopped on a mountain road?

The official NATO and French line that Gagović was directly threatening lives of soldiers suggested that he was driving toward them. But the car was fired on from the rear. The commander of SFOR in Bosnia, General Montgomery Meigs, demanded the French hand over video footage of the incident, but they refused.

In a report on war criminals at large written in November 2000, the International Crisis Group added to the intrigue surrounding Gagović death with this passage hinting at a French military conspiracy:

> Even more disturbing are allegations by highly placed sources both within the Bosnian jurisprudence system and close to the ICTY, that the action was taken to prevent Gagović from turning himself in to the ICTY. These sources asserted that Gagović was in contact with the ICTY at the time of his death, in an effort to arrange his surrender. Gagović's alleged wartime activities were rumoured to have included business dealings with the French UNPROFOR contingent. He had reportedly received anonymous threats that any attempt to turn himself in would cost him his life. The circumstances surrounding

*Gagović's death remain suspicious, and French refusal to give*
*a copy of the arrest videotape to NATO command can only fuel*
*speculation that the French Army is trying to hide something.*
*That videotape should be turned over without further delay.*[9]

Could the French military really have assassinated Gagović because he knew too much about the shoddy compromises
they made in the postwar Republika Srpska — compromises that
allowed atrocious war criminals to run many Serb towns years
after being indicted?

It is a far-fetched conspiracy theory for the same reasons it
was a deeply flawed arrest operation. Why choose a day when
there was a car full of witnesses, however young? And if you were
going to liquidate someone, would you use an entire squad of
paratroopers as your assassins?

More convincing than either the official version or the conspiracy theory is the possibility that the missed opportunity
to bring Gagović before a court and the unforgivable trauma
inflicted on five small children were the result of incompetence.
The decision to use a unit that specialized in shoot-to-kill operations significantly raised the likelihood that something would go
wrong during the arrest. In the wake of the shooting, the French
military belatedly decided that the First Marine Infantry Parachute Regiment was far too blunt an instrument for such tasks.
It was more accustomed to doing its work in remote corners of
Africa, away from civilian scrutiny and the media spotlight.

The debacle infuriated investigators at the ICTY, who
believed Gagović had been about to turn himself in with evidence
implicating more senior Serb officials who had orchestrated the
mass atrocities at Foča. Moreover, Gagović's death nearly caused
the deaths of the UN's police monitors in Foča. Their offices

were attacked by a nationalist mob looking for revenge. Five UN monitors were beaten and two were seriously injured before they could be rescued by SFOR soldiers.

Back in Paris, the French government was embarrassed and angry. If one of the bullets had gone an inch either way and any of the children had been killed, it could well have been the end of NATO's manhunt and the Hague Tribunal's arrest policy. Some in the French special forces feared the debacle would also shut down their Special Operations Command, a young organization that had only been formed in 1992. The reconnaissance and intelligence division was immediately placed under new leadership,[10] while new guidelines and procedures were put in place after a painful postmortem was held back at headquarters. France would stay in the hunt, but in the future, arrests would be performed by more subtle operators, the Marine Commandos.

# 9.
# THE SPYMASTER OF
# THE HÔTEL DE BRIENNE

There was a sense we were doing it because we had to do it,
but we were never given the critical means to achieve the goal.
There were limited resources, a limited team,
and the truth is we never really came close.
—*French intelligence officer*
*involved in the hunt for Radovan Karadžić*

**THE STRANGE AND BLOODY DEATH** of Dragan Gagović came within
an inch of bringing the Bosnian manhunt to a premature end.
The survival of the five young passengers in his car had more
to do with luck than the judgment of the French paratroopers
who shot him. If any of the children had been injured or killed,
the international uproar would not just have put France out of
the chase but would also have deterred other NATO member
states.

The near-disaster forced a pause in direct French involvement in arrests for nearly a year, while the military reorganized
and rethought its tactics. There was no tolerance for mistakes
in Paris, which had been ambivalent about the manhunt from
the start. It brought to the surface France's conflicting attitudes

toward the region and toward the whole notion of international justice.

At the beginning of the Balkan conflict, President François Mitterrand had declared: "As long as I live, never—mark my words well—never will France make war on Serbia."[1] The US and British governments were similarly loathe to get involved in a civil conflict in which they portrayed all sides as equally at fault. But they never expressed it so bluntly. Mitterrand's pledge reflected something deeper: a sentiment entrenched among French diplomats, senior officers, and intellectuals that the Serbs were natural allies.

The French revolution was an inspiration to the nineteenth-century Serb nationalists, who saw Paris as a counterweight to their Habsburg and Ottoman overlords. The Serbs and the French fought on the same side in two world wars, and Paris had entered into an alliance in 1921 with the first incarnation of Yugoslavia, the Kingdom of Serbs, Croats, and Slovenes. Along with Romania and Czechoslovakia, this Little Entente was designed to contain the influence of Germany and its Austro-Hungarian allies. The enduring image of Serbia in many French minds, as a vital link in the chain around the Germans, endured well into the Yugoslav wars in the 1990s. It was not unusual during those years of conflict for French officials to play down atrocities committed by Serbs, arguing they were explained, if not excused, by longer-term geopolitical perspectives.

Jacques Chirac, Mitterand's successor in the Élysée Palace, was not as encumbered by history's burdens. He was outraged by the massacres and the Serbs' seizure of French UN peacekeepers as hostages. Ten days after he took office in May 1995, Chirac ordered the recapture of a frontline French checkpoint on the Vrbanja bridge in Sarajevo, which had been seized by Serb soldiers disguised as French peacekeepers. For the first time in the Bosnian conflict the French fought back, with a hundred troops and supporting fire from half a dozen armored cars. Two French and four Serb soldiers were killed in the battle, which signaled a new posture in Paris.

Colonel Erik Sandahl, the commander of the Fourth French Battalion in Bosnia, declared at the time: "When the Serbs took our soldiers under their control by threat, by dirty tricks, they began to act as terrorists. You cannot support this. You must react. The moment comes when you have to stop it. Full stop. And we did."[2]

Three months later, Chirac backed NATO air strikes against the Bosnian Serbs. This fresh resolve in Paris had its limits and its nuances, however, particularly when it came to the pursuit of war crimes suspects. When Chirac discussed Operation Amber Star with Bill Clinton and Tony Blair in May 1997, he had appeared bullish about the possibilities of such a daring joint action. But his enthusiasm was fleeting and the idea went against the grain for many in the French state, particularly in the army.

Those mixed feelings expressed themselves in some striking cases of divided loyalty. A year after the Gourmelon affair poisoned Franco-American relations,* another French major, Pierre-Henri Bunel, was spotted in a Brussels restaurant passing NATO bombing plans to a Serbian military intelligence officer. Bunel insisted at his trial he had been acting on verbal instructions of military intelligence, but that defense was undermined by his initial claim immediately after arrest to be acting for "humanitarian reasons" to protect Serbia. In December 2001, he was sentenced to five years.

---

* See chapter 1.

A senior French peacekeeper, Colonel Patrick Barriot, was so persuaded by the Serb cause that he became an "ambassador" in France for the Serb Krajina enclave in Croatia.[3] Serb sympathies went all the way to the top. In December 1995, General Jean-René Bachelet, the commander of UN forces in Sarajevo, condemned the freshly signed Dayton peace agreement because it obliged Bosnian Serbs to give up suburbs of the capital they had occupied during the war. Bachelet described the Sarajevo settlement as a self-interested American imposition which would lead to an impasse, and he told journalists that it presented Serbs with "the alternatives of the suitcase or the coffin." He was immediately recalled for a dressing-down in Paris, where his embarrassed government was about to host the formal signing ceremony for the Dayton Accords.[4]

The attitudes of French officials and military officers were not just shaped by sentimentality for an old alliance. They also sensed a whiff of hypocrisy in the American enthusiasm for the pursuit of war criminals. From their point of view, the Americans had skipped the war and the long, troubled UNPROFOR peacekeeping operation, in which the French had paid the highest price, losing fifty-six soldiers. The United States had arrived only after the shooting had stopped and then had sought to monopolize the Dayton peace talks. Jacques Blot, the French negotiator in Ohio, felt so sidelined that at one point he threatened to walk out and return to Paris.

Moreover, the French military establishment was deeply suspicious of the philosophy and implications of the Hague Tribunal. It refused to allow its officers to appear as witnesses, lest cross-examination by defense counsels turn into a postmortem of their peacekeeping efforts in UNPROFOR.

When the defense minister, Alain Richard, described the

tribunal as a "show trial," he was expressing the deep unease among the top French brass. A senior French official told the American journalist Chuck Sudetic:

*The trial of Karadžić would be a trial of the inconsistencies, contradictions, failures, and hypocrisies of the entire Western world . . . If Mladić were brought to trial, his defense lawyers would be able to call half of the French army that served in Bosnia during the war to testify. He could not be denied the right to call them as witnesses. No one has worked out a strategy on how to handle Karadžić's prosecution if he is arrested. If he ever comes to trial, he'll say he was in permanent contact with all the countries of the Western world. He'll say he received permanent commitments.*[5]

The American and British military had similar concerns, but there were reasons for the French to be particularly worried. A French general, Bernard Janvier, was the UNPROFOR commander when Srebrenica fell, and he had held a series of meetings with the Bosnian Serb general, Ratko Mladić, in the weeks before the Muslim enclave was overrun. The talks were to negotiate the release of UNPROFOR peacekeepers taken hostage by Serb forces. Janvier's subsequent actions led to accusations that, as the price for recovering his men alive, he had given Mladić assurances that NATO airpower would not be used to defend Srebrenica or the other eastern Bosnian enclaves of Žepa and Goražde.* A French parliamentary inquiry in 2001 absolved Janvier of direct responsibility, but its report conceded that France "carries part of the blame" for the disaster.

*The allegations were made by the humanitarian group Médecins Sans Frontières, among others.

Encouraged by President Chirac, the French military took part in the Operation Amber Star planning exercise in Stuttgart, but the poisonous atmosphere created by the Gourmelon affair meant its readiness to carry out joint arrest operations was never put to the test. France's intelligence agencies were active, however, in tracking the high-value targets — it was a simple extension of what they had been doing all along during the war. The problem was there were too many spies from too many agencies.

The Directorate for Military Intelligence (Direction du Renseignement Militaire, or DRM) took the lead in tracking suspects, particularly in the immediate postwar years. Working in parallel was France's version of the CIA and MI6, the General Directorate for External Security (Direction Générale de la Sécurité Extérieure, or DGSE), whose headquarters on Paris's boulevard Mortier was colloquially known as La Piscine (swimming pool) because of its proximity to the French Swimming Federation. Initially its role was passive, confined to providing analysis and coordinating with other spy agencies. In the latter years of the chase the DGSE entered into direct tracking operations, spearheaded by the operations department, the Service Action.

The domestic intelligence agency, the Directorate for Territorial Surveillance (Direction de la Surveillance du Territoire, or DST), also played a role, when the suspects had French connections. Lastly, the country's gendarmes contributed their special operations group, the National Gendarmerie Intervention Group (Groupe d'Intervention de la Gendarmerie Nationale, or GIGN), which offered advice on how to track and capture a fugitive without killing the quarry or innocent bystanders.

Rivalry between these organizations was at times even worse in France than among their US and UK equivalents, in part because their territorial boundaries were not as clearly drawn.

An example of the knots the French agencies tied for themselves in pursuit of the war criminals is Operation Glaïeul, described in the memoirs of a former Service Action agent, Pierre Martinet. In the late 1990s Martinet took part in a stakeout at the Geneva home of a Serbian woman in her fifties, believed to be one of Radovan Karadžić's mistresses, code-named Glaïeul (Gladiolus). Martinet and a female agent kissed passionately at the entrance of the woman's apartment just as the postman arrived. They unclinched as soon as he left and picked Glaïeul's mailbox, taking the incoming mail and replacing it with the previous day's letters, which had already been scrutinized. Overnight DGSE specialists used stain remover, a dry iron, and a finely sharpened chopstick to open the envelopes. (Steaming open envelopes is hopeless, Martinet points out. It ruins the paper.)[6]

Operation Glaïeul produced useful intelligence on Karadžić's financial support network and his circle of closest conspirators. It could well have led to the man himself but for the failure of France's security agencies to cooperate. After two weeks under surveillance in Geneva, the woman left for Paris where DGSE tracked her to a hotel. There, agents broke into her room only to run into their rivals from the domestic counterintelligence agency, the DST.[7] Such was the raw competition between the two organizations that the Service Action burglars feared they might be arrested, perhaps exposing the whole operation. Rather than sharing the intelligence garnered thus far, the DGSE simply pulled out and a promising line of inquiry was abandoned.

In the summer of 1997, in order to avoid such self-defeating duplication, all operations targeting Balkan war criminals were formally placed under the control of one man, General Philippe Rondot.

Rondot was the son and grandson of military officers, and he was already a legend in his own right. He was one of very few spies to have served in both the DGSE's Service Action and the DST, and in 1994, he masterminded the intelligence coup of a generation, the capture in Sudan of Ilich Ramirez Sanchez, better known as "Carlos the Jackal."

For many years, Rondot was known inside the intelligence world only by his code name "Max," and few had any idea what he looked like.[8] Even his CIA counterparts rarely saw him. When the Americans flew through Paris in their periodic attempts to keep allied intelligence agencies on roughly the same page in the Balkans, Rondot would often send proxies to their meetings. A blurry black-and-white photo purporting to be him appeared in the press after the Carlos arrest, but it was so indistinct it could have been a lot of people. Rondot was from the old school—a true denizen of the shadows. The first time a clear image of him surfaced was in 2006, revealing a trim, bald man with steel-rimmed glasses, a suntan, and an amused smile twisting up the edges of his mouth. By then, he was seventy with a long cloak-and-dagger career behind him.

In the hunt for the Balkan war criminals, the veteran spy sought to centralize the flow of intelligence through his spartan office in the Hôtel de Brienne, the eighteenth-century headquarters of the Defense Ministry in Paris, where Charles de Gaulle had set up a provisional government after the 1944 liberation of Paris. From there, with carte blanche from both Chirac and Richard, Rondot could reach out through the secure telephones on his desk deep into the DRM, the DGSE, and the GIGN, giving him access to agents and officers who reported directly to him over the heads of their superiors.

Over the course of a year, Rondot built a web with himself at the center. He amassed dossiers on Karadžić and Mladić, on their routines, quirks, friends, and family, and did the same for all the other Hague indictees in the French zone in the southeastern third of postwar Bosnia. He started to develop substantial leads on where most of them were, yet still the French military remained reluctant to act on the intelligence he provided.

By 1999, the British had carried out half a dozen arrests, the Americans three, and the Dutch two. There were more war crimes suspects left in the French zone than anywhere else, but France had yet to capture a single one.

Its troops had handled one surrender, when Dragoljub "Zaga" Kunarac, an infamous paramilitary commander from Foča, contacted French officers in February 1998, offering to give himself up. But even then, the negotiations took more than a week.

Kunarac had been indicted for committing mass rape and torture as crimes against humanity. He told the French the birth of his son had persuaded him to hand himself in to face his accusers "for honor's sake," but he suggested his honor would be facilitated by money to cover his family's living expenses while he was in prison. Estimates of what was paid range from 80,000 to 800,000 French francs.[9] US officials claimed the French also cleared the deal with Bosnian Serb officials to ensure the surrender would not cause problems for the leadership.[10] Once a deal was struck, Kunarac arrived at the French base in his best suit and tie on March 4, and was flown to The Hague. He would eventually be sentenced to twenty-eight years in jail.[11]

The first genuine arrest operation in the French zone in Bosnia was carried out not by the French themselves but by the Germans. It took place on June 15, 1998, and represented a singular moment in history — the first time German soldiers had been in action since World War II.

Befitting the high stakes, Operation Precious Bounty was months in the planning and absolutely nothing was left to chance. It also marked the first significant operation carried out by the German Special Forces Command (Kommando Spezialkräfte, or KSK) set up only two years earlier. The target was Milorad Krnojelac, a high-school math teacher turned wartime commandant of one of the most brutal concentration camps in eastern Bosnia, Foča's KP Dom. Its inmates were selected at random for savage beatings under Krnojelac's regime. At least twenty-nine inmates died from torture or execution.

After the war, Krnolejac did not just keep his job at the high school—he was promoted to principal. But his savagery had not been forgotten. Camp survivors testified to the Hague Tribunal prosecutors and a sealed indictment for crimes against humanity was issued against him in June 1997. Starting in December, the Signals Corps of the German Bundeswehr listened in to Krnojelac's phone calls from its base in Mostar, and as summer approached, KSK reconnaissance teams watched him as he walked to school.

"Krnojelac was an elderly man, a former teacher with all the habits of a teacher," an officer involved in the operation recalled. "He was always on time, very organized, and following habits developed over decades. He behaved very predictably and was at home and on the street always at the same time. His POL* was easy to establish."[12]

With the approval of Chancellor Helmut Kohl, Operation Precious Bounty finally went into action on June 15 at 7:15 a.m. German commandos blocked off the streets and bridges in central Foča, surrounding Krnojelac midway on his walk to work. He gave up without a fight.

---

* Pattern of life.

In August of the following year, while the French were still reorganizing their special forces in the wake of the Gagović incident, the Germans struck again in Foča, arresting Radomir Kovač, another of the mass rape suspects. Kovač was at the other end of the personality spectrum from Krnojelac — an unemployed erratic drunk — and posed a much bigger operational headache for the Germans.

According to one of the German officers, "He could leave his apartment in the morning or he could stay in bed all day and get shit-faced at night. The only constant we were able to find was that he was in his apartment at around four o'clock every morning. We finally came up with the idea to snatch him at home rather than waiting for him on the streets of Foča. That…at first created a lot of resistance among the agencies involved. Finally we were able to prove that it was the only option and that it was feasible."[13]

The nervousness among the German intelligence agencies and political leadership was centered on the increased risk of civilian casualties posed by a capture operation inside a residential building. The KSK trained for the Kovač mission for weeks to try to minimize that risk. The group identified an abandoned apartment building in East Germany that had a similar Socialist-era design to Kovač's home in Foča, and military specialists blew dozens of doors off their hinges until they had learned precisely the right amount of explosive required. The blast had to be big enough to remove the door but not so large it would kill or injure people in the apartment. To be absolutely sure, the KSK commander, Brigadier General Hans-Heinrich Dieter, lay on a bed with another senior officer during final rehearsals, playing the roles of Kovač and his wife.

The meticulous preparation paid off, and Kovač was seized

on August 2, 1999, according to the plan rehearsed in East Germany. Kovač dissolved into tears when he was led away. His wife, Slavika, was another matter. With an attention to detail that bordered on the paranoid, the KSK had planned to take her into protective custody in case she was assaulted or worse by Serb nationalists and her injuries blamed on NATO. She walked away with the soldiers in silent resentment.

"I don't think she loved her husband for what he'd done but had no choice but to stay with him after the war," a German officer reflected. "But if her eyes would have been daggers she would have stabbed me a thousand times."[14]

The first two carefully orchestrated arrests gave the newly created KSK a huge boost of confidence. Too much confidence as it turned out. On its third arrest operation, the unit's commander cut some corners, with fatal results. The target was Janko "Tuta" Janjić, one of Gagović's comrades who had run a wartime rape camp at the edge of town. He was easy to identify from the death's-head tattoos on his eyelids and the bleak phrase "I was dead before I was born" inked on his forehead. Tuta did not bother to hide, relying instead on deterrence. He vowed never to be taken alive and let it be known he carried a live grenade on him at all times to fulfill the threat.

Buoyed by their earlier successes, the Germans tried anyway. They had found an observation post that allowed them to look straight into his apartment, which gave the German commanders confidence that they knew enough about their target to mitigate the risks. They proceeded despite obvious red flags that would normally have ruled out such an operation, a clear chance of death or injury to civilians and German soldiers. But the KSK officers gambled on the element of surprise and the presumption that Janjić would not detonate his grenade with his family around him. On October 12, 2000, the unit blew open the door of Tuta's brother's home and stormed in with full-body armor, helmets, and shields. Soldiers pushed his brother, sister-in-law, and mother to the floor, while a snatch squad surged into the bedroom for Tuta. However, they had misjudged Janjić, who pulled the pin of his grenade, killing himself instantly. His relatives were unscathed but three of the German soldiers were seriously wounded by shrapnel slicing between the ceramic plates of their flak jackets. They were Germany's first combat casualties since 1945, wounded in the course of bringing a concentration camp commander to justice.

As the German operations in the French zone and under French command steadily grew more daring, the pressure on the French forces to take action built up exponentially. The call to action came from home and abroad, from the press, public opinion, and, increasingly, the politicians.

There was no shortage of targets for the French to choose from. Their zone, Multinational Division Southeast, sat on the southern mountain stretch of the Drina, whose banks had become execution sites for the local Muslim population. At one point it was so clogged with bodies that the management of a hydroelectric plant at Višegrad complained they were choking its turbines.

Gagović was chosen as the first target at the beginning of 1999 principally because there was more intelligence data on him than any other suspect in the French zone, and because his travels were thought to make him more vulnerable to capture on the road. That assumption and the use of paratroopers proved fatal miscalculations.

The Gagović killing prompted a rethink of French tactics at the special forces headquarters, a set of old gypsum quarries in Taverny, twelve miles north of Paris. First, it was decided that the paratroopers would be replaced by marine commandos for future capture operations. They had trained for counterterrorist missions such as wresting back control of hijacked ships, and the skills involved in storming a fugitive's house and the bridge of an oil tanker were judged similar enough. Both required speed, timing, and the ability to make lightning decisions about when and whom to shoot. Second, advisers from GIGN were brought in help plan operations, with an emphasis on minimizing the risk of civilian casualties.

In the summer of 1999, under pressure to produce results and to make amends for the Gagović incident, the special forces commander, Major General Jacques Saleun, set a deadline for the first French arrest operation to be carried out by the end of the year.[15]

For their initial operation, the commandos chose a junior militiaman from Foča, Zoran Vuković, a sub-commander in the military police charged with raping a fifteen-year-old girl he had held captive in a detention camp. Four years after the end of the war, he presented a relatively easy target. Other than adopting an alias, he took no special precautions and lived a routine daily life in Foča. Supremely mindful of civilian casualties, the first few arrest operations were aborted because there were bystanders in the area, but the forty-four-year-old was eventually seized on a quiet street on December 23, 1999, barely a week before Saleun's deadline.

A month later, the French picked another low-level target in the nearby town of Višegrad. Mitar Vasiljević was a waiter who had been part of a paramilitary group variously calling themselves the Avengers and the White Eagles, who had terrorized the town's Bosniak majority, summarily executing many of them. Vasiljević had gone to ground in 1997 as soon as the tribunal began producing indictments for the Višegrad massacres, but French intelligence trapped him by the simple trick of having a local man lease the fugitive's apartment. They seized him on January 25, 2000, when he came to collect the rent.[16]

The French marines were hitting their stride, but it was still not enough to satisfy the Hague prosecutors and some of their allies, who complained that by arresting small fry like Vasiljević, the French had allowed a much bigger fish, Milan Lukić, the psychopathic leader of the Avengers, to escape. Lukić, who was just twenty-five at the start of the war, was indeed one of its monsters. He oversaw the mass killing of Muslim women and children in Višegrad, barricading them into two separate houses and then burning them alive. He fled to Serbia after the Vasiljević arrest and then to Argentina, where he was finally caught in August 2005.*

The disappointment over the failure to grab Lukić was forgotten a couple of months later, however, when French commandos succeeding in catching the biggest prize any NATO contingent ever managed to track down in Bosnia — Momčilo Krajišnik.

In the political pecking order of the wartime Republika Srpska, Krajišnik was second only to Karadžić. The two men had gone to jail together for an alleged construction scam in 1984 and had then been released together without conviction. They had been all but inseparable ever since. They were founding members of the SDS, which engineered the Serb breakaway from Bosnia in 1991. As the president of the Bosnian Serb assembly, Krajišnik took part in almost all leadership meetings. From Pale, the ski resort that served as the separatists' capital, he coordinated the Serb-run municipalities that were the epicenters of ethnic cleansing.

After Karadžić's genocide indictment ruled him out of the Dayton peace talks in 1995, Krajišnik went in his place and acquired the nickname of "Mr. No" for his intransigent approach.

* See chapter 7.

His reputation was heightened by his distinctive appearance. As the US Balkan envoy, Richard Holbrooke, noted: "Krajišnik had only one long and extraordinarily brushy eyebrow, which spanned his forehead, creating what looked like a permanent dark cloud over his deep-set eyes."[17]

The black unibrow and the brooding demeanor hung over Bosnia for two long years after the war ended. Krajišnik was elected as the Serb representative on Bosnia's three-seat presidency, creating an absurd situation. It put one of the architects of ethnic cleansing in a position to block international efforts to reintegrate the country. The travesty did not last, however. He was voted out of office in 1998 by a popular wave of repugnance against SDS corruption and cronyism.

By this time, however, Krajišnik had dropped from sight. He moved out of the family home in Pale and circulated between different houses and apartments. In his mind, he was taking sensible precautions, but he never really considered the French and Italian soldiers who patrolled the quiet streets of Pale to be a serious threat. After all, they had stood by and watched his closest friend and leader, Karadžić, drive around town attending political and business meetings for a full two years after his indictment for genocide. And Krajišnik reasoned that if the Hague Tribunal had not come looking for him thus far, the chances were that he had been overlooked by the prosecutors. He had largely steered clear of the killing fields, confining himself to running the bureaucracy of ethnic cleansing from drab smoke-filled committee rooms in Pale's political hubs, the Panorama Hotel at one end of town and the Famos auto-parts factory at the other.

"Since SFOR forces were often following me and my family and kids—following everyone I knew in fact—I decide to isolate myself. I started some private businesses," Krajišnik recounted fourteen years later. "People knew where I was but I was not publicly visible. I avoided any contacts with SFOR. It was not running away from being arrested. It was just that I was not going to get in their way. I never really thought I could be arrested."[18]

So he quietly resumed his money-making ventures beneath the radar, taking advantage of the shortages and high prices bequeathed by war and sanctions. At the beginning of April 2000, he was confident enough in his impunity to spend a few days with his children at his parents' house on the edge of Pale. He even gave his bodyguards the weekend off.

Krajišnik fell into a trap of his own complacency, failing to consider how the tide was turning against him. In The Hague, the tribunal's prosecutors were under the new leadership of Carla Del Ponte, who made it her policy to go after the bold-faced names of ethnic cleansing, men like Krajišnik who pulled the strings. On February 25, 2000, she issued a sealed indictment against him for genocide, crimes against humanity, deportation, and persecution, among other grave charges.

While focusing their arrest campaign in the Drina valley, the French had steered clear of leadership targets in Pale. But Krajišnik was a potential prize that was in danger of being snatched from them. The Americans were watching him and warned the French that unless they acted very soon, they would do the job themselves.

At the end of March 2000, someone threw a stone at a French Peugeot jeep while it was on patrol in Pale. It pinged off the steel plates and onto the road. Stopping to take a look, a French soldier saw the offending pebble had a folded piece of paper attached, with a message written in English. It said the man they were looking for, Momčilo Krajišnik, would be at his parents' house in Pale for a forty-eight-hour stay.[19]

Soldiers from the 13th Parachute Dragoons, a covert surveillance unit, set up a camouflaged observation post in an old tree on a hill overlooking the Krajišniks' house. On the first day of the stakeout, they photographed a familiar face at a bathroom window. There was no mistaking that ferocious brow. The alert traveled up the chain of command to the very top. A squad was flown out of Toulon made up of navy special forces from the Commando Hubert (France's answer to the SEALs) and a dozen or so specialists from the French navy's Close Quarters Combat Group (Groupement de Combat en Milieu Clos). The green light came directly from the Élysée Palace, along with a pointed message: "The president expects this mission to succeed."[20]

On the night of April 2, 2000, Krajišnik had guests at his parents' house. It was partly social but mainly business. As the men smoked and drank plum brandy, they noticed a couple of SFOR patrol cars parked nearby. They went outside to take a look but were unable to see through the vehicles' thick smoked-glass windows.

Krajišnik decided it was nothing out of the ordinary. After all, Pale probably had the heaviest military presence per capita of any town in Europe. He would later look back in regret at his complacency. "Those God wants to punish, he first robs of their reason," he observed.[21] The guests left around midnight. Krajišnik watched some television and then turned in. His children slept on the ground floor. His room was above them on the same floor as his parents.

At just past three in the morning the family dog started barking, and a few moments later, the house shook. The French commandos had blown open the front door and within a few seconds one of them was already upstairs in Krajišnik's room pointing a gun at him with one hand and brandishing plastic cuffs with the other. More French sailors arrived to put blackout glasses and earplugs on him, marching him out in his pajamas to a waiting helicopter for the short flight to the Sarajevo airport, where a plane was ready to take him to The Hague. It was all over in seconds.

Krajišnik was a man who had been the commissar for ethnic cleansing, overseeing the uprooting of hundreds of thousands of people from their homes. But he had done all that from a safe distance in the alpine tranquillity of Pale, far from the front lines. So his own forced removal in the middle of the night came as a rude shock. He even compared the initial blast to "an atomic bomb." He complained bitterly about his treatment: "It was horrible. They treated me like baggage. I was put in a military transport plane which was the size of a football field and just one chair, and I was to sit on it. There was just one line explaining my situation in ugly Serbian from a French soldier, and I was not properly charged until we arrived in The Hague, the next morning. When I got there, my blood pressure was very high. I was completely unwell."[22]

The Krajišnik operation in April 2000 represented the third French arrest and the peak of France's campaign. The coup appeared to sate the Élysée Palace and the pressure on the commandos to mount new operations waned. It was more than two years before the next French success, ticking another name off Foča's notorious list of rapists, Radovan Stanković, who surrendered after being tracked to a farmhouse outside town.

Between the Gagović debacle in January 1999 and the end of the NATO peacekeeping mandate in Bosnia in December 2004, French troops were directly responsible for the arrests of four of the suspects on the ICTY's list, and played a part in a handful more. For the military, a degree of honor was restored, but for the politicians, there were still unanswered questions.

These were the same questions that haunted the Americans: Why had they gone after mere cogs in the killing machine and not arrested Karadžić and Mladić? In the French case, the criticism was particularly acute because they had military control over Pale in the critical eighteen months after the war when Karadžić and Mladić, both indicted for genocide, lived openly and with seeming impunity. The failure to arrest them fed speculation of a secret deal made during in shadowy hostage negotiations toward the end of the war.

On August 30, 1995, NATO launched air strikes against the Bosnian Serbs in response to a particularly awful massacre, the killing of forty-three shoppers and stallholders in a Sarajevo market targeted by Serb artillery. Operation Deliberate Force was a huge undertaking, involving 400 planes, over 3,500 sorties, and more than a thousand bombs, targeting command centers, barracks, ammunition dumps, and radar stations. One plane was shot down on the first day, a French Mirage 2000. Its pilot and navigator, having bailed out over the Republika Srpska, were taken prisoner and held by Mladić's troops until the end of the war, during which time they were denied Red Cross visits and subjected to mock executions. During their 104 days of captivity, President Chirac launched several parallel efforts to negotiate their release, both overt and covert. Those initiatives were eventually successful, but what exactly the Bosnian Serb leadership received in return for the pilots remained a mystery.

The covert effort was led by Jean-Charles Marchiani, a retired intelligence officer who had experience infiltrating neo-Nazi networks in Western Europe and had helped negotiate the release of hostages in Lebanon.[23] Marchiani held a series of secret meetings with Karadžić and the Serbian intelligence chief, Jovica Stanišić, but he later denied that the Serbs had been offered any incentives. However, a later declassified inquiry revealed that there had been an unexplained transfer of twenty-one million francs in government funds to Swiss bank accounts under Marchiani's control in October 1995 at the height of the negotiations. Charles Millon, the defense minister at the time, later admitted "there was some sort of compensation."[24]

British intelligence suspected the French had also supplied Mladić's forces with arms as part of the hostage package. But did Chirac give even more than that? Did he offer immunity from prosecution? An intercepted conversation between senior Serbian officials just two days before the release of the pilots suggested they, at least, had that impression. In the December 1995 conversation — intercepted by Croatian intelligence and provided to the ICTY — Zoran Lilić, a former Yugoslav president, is passing on a message from Milošević to the army chief, Momčilo Perišić, who is in turn trying to persuade Mladić to give him the French captives:

> Perišić: The important thing for [Mladić] is that the
> [tribunal] take this off his shoulders, you get what I mean?
> Lilić: Fine, everyone has promised it to him, damn
> [Momčilo]...
> Perišić (later in the conversation): Look at what he says.
> If they drop the [tribunal's] charges against him,
> there is no problem. He is prepared to resolve the problem
> immediately. I said to him that —
> Lilić: Are your word and mine not enough? And those of
> Chirac and Slobodan [Milošević], are they are they not
> enough?
> Perišić: OK. I'll check it.

Some eight years later, Del Ponte challenged Chirac directly in his Élysée office about the allegations of an immunity deal. Chirac responded with a little piece of absurdist theater that left plenty of room for reasonable doubt.

*I asked Chirac, "Is the suggestion in this document true, that you promised not to arrest Mladić if the pilots were freed?" Chirac has very sincere-looking eyes. Women love his eyes. And he look at me and answered, "Absolutely not."*

*Chirac admitted that he had spoken with Milošević about the release of the pilots. But he denied having made any deal . . .*

*It was as if he wanted to prove concretely to me that no deal existed. He immediately stood up, strode to his desk, picked up the telephone, and called the commander of the Army of the Republic of France.*

*"Alors General," he said, "Mladić, he is still at large. This is unacceptable. He must be arrested immediately. France must do everything necessary to have him arrested." Chirac ordered a search of a specific location.[25]*

Even members of the French government were unconvinced by the denials. Louis Gautier, a foreign affairs adviser to the Socialist prime minister Lionel Jospin, revealed that when the party took office in 1997 at the beginning of a long period of uneasy "cohabitation" with the conservative president, they could find no credible documentation of the negotiations for the pilots.

"Were there assurances given to Mladić under a deal between Chirac and the Serbs? Nothing is clear and we never really wanted to know. To avoid it becoming a political problem in the middle of cohabitation," Gautier told the French investigative journalist Jacques Massé. "It's true we only engaged timidly in the hunt for the war criminals. Because we had the clear impression that we had inherited a situation of which we were not the masters."[26]

There has never been any documentary proof of French offers of immunity, nor was a comprehensive guarantee within Chirac's power to give. But it is equally undeniable that under Chirac's presidency, finding Karadžić and Mladić was never a priority.

"Karadžić was supposed to be the DGSE's focus, but we never went too far, and I was never convinced by the effort," said a former French intelligence official involved in the manhunt. "There was a sense we were doing it because we had to do it, but we were never given the critical means to achieve the goal. There were limited resources, a limited team, and the truth is we never really came close."

From his little office in the Hôtel de Brienne, Rondot faced a near-impossible task. He was under constant pressure to track down fugitives by a president whose own commitment to the mission constantly wavered and who never provided sufficient resources to do the job. The general's long career in the shadow world ended in indignity in 2006 when he was hauled in to testify in a convoluted scandal called the Clearstream affair, involving alleged bribes paid in the sale of French frigates to Taiwan and a political smear campaign based on a forged list of tax evaders. Rondot was extensively interrogated by a parliamentary committee on whether he had been tasked in 2004 by the then foreign minister Dominique de Villepin to spy on his future (successful) rival for the presidency, Nicolas Sarkozy.[27]

Standing in the dock, the man who had spent his life unseen was made to endure the humiliation of public interrogation.

"I am a soldier," he declared, looking the judges in the eye. "When you're a soldier, you don't have much. Except honor. And in this affair my honor is at stake."

The affair revealed something quite unexpected about Rondot. This secretive, security-obsessed man harbored a highly insecure habit. He kept a meticulous diary of his career in espionage, written out in longhand in a set of notebooks. A court clerk stumbled on them by chance during a search of Rondot's country house at Meudon, southwest of Paris. The clerk was about to leave empty-handed when he pulled aside a curtain exposing the reinforced steel door of a vault in which Rondot's secrets lay. Among much else, they showed his frustration at being sent on the Balkan manhunt in competition with the Americans but with limited and dwindling support.

In a 2003 entry, he complained: "Our resources are being depleted. Carla Del Ponte, the prosecutor at the International Criminal Tribunal for ex-Yugoslavia, is irritated. The cabinet secretary thinks that this portfolio is of less interest to the President and the Defense Minister."

Rondot estimated that 80 percent of his time was taken up following dubious leads that led nowhere. But worse than the prospect of failing to find Mladić or Karadžić, was the fear that the CIA might beat him to it.

In 2005, Rondot fretted: "The president would be furious if the capture/rendition of M and K were to happen without us."

In the end, it did happen without them or the CIA. Rondot had ended his illustrious career long before Karadžić and Mladić were finally tracked down in Serbia. The French spymaster was just the latest in a multinational cast of seasoned manhunters to abandon the quest, exhausted and defeated.

# 10.
# SLOBODAVIA: THE FALL OF MILOŠEVIĆ AND THE UNRAVELING OF SERBIA

I thought myself that Milošević, Karadžić, and Mladić should all
have committed suicide. They would have gone into history.
Thousands of people died for them, and if you are sending people's
children to their death, you should know how to leave yourself.
—*Toma Fila, Slobodan Milošević's lawyer*

Slobodan, kill yourself and save Serbia!
—*Red Star Belgrade fans*

**IT IS THE MIDDLE OF A WINTER'S NIGHT,** and Slobodan Milošević
wakes up to see uniformed men outside his Belgrade villa. He
rouses his sleeping wife, Mira, shouting, "They've come! They've
come to take me to The Hague!" Mira takes one look through
the window before going to back to bed. "Relax," she tells her
trembling husband. "They're just customs men policing the
new border."

This was the funny story going around Belgrade in early
2001, and the joke was entirely on the fallen dictator. The
would-be overlord of the Balkans had first sought to master all
of Yugoslavia, then—when the country fell apart—to carve out
Greater Serbia with a meat cleaver. The more he fought to gain

territory, the more he lost. He lost in Slovenia, Croatia, Bosnia, and Kosovo. By now, even long-faithful Montenegro was edging nervously toward the exit, leaving only a withered stump of a country, impoverished and disoriented.

And even in this amputated Serbia, Milošević's domain had shriveled. NATO had bombed him out of the mock-classical White Palace, once Tito's residence in Belgrade's diplomatic district of Dedinje, forcing him and his family into more modest accommodations next door. He had been beaten in the presidential election of 2000 and then ousted in an uprising on October 5 of that year when he tried to annul the result. Within a few months, this walled villa at 11 Užička Street, known as the Oval House, was all that remained of his territorial pretensions. It was the last redoubt of Slobodavia. Like a miniature version of Milošević's Yugoslavia, it was a state built on delusion, crime, and violence.

After recovering from the shock of being shrugged off by his former acolytes in the army and the police, the ex-president had yanked himself out of depression by the end of 2000 and began a comeback campaign by telephone, plotting with loyalists and berating the waverers. But the former were a fast-dwindling band and the latter were gaining in number exponentially with every passing day. Milošević was oblivious to the odds. Like many tyrants past their peak, he seemed to be the last person in the country to realize his day was done, as if the downward plunge was so fast he had become giddy with weightlessness.

There were those in Milošević's inner circle who could see what was coming, and they were busy squeezing the last drops from an already plundered country. But at home on Užička Street, the Milošević family prepared for battle. They had stockpiled a small arsenal: a rocket launcher, two cases of hand grenades, two machine guns, thirty assault rifles, a sniper rifle, ten cases of ammo, and twenty-three pistols. Milošević's thirty-four-year-old daughter, Marija, was packing three handguns of her own—a Beretta, a Walther, and a Derringer[1]—and she was clearly not shy about using them. Once, on breaking up with a boyfriend, she shot his dog.[2] Long-term relationships, she once explained, were not for her. "Holding a gun in one hand and a baby in the other is a little complicated and awkward," she told an interviewer.[3]

This is how the tiny remnant of Slobo's empire dug in, a collection of damaged people clinging together, braced for redemption or Armageddon, whichever came first. They girded themselves with copious amounts of booze and pills. Milošević was "drunk most of the time," a domestic employee told the press. "He drinks lots of expensive whisky and makes long phone calls," the servant reported.[4]

Meanwhile, Mira Marković, who had helped rule Yugoslavia for thirteen years at Slobodan's side as the largely unseen half of a ruthless diarchy, had sunk into a deep gloom, gulping down tranquilizers and sleeping pills.

Milošević had never really had friends. The only person he trusted fully was Mira. They had presided over the destruction of a country while gazing into each other's eyes. Even as Yugoslavia was being whittled away by Milošević's disastrous military adventures, they had worked ceaselessly to monopolize power over what remained. If Yugoslavia had been a mighty ocean liner fast disintegrating into a leaky Serbian life raft, the response of captains Slobo and Mira was to lash the passengers and crew all the harder and throw suspected mutineers to the sharks.

They even had his and hers political parties: Slobodan ran the Socialists while Mira led the Yugoslav Left (Jugoslovenska

Levica, or JUL). It was the first couple's version of pluralism and together they controlled parliament, which was constantly ready to vote them greater powers. Their domination of the media was just as complete, enforced with bullets and high explosives. The one relatively independent-minded television station, Studio B, had had its transmitter and repeater towers blown up. The founder of the country's first privately owned newspaper since World War II, a prominent journalist named Slavko Ćuruvija, was denounced as a traitor by Mira Marković. A few days later, in April 1999, someone shot him in the back seventeen times outside his house.

Consuming their own carefully curated news, and listening solely to advisers handpicked for their readiness to please, Yugoslavia's first family failed to notice the hollowing out of the regime. Mira had busied herself gutting Tito's White Palace, burning Persian silk carpets in the garden and redecorating to her own taste, until she was interrupted by NATO, which put a bomb through one wing of the mansion at the height of its aerial campaign in the spring of 1999. Meanwhile, the couple's twenty-five-year-old son, Marko, embarked on a quixotic but costly project, building a ten-acre amusement park called Bambiland in the family's hometown of Požarevac, complete with a cement ziggurat and a pirate ship. It opened in June 1999, in what was intended to be a show of defiance after the NATO bombing and the loss of Kosovo. But to most of Serbia, Bambiland's gaudy painted rainbows and neon fawns just looked like Slobodavia's delusions set in concrete.

The Milošević family might not have been so deaf and blind if they had gone to a soccer game at Red Star Belgrade, where the chant had changed since the NATO bombing and the defeat in Kosovo from "Serbian Slobo, Serbia is with you!" to "Slobodan, kill yourself and save Serbia!" The bread and circuses were over and Milošević had lost the mob. The hard-core Red Star fans, the Delije (Heroes), who had been the shock troops in Milošević's ethnic cleansing campaigns, had defected after the violent death of their leader, Željko "Arkan" Ražnatović. On January 15, 2000, Arkan had been gunned down in the lobby of the Intercontinental Hotel in Belgrade. The speculation, particularly among the Delije, was that their leader had been eliminated on the orders of Slobodan Milošević, possibly because he had begun to talk to the Hague Tribunal (his lawyer had unsuccessfully tried to cut a deal with the prosecutors).[5]

Arkan's death, by machine gun at close range, was just one of a spate of gangland murders in Belgrade at the time. The city was run by mobs struggling for shares in the black market under sanctions, who had ample access to guns and a pool of young war veterans who had no compunction about using them. But there was something systematic and coldly professional about the string of assassinations around the turn of the millennium that suggested the hand of a disciplined state-run force. It was a suspicion reinforced by later trials, which found that the security services had been involved in a number of the killings, including that of Milošević's former mentor and potential presidential rival, Ivan Stambolić. He went missing while out jogging in August 2000, not to be seen again until his remains were found three years later buried in quicklime in a national park. His hands had been taped behind his back and he had been shot twice in the head. A Belgrade court ruled Stambolić had been executed by special forces soldiers on direct orders from Milošević.

As many a mob boss and despot has discovered, a reign of terror works perfectly, up to the moment when it backfires totally. At some critical point in 2000 the calculus of fear flipped, and

Milošević's lieutenants started to suspect they might end up in a shallow grave, whether they stayed loyal or not. At that point they no longer had anything to lose.

The worm turned — critically for Yugoslavia and terminally for Milošević's grip on power — for Milorad Ulemek, a failed thief from the tower blocks of New Belgrade who became, by force of arms, the most influential kingmaker in modern Serbian history.

Ulemek was a classic product of Milošević's Yugoslavia — a petty criminal raised high by the career opportunities offered by war. After a botched robbery in 1985, he fled to France and the next year, at the age of thirty-one, joined the French Foreign Legion. It was a popular choice for young Yugoslavs on the run. There were no questions asked about criminal records, and the recruits were allowed to choose a new name. After tours in Chad and French Guyana, and a spell as a French army translator in Yugoslavia, Ulemek emerged with the nom de guerre of Legija and a taste for battle.

When the war started in Yugoslavia, Legija deserted from the legion and returned home where he rose rapidly to become Arkan's right-hand man. And at the war's end, he was the perfect choice to run the Milošević's praetorian guard, the Unit for Special Operations (Jedinica za Specijalne Operacije, or JSO). But there was a limit to the Serb blood Legija was prepared to spill for his master, a limit that only became clear when the regime was hanging by a thread.

Milošević had every reason to believe he would win the elections of September 2000. The eighteen parties that made up the Democratic Opposition of Serbia had a history of squabbling. So Milošević was caught unawares by the emergence of a compromise candidate, a soft-spoken and obscure law professor named Vojislav Koštunica.

An uncharismatic man who rarely smiled, Koštunica none-theless represented a potent threat, embodying both liberal and nationalist strands of the opposition. He denounced the blood-lust of the Milošević regime while maintaining an instinctive dis-trust of the West, which took visceral form after the 1999 NATO bombing. For Koštunica, getting rid of Milošević was a means not to enter the European embrace but to rejuvenate the Serbian nation, one that looked inward and eastward for its inspiration. In his view, the Hague Tribunal was illegal and anti-Serbian.[6]

As Serbia's sanctions-induced economic malaise deepened, repugnance for the Milošević family became tangible on the streets. Otpor (Resistance), a loose student opposition net-work, spread across the country. It was made up of disparate cells with no leaders or heirarchy and so was impossible to eradi-cate. When the police beat up its young members, their parents took to the streets, shamed out of their apathy by the courage of their sons and daughters. The Otpor logo was stenciled every-where — a clenched fist and the words "*Gotov je*" (He's finished). It was so ubiquitous that people stopped noticing it, but the words nonetheless seeped under their skin and took root in their heads. Maybe Milošević was not indestructible after all. Perhaps the regime was finished. As the September election drew closer, the chants of "*Gotov je*" grew louder.

After the polls closed on September 24, there was a deafen-ing silence from the regime. It was clear that the Socialists and the JUL had been beaten, and they were in shock. They tried to cover up the scale of the defeat and prepared for a second round. The Koštunica camp called for a general strike and the struggle went into the streets. The opposition strategist, Zoran Djindjić, who had made his name leading urban protests, was prepared for this moment. He organized columns of opposition supporters to converge on Belgrade from five directions on October 5, in convoys of cars, buses, trucks, and bulldozers. These would be no pacifist, egg-throwing protests like earlier antigovernment demonstrations. The convoys carried striking miners with crowbars and off-duty policemen with guns hidden in their coats. The flimsy police roadblocks they met along the way were no match for that kind of determination. Along the five highways to Belgrade, the police stood aside, in some cases waving the three-fingered Serb salute (thumb, index, and middle fingers) as the convoys rolled by.

Milošević had initially been unconcerned by the unrest, assuming he was well protected by several rings of security forces. It was a complete miscalculation. Here again Djindjić and his colleagues had done their homework, sounding out the police and army in advance, both in the provinces and the capital. What they heard in the ranks of the security forces was disgust and disillusionment with the regime. It had rotted from the inside out and the façade that remained was thin and brittle. The head of the army, General Nebojša Pavković, had no intention of sending his troops to kill other Serbs, a decision born out of uncertainty over whether his men would obey. Pavković planned to sleep in on October 5.

There was just one more powerful piece on the board to take out of the game. Late on the night of October 4, Djindjić drove to Admiral Geprat Street in central Belgrade for an extremely delicate and rather risky meeting. When he arrived, there was an armored SUV parked at the side of the road, watched over by armed men loitering in the doorways of nearby buildings. Djindjić got in the vehicle. The man waiting for him was Legija, the head of the JSO special forces. This backstreet audience with the regime's praetorian-in-chief was the biggest gamble of Djindjić's life.

The two men talked as Legija drove around the empty city streets.

"It's going to be a mess. The orders are extreme," the commander said.

Djindjić already knew this, but what he wanted was advice. Legija told him not to allow the demonstrators to open fire on the police or attempt to storm police barracks.

Djindjić agreed and asked for Legija's word that if those terms were met, his Red Berets would not enter the fray. Legija gave his word.[7] They shook hands and that was that. Milošević's secret weapon was still secret, but it was no longer under his control.

At the climax of the revolution, on the evening of October 5, when the five rebel columns had converged on Belgrade and opposition demonstrators were laying siege to the state television center, Legija, the wellspring of Milošević's power, arrived on the scene at the head of a convoy of armored cars, two pistols stuffed into holsters at his chest. Witnessing the arrival of the JSO fighters, the protestors were sure they would be mowed down.

But instead Legija did something that—more than any other single action—marked the end of the Milošević regime. He raised his arm and gave the three-finger salute to the crowd. His men removed their balaclavas and did the same. The protesters roared and triumphantly clambered onto the armored cars. The revolution had won the day.

Boško Buha, the Belgrade police chief, provided an account of what happened next: "Then Legija received a phone call from Milošević himself and from that point on the former president's link to the police was broken. In the presence of one of my men who were guarding those vehicles of his, he threw his mobile or his walkie-talkie, whatever he was using, down and smashed it to pieces."

Half an hour later, parked near the burning parliament building, Legija held another impromptu conference with Djindjić in his vehicle. "As far as I'm concerned…this business is over. Milošević is out. There's no going back, the people have won themselves a victory."

Djindjić was still concerned. He asked about the army. Legija told him: "I'll let them know that if they intervene, we'll intervene against them. I have twelve hundred men."[8]

The warning was unnecessary. The army had no intention of leaving its barracks. By six o'clock on the evening of October 5, after less than three hours of street fighting, the revolution was over. Just over a hundred people had been injured, five with gunshot wounds. Only two people had died: one run over by a truck, the other of a heart attack.

"The new government was mostly created by the disintegration of the old. The terrified establishment had simply fled. There was no government, no police, no state media, no ruling party," the journalists Dragan Bujošević and Ivan Radovanović wrote.[9] It was one of the most perfectly executed revolutions in modern history.

The next morning, October 6, 2000, as the tear gas was clearing, Koštunica woke to find himself president. There was one unresolved question, however: Was Milošević even aware he was no longer in charge? He would have to be told. General Pavković set up a meeting between the new president and the deposed leader at the Oval House. For a few minutes the three sat in silence. Each had been expecting the other to speak first. Eventually Pavković made an awkward attempt to break the impasse. "Well, here we are," he said. There was more silence, and Pavković opted to leave the room and close the door behind him.[10]

The two men talked for an hour. Whatever they agreed in private, the upshot was that Milošević went on television later that night, conceding defeat and expressing jocular relief he could now spend more time with Marko, his grandson. In return, Koštunica allowed Milošević to remain at home with his family. And when the Hague prosecutor Carla Del Ponte called the new president to congratulate him on his victory, Koštunica made it clear she would not be getting her most coveted prize.

This fragile modus vivendi held for six months, but it could never last. While Koštunica had taken over the Yugoslav presidency, Djindjić was the prime minister of the Serbian Republic, with far more influence over judicial affairs in Belgrade. He was not going to let Milošević get off scot-free for more than a decade of misrule. As with Al Capone, Milošević would be charged not for the long trail of bodies he had left in his wake but for financial irregularities. In the Serbian's case he was indicted for alleged improprieties in the purchase of a garden next door to his Dedinje villa, along with other financial misdeeds.[11]

A warrant was issued for Milošević's arrest. He now faced a dilemma. With an eye on the history books, he and his supporters had imagined a climactic shootout to prevent him being snatched by foreign agents and smuggled to The Hague. Resisting arrest for financial fraud did not have quite the same heroic ring to it.

Milošević did not want to decide on a course of action without his lawyer, Toma Fila, who was called back from The Hague where he was representing other Serb defendants at the tribunal. He landed at 9:00 p.m. on March 31, 2001, and was summoned to Užička Street immediately. But how was the fifty-nine-year-old lawyer going to cross the police lines at Milošević's house? It had become a war zone with jumpy — and in some cases drunk — combatants at the barricades. Fila contacted Legija and arranged to meet in a central Belgrade square. Not long after, the soldier was waiting in his armored SUV for the lawyer.

"What should I do?" Legija asked plaintively as he drove. He knew and trusted Fila—a blunt defense lawyer with a fondness for bawdy humor. He had specialized in death penalty cases in Tito's Yugoslavia before making the transition to a counsel for war crimes defendants under Milošević.

"Don't even think about shooting," Fila insisted, as they approached the Oval House.

"You should know I have made an oath," Legija insisted. "A Serb doesn't kill another Serb."

As future court cases were to prove, it was an oath with many exceptions. But at three in the morning on April Fool's Day 2001, Fila took him at his word. When they arrived in Užička Street, the lawyer tentatively made his way up the drive shouting "Don't shoot" to the gunmen he imagined fixing their sights on him. On reaching the front door alive, the first thing he noticed was the smell. The police had cut off the water six days earlier and no one in the house had washed since then. Fila's second impression was that the whole family was ready to snap under the pressure, starting with Milošević's daughter, Marija.

Some time after three o'clock in the morning on April 1, Čedomir Jovanović, a Djindjić aide, arrived at the house to negotiate Milošević's surrender. He had brought along three documents for Milošević, offering guarantees in return for a peaceful arrest. The first was a statement promising that the charges against him were not prompted by the demands of the Hague Tribunal but by "reasonable suspicion" that he had committed crimes under the Yugoslav penal code, a reference to the financial fraud charges. The case would be heard in a Yugoslav court, and Milošević would have "unimpeded communication" with his family throughout the proceedings. It was signed by the Yugoslav president Koštunica, the Serbian prime minister Zoran Djindjić, and Milan Milutinović, a Milošević crony who still occupied the largely empty post of Serbian president.

The other two documents Jovanović brought were short annexes. One stated: "Slobodan Milošević will not be handed to any judicial or other institution outside the country." The other promised he could receive daily visits. Jovanović had persuaded Djindjić to approve these hastily typed addenda in order to clinch the deal. Time was of the essence. Djindjić and Jovanović were racing to get Milošević into custody before a March 31 deadline expired at midnight Washington time, six o'clock in the morning in Belgrade, cutting off US economic aid.

In the Oval House the ex-president read through the papers and looked up at his lawyer. "Will this hold?" he asked. Fila's reply was characteristically blunt. Sure it would hold, for one night.

"It was obvious he would go to The Hague. Without Milošević, The Hague would make no sense," Fila recalled.

Fila then left the fallen dictator alone with his thoughts in his study, half expecting that his client would take the opportunity to find an honorable exit from his predicament.

"I thought myself that Milošević, Karadžić, and Mladić should all have committed suicide. They would have gone into history. Thousands of people died for them, and if you are sending people's children to their death, you should know how to leave yourself," Fila said. "I left Milošević alone for half an hour so he could do that. Both his father and mother had done it."[12]

ALL OF THE MISERIES of Yugoslavia's postwar history seemed to have been condensed into Milošević's unhappy early life. His mother, Stanislava, was a committed partisan and a zealous Communist. His father, Svetozar, was by contrast a melancholy, spiritual man, a high-school religious studies teacher, devoted to the Orthodox church. The marriage was doomed, and Svetozar left to live a life of introspection in Montenegro, leaving Stanislava to raise Slobodan and his brother, Borislav, alone and in poverty. In 1962, adrift and depressed in the new Yugoslavia, Svetozar shot himself. Slobodan was away on a study trip in Moscow at the time and did not attend the funeral, nor did he ever mention his father or the suicide to his friends. He never visited the grave.

His reaction was quite different twelve years later when Stanislava followed the same path and hanged herself from a light fixture. Slobodan was reportedly distraught and racked with guilt for having neglected her.[13] His hermetically sealed world with Mira did not allow emotional attachments to anyone else, and he had rarely visited his mother in Požarevac. When Stanislava went to visit Slobodan in Belgrade, Mira would leave the apartment as soon as her mother-in-law arrived. Stanislava got the message. There was room for only one woman in Slobo's life.

Unlike his parents, Slobodan Milošević was not cut out for suicide. After being left with his thoughts in the study on Užička Street in the predawn hours of April 1, he emerged a defeated man and agreed to the terms of his surrender. At this point, according to Fila, Marija lunged furiously for Jovanović, the messenger sent to negotiate her father's surrender. She chased him around the room, as he appealed for help from Fila who hustled him out of the house.

Waiting to enter as Jovanović left were a judge and police officer who had been assigned to carry out the actual arrest. Fila took them upstairs, introducing the police officer as a prosecutor (a subterfuge that may have saved the man's live given the febrile atmosphere inside the house and the palpable hatred of its occupants toward the police). As they escorted Milošević out of the house to a waiting car, the melodrama had one last surprise to offer.

Marija suddenly produced one of her pistols and fired wildly into the ceiling five times, narrowly missing the judge — a final act of inchoate violent despair. The delusion that Milošević would magically bounce back had evaporated forever.

At 4:30 a.m., April 1, Milošević emerged from the gates of his house on Užička Street and into a waiting BMW with tinted windows. He was driven with a State Security Service escort across Belgrade to Central Prison.

Milošević was assigned the most comfortable block, generally known to the prison population as "The Hyatt" for its fourteen-square-meter cells with en suite showers and hot water. At the admissions desk, his belt, tie, and shoelaces were taken from him. "Don't worry — I won't hang myself," he assured the prison governor. He was put on twenty-four-hour suicide watch nonetheless, and given a number. The champion of Greater Serbia was now prisoner 101980. On entering the cell, he took off his coat, washed his face, and lay down on a lower bunk, falling asleep almost immediately.[14]

Milošević's kingdom had been stripped away piece by piece, but inmate 101980 was still a disciplined master of his cell. He kept it perfectly organized, leaving his clothes neatly folded in his suitcase, disdaining the cell locker.[15] Unpacking perhaps would have conceded too much to his jailers. He read widely in Serbian and English, crime novels, spy thrillers, C. S. Forester's Napoleonic saga of Horatio Hornblower, as well as John Steinbeck's *Grapes of Wrath*. Every day he fed the pigeons in the courtyard, and every day, at noon exactly, Mira would visit, bringing a packed lunch and an occasional gift, like painted Easter eggs.

They spent their hour together holding hands, kissing, and stroking each other's faces.

In conversations with his head jailer, Dragiša Blanuša, about the Yugoslav wars that had left more than 130,000 of his fellow countrymen dead, Milošević betrayed almost no regrets, certainly no remorse. Describing himself as the "moral victor" who had stood up to dark forces abroad, he placed the blame for the catastrophe that had befallen Yugoslavia exclusively on foreign powers. Somehow the whole bloodbath had been Germany's fault, a way "to get back at us for the defeats in past wars."[16]

Only once did the thick veil of denial slip. In what would turn out to be one of Milošević's last days in Belgrade, Blanuša poured them both a glass of whisky (allowing the prisoner to choose his glass lest he imagine it was poisoned) and asked him, "Why didn't you quit while you were ahead, while you were still popular? You could be lying on a beach somewhere now."

Milošević began to embark on a speech about his duty to the Serb nation, but after a few moments he seemed to lack the energy to finish it. A different man, frightened and tired, appeared.

"Yes, you're right. I did make a mistake," he told Blanuša. But that was it. He never admitted fault in public again. Even this fleeting concession concerned his own career rather than the lost or ruined lives of others.

Fila had been right. The signed guarantees promising Milošević would not be extradited were valid only as long as it took to get the ousted leader out of his barricaded home. Djindjić's cabinet knew full well that the crippled, pillaged country would never get the financial relief it desperately needed without surrendering Milošević. A donor's conference was looming on June 29, at which Yugoslavia hoped to raise $1 billion, and the United States was threatening not to show up unless

Milošević was sent to The Hague. But getting him out of the country was a risky undertaking. Many of those who took part in the October 5 revolution, including some of the best-armed, were set against it. The deed would have be done quickly and as discreetly as possible.

The Djindjić government made an abortive effort to open a loophole in the constitutional ban on extradition, making an exception for the Hague Tribunal. Parliament would not accept it. So on Saturday, June 23, 2001, the cabinet simply sidestepped parliament and issued a decree to the same effect.

At the time Djindjić could sense that public opinion was shifting in his favor. Mass graves had recently been found in Serbia containing the remains of hundreds of Albanians. They had been slaughtered in Kosovo in the murderous counterinsurgency campaigns of 1998 and 1999. When peace was imposed by NATO and Western troops were on the verge of deploying in Kosovo in the summer of 1999, the graves were dug up and their contents driven north toward Belgrade in refrigerated trucks. The gruesome operation had come to light because one of the trucks slid off the road into a river. The vehicle and its cargo of bones were discovered four years later. For once, the skeletons were too close to home for the people of Serbia to ignore. In a poll published on the day of the decree, 46 percent of those questioned backed full cooperation with the ICTY, compared to 36 percent against.[17] The tide had turned.

Even President Koštunica, the most skeptical of all the country's leaders about cooperating with The Hague, told a Socialist Party delegation that extradition was now the "lesser of two evils" (though he was to complain bitterly about it after the event).[18]

Milošević supporters made a last-ditch effort at the constitutional court to try to stop the transfer, but the government had made up its mind. An operation, code-named Dove, was aimed at hustling him out of the country by the June 29 international donor conference. At noon on June 28, Mira came to the prison for the last time, accompanied by their daughter-in-law, Milica. At the end of the visit, Milošević, who had been told that extradition was imminent, produced seven paper boats from his pocket and asked that they be given to his grandson. A single tear ran down the ex-dictator's cheek.[19]

At six o'clock that evening, Blanuša and six guards came back to get Milošević, who had assumed the extradition process would take days. He was in his pajamas, reading.

"Get up and get ready," Blanuša said.

"Where am I going? Where are you taking me?"

"To The Hague."

Milošević asked to call his wife and his lawyer, but the request was refused. Blanuša took him by the arm and told him to hurry.

"Be human. Let me at least dress," Milošević pleaded. He packed his case, taking his coat and four books chosen at random. He was walked down to the courtyard where there was a blue police van waiting. On seeing it, Milošević balked. He had expected greater ceremony.

"Warden, what is this?" he demanded. "This is not in order. This is an abduction. May I call my wife now?"

"Later," Blanuša answered. Milošević was helped into the van which drove across a city sweltering in a heat wave with a single unmarked Mercedes van as a discreet escort. There would be no flashing lights or motorcade.[20]

In fifteen minutes, at about 7:00 p.m., they had reached Banjica, a district south of Belgrade's center and home to the Security Institute, the headquarters of the State Security Service, which had been bombed and partly destroyed by NATO in 1999. As the cars pulled up, there were three helicopters waiting for them. Fearful that some in the military establishment might try to shoot down any aircraft carrying Milošević out of the country rather than allow him to give incriminating evidence, the new government had arranged for two decoy choppers, though the subterfuge was undermined by the fact that the decoys were puny two-seaters. It was obvious that the bigger military helicopter would be carrying Milošević.

Kevin Curtis, an ICTY investigator, was waiting with a translator. The policeman from Stratford-upon-Avon had been instrumental in the first armed arrest of an ICTY suspect in 1997.* He too had been taken by surprise by the speed of the events. Curtis had left the tribunal's Belgrade office before five o'clock that day to take refuge from the unbearable heat in his air-conditioned hotel room. But as soon as he got there, there was a call from the Foreign Ministry, saying he was needed. A car was waiting outside to take him to the Security Institute.

Dušan Mihajlović, the new interior minister and deputy prime minister, was waiting for him in a large room. He immediately wanted to know how long it would take, if they brought Milošević right away, to charge him and fly him out of town. Curtis estimated about twenty minutes. Mihajlović said that was too long. He was jumpy. The newly elected government had only a tentative grip on the real levers of power in the security establishment and feared an ambush at any time.

Curtis insisted that there had to be a proper arrest, which involved Milošević being read his rights. At that point there was a murmur among the government officials and one of them

* See chapter 2.

Slobodan Milošević's final defeat, being read his rights by British ex-policeman Kevin Curtis on June 28, 2001. Standing alongside the ousted president is his jailer, Dragiša Blanuša.

rushed out of the room. They had forgotten to tell President Koštunica what was going on, and someone was hastily dispatched to call him.

Curtis, the translator, and his security officer were then walked out the back of the building just as the two vans from Central Prison pulled up. Milošević was in the second one. He climbed out and looked about him, nodding his head as if finally comprehending the scale of the conspiracy against him.

"Congratulations. Job well done. You may pay out these people," he declared with theatrical sarcasm, pointing at the prison staff and guards.

Milošević was playing his part on the stage of history, fully aware that his words would be recorded for posterity. But if this was theater, not everyone knew their lines and there followed an awkward moment of silence. Curtis had expected Milošević to be walked over to the institute's steps where he had set up a recording device, but nobody moved. In the end, Curtis walked over to the prisoner to read him his rights.

Milošević scoffed at Curtis, declaring he had no authority to issue charges against him as he did not recognize the Hague Tribunal. The recitation went on anyway and Milošević affected insouciance, asking his guards for a cigarette and interrupting the translator to inquire where she learned such good English. She looked at Curtis for permission to reply but the detective shook his head.

Milošević then had to be searched by the ICTY security officer, which brought more complaints. He had just come from the prison system so why did he need to be frisked again, he demanded to know.

"You are my prisoner now and you will be searched," Curtis insisted.

As they walked toward the helicopter, Milošević stopped abruptly once more, remembering the date. "Do you know that today is Vidovdan, Serbs?" he asked Blanuša and his guards. Vidovdan is the most sacred day in the Serbian nationalist calendar, the day Prince Lazar was killed at the battle of Kosovo Polje in 1389 as he fought to hold back the Ottoman advance into the Balkans. It is the apotheosis of Serb victimhood. Milošević had chosen the six-hundredth anniversary of the battle for a speech at the historic site, designed to reignite the flame of Serb nationalism with him at the helm. The choice of this particular day, twelve years on, to fly him out of the country appeared to him as a final twist of the knife by his enemies.

For all his efforts to leave something resonant for the history books, Milošević's last words on the territory he sought to dominate for so long were mundane.

On being helped into the helicopter he called out, "Warden, where are my coat and my things?"

"There, next to you," Blanuša said. The roar of the chopper's blades blocked everything else out. The governor looked at his watch. It was three minutes to seven in the evening.

As soon as the helicopter lifted off, Milošević switched to English.

"How long have you been doing this?" he asked Curtis. "Do you like the job? What do you do when you're not arresting innocent people like me?"

He was looking back at Belgrade as the helicopter followed the Sava River south, then asked for a cigarette. Curtis said smoking was not allowed but Milošević was not to be put off, pointing to the ashtray in the cockpit. Even as he was being flown into exile and incarceration, Milošević sought to assert his authority.

"I own this helicopter anyway," he said sourly.

Curtis relented and the two of them chain-smoked as they flew over Serbia.

Milošević asked where they were going, and on being informed the first stop would be Bosnia, he snorted the word contemptuously, as if it were an unworthy destination for such a momentous journey. To labor the point, when they landed at the US-run Camp Eagle in Tuzla, he took out a handkerchief and wiped his shoes, as if the very ground was contaminated.

A squad of US special forces was on the runway to meet the prisoner and took them to a concrete-floored ammunition bunker at one end of the airstrip, which had been converted into a spartan transit lounge for war crimes suspects on the way to The Hague. There was a desk and chair inside where the detainees could be asked basic questions and given a medical examination before the flight.

Once inside, Milošević tried to take charge once more. He affected a jovial nonchalance, handing out a stick of chewing gum to Lieutenant Colonel Andy Milani, the newly arrived head of the Delta Force manhunting team based in Sarajevo, who had come to witness the historic transfer.

Milošević then started pacing up and down, forcing an American soldier trying to video the proceedings to keep pace alongside him. Milošević stopped to give instructions on the proper use of the camera's zoom function and the relative merits of different brands of camera.

A few minutes later there was a new argument, about going to the toilet. The Americans said he could go, but the door would have to remain open. Milošević complained bitterly at the humiliation, but he lost. Later, in The Hague, he would salvage some pride, holding his chin up combatively in court, pouring contempt on the judges, while playing the role of the Mafia don in the prison common room—courtly, feared and respected in equal measure. But that was all to come. This moment in Tuzla was surely his nadir. The erstwhile despot, who had once held the whole region in the palm of his hand, was sitting on a toilet in full view of American soldiers in a disused military bunker.

The wait in Tuzla began to seem interminable. Having won the diplomatic squabble over who would have the honor of flying the Butcher of the Balkans to justice, the British were two hours late. In drawing up their plans, Curtis later discovered, they had miscalculated the time difference between the United Kingdom and Bosnia.

Finally, a BAE 146 short-haul jet from the Royal Squadron—which Curtis was told was the same aircraft that brought Princess Diana's body back to Britain from Paris after her fatal car crash in 1997—landed and taxied up to the bunker. Curtis boarded with his prisoner. The aircraft was manned by a mix of MI6 officials and SAS soldiers in plain clothes, who chatted casually on the two-hour flight to the Netherlands. Curtis would have liked to have seen a greater sense of occasion.

"It pissed me off," he recalled. "They were talking about the nights out they'd had, shagging and drinking, which I thought was unprofessional."[21]

They landed at the Royal Netherlands Air Force sector of Eindhoven Airport near the Dutch-Belgian border, a destination known only to a handful of people to ensure it would not be mobbed by the press. The only photographer there was from the ICTY, but in the excitement he had forgotten to put film in his cameras. There would be no photographs of Milošević's arrival for the history books.

With this precarious delivery nearly completed, the Dutch took every security precaution they could think of. A Dutch police helicopter landed nearby with its lights off to take custody of the prisoner and — according to Dutch aviation buffs[22] — was cleared for takeoff with a flare so the control tower could maintain radio silence. At a quarter past one in the morning, the chopper deposited Milošević inside the grounds of Scheveningen prison, which would be his home for the last five years of his life.

Eight years after it was established, this was the ICTY's defining moment. "This tribunal was set up to investigate and prosecute as high up the chain of command as the evidence will allow, and I think this is the ultimate case," the tribunal spokesman, Jim Landale, said.[23]

The last and only time a head of state had stood before an international tribunal was Admiral Karl Doenitz's appearance at Nuremberg, and he hardly counted. Doenitz had been Germany's stopgap leader for less than a month after Hitler's suicide. Milošević had been in command of Yugoslavia for thirteen years and was the main protagonist in four disastrous wars, the author of human suffering on a scale not seen in Europe since the Third Reich. His arrival at The Hague was a unique moment.

"The transfer of Slobodan Milošević to the tribunal is a turning point and the beginning of a new era in the development of international criminal justice," Claude Jorda, the tribunal president, said in a statement.[24]

That night, many of the prosecutors also felt a corner had been turned and the remaining fugitives would arrive in The Hague in quick succession. The head of investigations, Patrick Lopez-Terres, remembered walking home from the tribunal headquarters at three in the morning after Milošević had been safely delivered. A big staff reception had been planned at the tribunal for a few nights later.

"It was a feeling something really important had happened, and it was the start of something. There was a hope that it would snowball. But I was wrong," Lopez-Terres recalled.[25] History turned out to be more complicated. The manhunt had another decade to run.

CURTIS ALSO REACHED HOME in The Hague in the early-morning hours. It was barely worth going to sleep. Del Ponte wanted him in the office at eight in the morning and a full report on the arrest within twenty-four hours. However, when he got to the tribunal, she walked past him as if she did not recognize him. She was not known for being effusive with praise or recognition for her employees, and he had expected none. But he kept the handcuffs he had clapped on Milošević's wrists as a souvenir.

# 11.
# RADOVAN KARADŽIĆ:
# THE SHAMAN IN THE MADHOUSE

Oh Radovan, you man of steel…
—*poem in praise of Radovan Karadžić, 1992*

**BY 2008,** Radovan Karadžić was Europe's most wanted man and its greatest embarrassment. The self-declared republic the former psychiatrist and poet had carved out of Bosnia had brought death camps, mass executions, and genocide back to the heart of a continent that had fooled itself into thinking it had left such abominations behind.

The atrocities in Bosnia had drawn expressions of horror and outrage from the capitals of Europe, yet it had taken three years to stop the killing and twelve more years had slipped by in which the West's combined intelligence agencies supposedly stretched every sinew to find the perpetrators. Yet Karadžić, the wartime president of Bosnia's Serb Republic and high priest of ethnic cleansing, remained at large. And every day he was at liberty called into question the world's promises to sit in judgment on the killings it had failed to stop.

The pursuit of Karadžić had been marked by false starts, blunders, betrayals, and near misses, from the abortive negotiations over surrender, the spy drama of the Gourmelon affair and the consequent long-running Franco-American spat, followed by a series of would-be American ambushes that the fugitive always managed to avoid, either by blind luck, tip-offs, or a highly sensitive nose for danger.

As the years went by, the sense of urgency had ebbed. Washington and its allies had fought new wars, chasing new fugitives and nonexistent weapons of mass destruction. Diplomats speculated Karadžić was dead. His family was even trying to obtain a death certificate.

For many Bosnian Muslims, outrage at the failure to find their former tormentor had given way to cynicism and despair. Meanwhile in Belgrade, the reforming president Boris Tadić had vowed to track down the remaining fugitives. The European Union had made it a condition for Serbia's further progress toward membership. Elections in May 2008 had shown growing support for Tadić's promise of prosperity tomorrow in return for Westernization today. He would never again have such a strong mandate, but neither the president nor the Serbian assembly controlled the Security Information Agency (Bezbednosno-Informativna Agencija, or BIA), whose job was it was to find the wanted men. The BIA was still run by people put in place by Tadić's predecessor, Vojislav Koštunica, a nationalist opposed in principle to cooperation with the Hague Tribunal, particularly when it came to handing over Serb leaders. Rade Bulatović, the BIA director, had been Koštunica's national security adviser.

Every few weeks, investigators from the ICTY tracking unit would fly to Belgrade with spreadsheets listing Karadžić contacts and possible leads. They would sit around a table with their Serbian counterparts on the Belgrade "action team" and grade their homework. Had the BIA checked this cousin, visited this associate or supporter? Had these doors been knocked on recently?

Were they were making good use of the electronic surveillance equipment provided by the Americans, British, and French? Were they still listening in case someone dialed any of the long list of cell-phone numbers linked to Karadžić's family and closest associates? The Serbian secret policemen would accept these assignments sourly, grumbling that they had no need of lectures from foreigners on how to do their jobs.

This was the frustrating state of affairs in early 2008 when out of the blue, luck for once abandoned the fugitive in favor of his pursuers. One of the many dormant phone numbers on the BIA's list suddenly rang after four years of silence. More interesting still, the person using the SIM card in question was Luka Karadžić, Radovan's younger brother and staunchest defender. Luka was a blustering small-time businessman preoccupied at the time with defending himself against charges of killing a young woman in a drunk-driving incident in 2005.[1] But who was Luka calling?[2]

The voice on the other end of the line was unfamiliar to the BIA eavesdroppers. It was male but high-pitched with a Belgrade accent, but the stilted, perfunctory conversation told them nothing more. A couple of investigators were sent to take a look at the address to which the mystery man's phone number was registered. They returned having discovered his name was Dragan David Dabić, a somewhat eccentric old character who lived in one of the high-rise apartment blocks that lined Yuri Gagarin Street, named in honor of the first man in space, in the shabby remains of the concrete Socialist dream that was New Belgrade. Above a bushy white beard and glasses, he sported a topknot tied with a black bow perched distractingly on his snowy hair.

Dabić made a living as a New Age mystic, offering spiritual cures for chronic diseases and everyday maladies. In the world of alternative medicine, he was a minor celebrity with a regular column in the national magazine *Healthy Living*, a part-time gig representing the Connecticut-based vitamin company CaliVita, and a joint project with a well-known sexologist aimed at rejuvenating the sperm of infertile men. The therapist in question, Savo Bojović, claimed that sluggish sperm would start moving faster if Dabić placed his hands in their vicinity.[3]

Dabić seemed an unlikely acquaintance for the hard-drinking, splenetic Luka Karadžić, who had hitherto shown little interest in healthy alternative lifestyles. So the BIA officers dug a little deeper, and the more they looked into the life of the white-haired shaman, the stranger he appeared. According to his identity records, Dabić came from a town called Ruma west of Belgrade, halfway to the Croatian border, but there was one rather glaring discrepancy. There was another Dragan Dabić in Ruma with exactly the same date of birth. This version looked nothing like the looming Gandalf-like figure in New Belgrade. He was a squat former construction worker with short gray hair and a drooping mustache who grew tomatoes and made plum brandy. He had barely strayed more than five miles from his birthplace in his entire life and did not even own a mobile phone. The records showed only one Dragan Dabić had been born in Ruma in the 1940s, so one of these two men was clearly an impostor, and it did not take a Sherlock Holmes to deduce which.

There were other aspects of Dabić which did not fit the lifestyle of spiritual healer. He carried half a dozen mobile phones and used some of them to maintain contact with hardline Serb nationalists campaigning against the Hague Tribunal. A BIA officer was sent back to 267 Yuri Gagarin Street to hang around and take a closer look, strolling past him in the street. The officer returned with a startling suggestion. Perhaps this hairy spiritualist was *not* the mysterious link to Radovan Karadžić the surveillance team had suspected. If you cut off the topknot, shaved the beard, and removed the glasses, Dabić could be Karadžić himself!

This startling possibility brought with it a dilemma. The Tadić government said it wanted to catch Karadžić, but it was not clear whether the BIA leadership shared its enthusiasm. By May 2008, however, Bulatović's future was unclear. It was no secret that Tadić wanted to replace him, and after the parliamentary elections his supporters were close to putting together a majority coalition. If they succeeded the president would have the votes he needed to remake Serbia's security services. The country had reached a tipping point, and the BIA officers on the Dabić case made a calculated gamble on which way it would tilt. Instead of going to their boss, the BIA officers took their story straight to the president's office, to a man called Miodrag "Miki" Rakić. Rakić was a chubby, keenly intelligent strategist who was the power behind the throne in the presidency. Since 2008, he had been given an urgent new task: cutting through the inertia and resistance of the security services to catch the last handful of war crimes fugitives.

"Some of the guys we were working with approached me and said they had someone under long-distance surveillance," Rakić recalled. "They said, We don't know who it is but we know he's not the guy he's pretending to be. He's hiding his identity and maybe it's Karadžić himself."[4]

A few weeks later, the BIA men returned. They had been watching Dabić closely and were almost sure he was Karadžić in disguise. They still had not told their bosses what they were doing and were therefore risking their jobs. They wanted to know whether, in the event they were found out, Rakić would protect them.

At that moment, this was a guarantee Rakić was not in a position to offer. The fate of the investigation — and by extension, Karadžić's destiny — was being determined elsewhere in Belgrade, in the corridors of Serbia's national assembly. The general election in May had produced a hung parliament. The generally Western-oriented pro-European parties clustered around President Tadić had emerged as the biggest single bloc, but it was outweighed by the combined strength of the two leading nationalist parties, the Radicals and the Democratic Party of Serbia led by Tadić's predecessor and fiercest rival, Koštunica. When it came to forming a majority coalition, the final say belonged to the Socialist Party.

On July 7, the Socialist Party of Serbia finally swung its twenty votes behind the pro-European bloc, and in doing so sealed Karadžić's fate. The party of Slobodan Milošević, who had raised Karadžić to his wartime zenith, struck the blow that would complete his downfall, bringing him to justice in a matter of days.

The formation of a government allowed President Tadić, for the first time since he was elected in 2004, to reshuffle the leadership at the BIA. He replaced Bulatović with the thirty-six-year-old career policeman Saša Vukadinović, who had led the fight against organized crime in the provinces and then run Serbia's prisons for a year. He was smart, ambitious, and unburdened by nationalist political allegiances.

When Vukadinović met Bulatović to discuss the transition, the outgoing spy chief never raised the subject of the Karadžić file, and his younger successor did not press him. Bulatović handed over his office keys and computer passwords, and left.

By this time, word had reached Karadžić he was being watched. According to his lawyer, Sveta Vujačić, the fugitive began to spot unfamiliar faces in mid-July, brushing past him on the stairwell at his apartment block or at his favorite bar, the Luda Kuća (the Madhouse). "He knew he was encircled," Vujačić said.[5]

The endgame had begun, in which the fugitive king was running out of pawns to shield himself from his hunters. But he was not prepared to simply wait for them to come knocking on his door. On July 17, the BIA surveillance team sounded the alarm after seeing two unidentified men enter the Dabić apartment with large bags. It looked like the old man was getting ready to run.

The next evening, Dabić left 267 Yuri Gagarin Street in a light blue T-shirt and a broad-brimmed straw hat that was pulled low over his face. He was weighed down with baggage: a white plastic bag, a raffia shopping basket, and a knapsack, all of which appeared to be full. He walked to a nearby bus stop where he was soon discreetly joined by one of his BIA trackers. They boarded the number 73 bus bound for the suburb of Batajnica about eight miles to the northwest. Dabić sat near the front. His shadow was several seats back.

Dabić's intentions were obscure. He had told friends he was going on holiday in Croatia. His lawyer later claimed he was heading for a spa at Vrdnik, northwest of Belgrade. The old man had indeed packed swimming shorts and a cap, along with his laptop, CD-ROMs, and at least some of his mobile phones. But reaching Croatia or Vrdnik would normally have entailed a long-distance coach trip, rather than the number 73 bus. Some of Karadžić's pursuers theorized there must have been an accomplice waiting in a car somewhere along the bus route, ready to take him to another hideout. If so, the accomplice went undiscovered. Dabić never got that far.

As the bus lumbered through the streets from the concrete towers of New Belgrade into the older, richer, and leafier district of Zemun, the eccentric, confected character known as Dragan

Dabić, now in his last minutes of a long-running performance, put on his clear-glass spectacles and opened a spiritual text.[6] Through the window, city blocks gave way to green fields turning gold in the light of a Balkan summer evening.

The unhurried calm inside the bus contrasted with the hectic activity in the surrounding streets triggered by Dabić's departure from New Belgrade. Vukadinović had set a snatch plan in motion. A few stops before Batajnica, in the greenbelt around Belgrade, a couple of patrol cars steered in front of the bus and four plainclothes policemen got on, two in the front and two in the back. They made their way toward the middle seats, posing as inspectors, showing their badges and asking to see tickets. The old man in the straw hat was reaching into his pocket for his fare when he felt a policeman's grip around his arm.

"Dr. Karadžić?" the policeman asked.

"No, it's Dragan Dabić," the man protested.

"No, it's Radovan Karadžić," the policeman insisted.

"Are your superiors aware of what you are doing?" the man asked.

"Yes, fully."[7]

The officer ordered the driver to stop the bus and the captive was escorted onto the grass shoulder. At 9:30 p.m. on July 18, 2008, the flamboyant fiction that had been Dragan David Dabić evaporated. In his place, the ghost of Radovan Karadžić, who had haunted the Balkans for a decade, rematerialized on a Belgrade roadside as a flustered old man, his straw hat askew, clutching a white plastic bag to his breast.

It was a banal end to a life on the run that Karadžić himself had envisioned in almost mythical terms, his people's last hope hiding in plain sight from a legion of oppressive foes. As he grew older and more isolated, he drew increasing comfort from the

Three faces of Radovan Karadžić: at the height of his power, as the spiritual healer Dragan Dabić, and standing before the Hague tribunal, beardless and dapper once more.

notion that he was the spiritual reincarnation of Serb heroes of a bygone age. He wove his own legend, drawing on a life immersed in a cultural tradition in which mysticism, epic storytelling, warfare, and politics were all tightly enmeshed.

RADOVAN KARADŽIĆ was born in Petnjica, a mountain village in Montenegro, at the very end of the Second World War. The conflict left a deep imprint on the Karadžić family as it did on the rest of Yugoslavia, and the family, like the country, was never able to shake it off. Eight members of the clan were killed by Partisans in 1942 and their bodies thrown down a well.[8] Radovan's father, Vuko, a village cobbler, was part of the flotsam of conflict. He joined the Chetniks, monarchist paramilitaries who fought on both sides in the war. They initially resisted occupation by the Axis powers, but as the conflict wore on, they found more and more reasons to collaborate with the Germans and Italians, allowing them to settle old ethnic scores with Bosnia's Muslims and fight new ideological enemies: the Partisans led by Josip Broz Tito.

In the closing stages of the war, as it became clear the Partisans would emerge the victors, Vuko went home to Petnjica, only to be drafted as a Partisan cobbler, mending the worn boots of Tito's guerrilla fighters. He no doubt hoped his services would excuse him for his time in the Chetnik ranks, but he was wrong. The Communist secret police sought him out after the war and he only narrowly escaped execution. Instead, he was locked up for five years, leaving behind an infant son he hardly knew, a boy called Radovan. The child was raised for his first five years by his mother, Jovanka, who struggled to grow enough potatoes and grain for them to survive. As an adult, he would make many boastful and dubious claims about his life, but his accounts of rural destitution were no exaggeration.

Karadžić seems to have long harbored ambitions of acting out his life in a bigger arena than the one he was born into. Even when his father returned from jail, he looked elsewhere for male role models, back in time to the godfather of romantic Serb nationalism who bore the same family name, Vuk Karadžić.

In the nineteenth century, Vuk Karadžić had modernized the Serbian language and rescued Serb culture from the doldrums of Ottoman subjugation, resurrecting the tradition of the epic poem. Radovan would come to see himself walking the same path as his nation's statesman-poet, and he would present his own life story as an epic, a fateful trajectory from humble village origins to reluctant national leader to martyrdom on the world stage.

The biographical facts are less straightforward. The ambition was always there, but his sense of national destiny was slow to arrive. In 1960, when he was fifteen, he persuaded his parents to let him leave home in search of a better education. But instead of heading for Belgrade, the capital of Yugoslavia and of all things Serb, he went to study in Sarajevo, the ethnically diverse capital of Bosnia and Herzegovina, the only one of the six constituent republics of the Socialist Federal Republic of Yugoslavia that was not defined by a dominant ethnic group.

As a young man in 1960s, Karadžić thrived in Sarajevo. He qualified as a psychiatrist and at the same time met his future wife, Ljiljana Zelen, in medical school, launching a career and a family all at once. Throughout, there was no hint that he was destined to become a nationalist ideologue. Sarajevo was not the place to go to avoid Muslims or Croats. It was where national or religious identity was of passing interest or no interest at all.

Karadžić worked for a time as the in-house psychiatrist to

Sarajevo's multiethnic soccer team, trying with limited success to instill in them a will to win. The players struggled to take his "psycho-training" sessions seriously. On one occasion, he got them to lie on the floor in a darkened room while he played taped music and told them to imagine themselves as bumblebees flying from flower to flower. As the team captain at the time, Predrag Pašić, recalled the players' responses: "someone was sleeping, someone snoring, someone else was farting and someone cursing about bumblebees. The whole bumblebee thing was a huge joke to us."[9]

They may have laughed at him but none of the players ever took him for a nationalist. "Looked on from that perspective," Pašić said many years later, "it seems strange that there was such a huge contrast with what Radovan would later become."

In retrospect, Jovanka Karadžić would declare herself equally taken aback by her son's career. "I tried to teach him to be honest and law-abiding. I educated him under adverse circumstances to live as a doctor and a gentleman," she would recall wistfully. "I never for a single second thought he would go into politics. I always knew politics was not good, and I never wanted him to do it. Oh, how I wish he hadn't."[10]

Throughout the 1970s, he showed no signs that he would follow such a route. In 1974, he won a one-year fellowship in New York at Columbia University, working on a thesis that sought to synthesize the two passions in his life at that time, psychology and poetry, exploring how the former underpinned the latter. The following year he spent in Belgrade, trying to further his career in sports psychiatry and living in an apartment block on Yuri Gagarin Street, the same road he would later inhabit during his last days as a fugitive. The wanderings suggest a man searching for a niche in which he could excel. But the pull of family and his Sarajevo home kept bringing him back to Bosnia.

It is hard to scan Karadžić's biography and find a starting point for the path that would one day bring him before a war crimes tribunal. He did spend a year in jail and was clearly embittered by the experience, though not noticeably radicalized. In 1984, he was accused of involvement in a construction scam. Along with Momčilo Krajišnik (a close friend destined to be the Bosnian Serb parliamentary speaker and a fellow war crimes defendant), he was alleged to have diverted building materials from a state enterprise to his own chicken farm, Karadžić's bid to cash in on hungry tourists coming to the Sarajevo Winter Olympics.[11] He was finally released for lack of evidence but only after spending twelve months behind bars without a trial. Yet there is no outward sign his jail time awoke the rebel in him. Far from it. He returned quietly to his psychiatric practice.

If there is a trace of inner tumult anywhere in Karadžić's life it is in his poetry, the one constant through the decades. From a young age, he wrote verse in prodigious quantities, with imagery that was mostly romantic but with decidedly violent undertones. And that was just his poetry for children. In his 1982 collection for young readers, *There's a Miracle, There's No Miracle*, a poem called "War Shoes" is decorated with childish renderings of houses and clouds, tanks and cannons blasting away merrily in between, all on a purple background. In the poem, the shoes are dozing but watchful. If a foreign army should approach, the little readers will have to defend their playgrounds and picnic spots. The verses warn the reader there will be "Days of heroism, nights of chivalry" ahead, when the time came "for the gun barrels to speak."

Another of Karadžić's poems, "Sarajevo," published in his first book in 1971, presciently talks of the Bosnian capital burning "like a stick of incense." A verse from the same period urges spiritual catharsis through violence: "Let's go down to the cities / To beat up the bastards." It makes a rhyming couplet in Serbian, but just who the "bastards" were supposed to be and who was supposed to beat them up was left unspecified.

The reaction to Karadžić's poetry in Sarajevo's literary circles was mixed. One critic in the mid-1980s accused him of engaging in "verbal narcissism." Karadžić's sense of destiny remained intact, however. He informed the chief psychiatrist at the clinic where he worked that he was destined to become "one of the three most important poets writing in the Serbian language."[12]

The foreboding tone of his work, coupled with the disconnect between Karadžić's certainty in his own genius and society's indifference, raises the question of whether he had harbored destructive feelings for his adopted hometown long before the collapse of Yugoslavia. His wife rejected the suggestion. "They say in the West that Radovan wanted to destroy Sarajevo in revenge because he was marginalized as a Montenegrin at parties," Ljiljana said. It was an illuminating insight, as few had previously been aware that her husband had felt snubbed at gatherings of the Bosnian intelligentsia. Ljiljana insisted the infamous Sarajevo-in-flames poem had not been a statement of intent but "just a moment of depression." "Why don't they ever mention his poems about nature and children?" she asked an interviewer.[13]

It was Yugoslavia's violent implosion that gave Karadžić the chance to escape mediocrity and live his life on the heroic scale envisaged in his poetry. Yet his first tentative venture into politics was hardly headed toward militant Serb nationalism. He had a brief flirtation with the embryonic Green Party, during which he declared "Bolshevism is bad, but nationalism is even worse" and was remembered principally for making suggestions about environmentally responsible food labeling.[14]

In early 1990, the possibilities offered by the collapse of Communism seemed dizzying. New parties of all complexions were springing up everywhere. Karadžić and his circle of Serb intellectuals knew they wanted to be part of it. They were just unsure what sort of party it should be.[15]

The story of Karadžić's sudden political ascent is a reminder that there was nothing inevitable about Bosnia's plunge into ethnic violence. The man who would emerge as the central protagonist in the tragedy was dithering about what he wanted and what he stood for. He initially ruled himself out of the leadership of any Serb national party, arguing his life was already too full of family and professional commitments. But no one else emerged who was acceptable to Belgrade, where the nationalist writer and ardent Milošević supporter Dobrica Ćosić was holding auditions for the post. Ćosić was a dominant figure in post-Communist cultural life and his iconic status in the nationalist pantheon would be confirmed two years later when he was elected as the Yugoslav president. At the beginning of 1990 he was looking for someone suitable to carry the Serb flag in Bosnia and picked Karadžić only after several other more prominent figures had dropped out.[16]

Once Karadžić accepted the task, a path through the thickets of post-Yugoslav politics was cleared for him by his new friends in Belgrade. Ćosić advised him on how to organize the new Serb Democratic Party (SDS), emulating the title, flag, and emblems of a parallel Belgrade-backed group that was proving successful in Croatia. Would-be rivals in Bosnian Serb politics were persuaded to step aside.

Throughout the election campaign of 1990, Karadžić's instincts were to treat the other nationalists parties, the Muslim

Democratic Action Party and the Croatian Democratic Union, as partners in opposition to the Communists. He went out of his way to refute the sort of alarmist claims of a radical Islamic threat to Europe that he would be championing before long.

The abrupt change from ambivalence to demagoguery might be explained in part by the circumstances. The old League of Communists and its offspring were destroyed at the polls, and without this common enemy the nationalist parties discovered they had very different visions for their country. The Croats wanted Yugoslavia to devolve into a loose confederation of largely independent republics. The Serbs wanted the opposite, a federation with a strong center in Belgrade, run by them. The Bosniaks, anxious to avoid conflict, opted for a vague compromise between the two.

While the outside environment was in convulsions, there were dramatic changes in Karadžić himself. He had hesitated over taking up the burden of leadership, but once it was placed in his hands he was captivated by the power it brought. He was stunned by the sudden adulation of Serb voters for a previously unknown psychiatrist who they now hailed as a savior from the anxieties of post-Communist existence.

Once he had tasted the thrill of political potency, he was prepared to do whatever was necessary to keep it. First of all, that meant bowing to Milošević. He first met the Serbian president in September 1990 and quickly fell into step as a loyal lieutenant.[17] There was little choice. Serb leaders in Croatia who had not been sufficiently aggressive in demanding full self-government for Serb areas were unceremoniously dumped by Milošević and disappeared into obscurity.

Karadžić always presented the relationship as a partnership of equals, but it was closer to patron-client. His biographer,

Robert Donia, notes that Milošević would call him "Radovan," while Karadžić never dared to copy such familiarity. He addressed Milošević as "President": "Milošević frequently summoned Karadžić to Belgrade and Karadžić invariably cancelled or rearranged other plans to make the short trip to meet in Milošević's private office. Milošević only occasionally gave Karadžić direct orders, but when he did, Karadžić obeyed them."[18]

In 1991 Karadžić began to push autonomy for Serb majority municipalities from the republic's government in Sarajevo, cranking up the tensions in Bosnia, as Yugoslavia began to break apart from its western end. Slovenia and Croatia fought for and won their independence, but Croatia only got away at a price. Under Milošević's guidance, Croatian Serbs seceded and declared their own republic.

When Bosnia's moment of decision approached in the spring of 1992, Karadžić prepared to follow the same course, stockpiling the weapons that arrived in a constant flow on night convoys from Belgrade.

By the hot summer of that year, Karadžić dominated the self-proclaimed Republika Srpska that had wrenched itself away from a newly independent Bosnia. He looked down from the heights around Sarajevo as his artillery poured shells into the heart of the city that had been his home for almost all his adult life.

For the benefit of the cameras, he invited a Russian nationalist writer, Eduard Limonov, to join him on the crags. Performing for the famous visitor, Karadžić embarked on a soliloquy on the great geopolitical game that he claimed was under way below them. The Muslims might be the urban majority, he told the Russian, but the land beneath their feet belonged to the Serbs.

"We may be negotiating about territory but we own this country. This is our country," Karadžić said. And while Limonov, apparently inspired by the spirit of Orthodox Slav unity, is allowed to fire off a few machine-gun rounds at the city below, the Bosnian Serb leader takes the opportunity to recite his Sarajevo poem, imagining the city as flaming incense, where disaster is stalking the streets and even the trees are armed.[19]

"Everything I saw in terms of war," he tells Limonov. "That was twenty-three years ago...And many other poems I wrote have something of prediction which frightens me sometimes."

On the way to doomed peace talks in Geneva in 1993, Karadžić had a verse sung in his honor to the accompaniment of a gusle, a single-stringed Serb fiddle. It compared the chubby president, girded with his ever-present white scarf, to the dashing Karadjordje, the warlike founder of modern Serbia who had led a Napoleon-era uprising against the Ottoman Empire.

"Oh Radovan, you man of steel, the greatest leader since Karadjordje, defend our freedom and our faith, on the shores of Lake Geneva" the gusle player sang for the Serbs' latter-day liberator.[20]

He cut such a plump, vainglorious figure, with his trademark vertical quiff like a gray cockatoo, that Western reporters who witnessed these performances initially had trouble taking him seriously. Distracted by the poetry, the self-regard, and the colorful silk ties, they did not pay enough attention to what he was saying. In a chilling speech to Bosnia's parliament six months before the shooting started, he warned Bosnia's Muslims they could "disappear" in a war, having no means to defend themselves.

In an intercepted telephone call later produced as evidence in his trial, he told a party colleague: "They have to know there are 20,000 armed Serbs around Sarajevo...Sarajevo will be a *karakazan* [black cauldron], where 300,000 Muslims will die."[21]

At the beginning of the conflict, the Republika Srpska was run by a triumvirate. Besides Karadžić, it included Nikola Koljević,

Yugoslavia's foremost Shakespearean scholar, an urbane but tragic figure whose son was killed in an accident before the war and who went on to shoot himself in January 1997; and Biljana Plavšić, a stern biology professor and advocate of the pseudoscience of racial genetics.

"It was genetically deformed material that embraced Islam. And now, of course, with each successive generation it simply becomes concentrated," Plavšić explained in 1994.[22]

By the end of 1992, Koljević and Plavšić had been relegated to the role of deputies. Karadžić emerged as sole president and supreme commander of the armed forces, a title that would eventually constitute the point of departure for his indictment for genocide and crimes against humanity in The Hague. The indictment notes that from at least March 1992 until about July 19, 1996, Karadžić was the highest civilian and military authority in the Republika Srpska.

In his years in the dock following his capture, Karadžić had reason to regret his many past vanities. His coveting of imperious titles, grandstanding, playing Nero above Sarajevo, intoning verses while the smoke rose from the city—it all came back to haunt him. So did his boasting to the Republika Srpska parliament in the summer of 1995 that he had ordered the Srebrenica massacre in his "Directive 7" to General Mladić. "I was in favor of all decisions made and I support them. The time had come," Karadžić told the assembly.

In court, his best defense lay in the carping of his detractors, those around him who had sought to portray him as cowardly; intimidated by his military commander, Ratko Mladić; and out of touch at the height of the war, when he was often to be found gambling at the Hotel Metropol Palace in Belgrade or skulking at home.

In her 2005 jailhouse memoir, *I Testify*, Plavšić complained about

> *the continuous picking of his ears with a pencil, spreading*
> *dandruff from his hair, biting his nails until they bled and*
> *his changing day to night, was drawing more and more*
> *attention from people ... Presidency meetings were supposed*
> *to be held every day at 11 a.m. Everybody was on time, except*
> *the President ... who was regularly late between one and*
> *two hours ... On two or three occasions, I personally called*
> *his house and his wife always gave the same short answer*
> *"Radovan is sleeping" and then she would just hang up.*[23]

No matter how dysfunctional and erratic his leadership style may have been, Karadžić proved extraordinarily hard to dislodge from power, even after NATO arrived to keep the peace. When he realized that Western commanders were unwilling to have him arrested, he became steadily more brazen, testing the West's resolve in enforcing the basic terms of the Dayton Accords that subordinated the Republika Srpska to an overarching Bosnian state and allowed the return of deported communities to their homes. All three parties to the Bosnian conflict dragged their heels in implementing different parts of the agreement, but the scale of Serb obstructionism soon became a serious challenge both to the peace and to its American backers.

In June 1996, Richard Holbrooke, the former American envoy who had left government after Dayton to go into banking, wrote to President Clinton to warn him about the consequences of the unraveling of the Dayton Accords: "The implications of Karadžić's defiance go far beyond Bosnia itself. If he succeeds, basic issues of American leadership that seemed settled in the public's eye after Dayton will re-emerge. Having reasserted American leadership in Europe, it would be a tragedy if we let it slip away again."[24]

The White House was duly alarmed. Holbrooke was pulled back into government service and sent to Belgrade to salvage Dayton. There he met Milošević and two Karadžić lieutenants, Momčilo Krajišnik and Aleksa Buha, the Serb statelet's parliamentary speaker and foreign minister, respectively. They struck a deal that removed Karadžić from power in exchange for allowing his party, the SDS, to continue to function and to take part in that year's elections. Milošević's intelligence chief, Jovica Stanišić, was dispatched by helicopter to Pale to secure Karadžić's signature on his political suicide late at night on July 18, while Holbrooke and his team were treated to a dinner of lamb, yogurt, and spinach as they waited at Milošević's Belgrade villa.

Stanišić returned with the signed document at two o'clock in the morning, and the deal was done. Karadžić would later claim that Holbrooke had promised Krajišnik and Buha that immunity from prosecution was part of the bargain, something Holbrooke always vehemently denied.

"That is...C-R-A-P...crap," he told the BBC in 1995. "It is something that Mr. Karadžić put out in order to cover his massive humiliation at being forced to give up his two titles, president of Srpska and president of his party. So he put this lie out, and because he hasn't been captured some people still believe it. But it isn't true."[25]

Karadžić and his supporters frequently suggested that they had documentary evidence to prove Holbrooke's alleged pledge of immunity but never produced it during the five years of his trial. On the other hand, several US officials, including those who worked with Holbrooke, say it is quite possible the dogged, overbearing negotiator may have deliberately given the impression that the indictments were nothing to worry about in order to secure the deal, while committing nothing to paper.

The Hague was not the only option Karadžić explored in the uneasy transition between war and NATO-enforced peace. Boris Yeltsin told his French counterpart, Jacques Chirac, that after Dayton the Russians had arranged for Karadžić to be flown to Belarus in a bid to sell it to him as a potential seat of exile. Karadžić took one look at the country's grim capital, Minsk, and asked to be flown home.[26]

In Pale, Karadžić withdrew from public view and concentrated on making money from the black-market trade in fuel and timber, while seeking to control Bosnian Serb politics from behind the scenes. Under his sway, the SDS continued to prevent Bosniaks and Croats from returning to their villages and persisted in the harassment of Serb opponents.

The root of the problem was a lack of political will in the Western capitals where an arrest operation would have to be authorized. And even when the realization dawned that Karadžić's presence was poisoning the peace settlement and substantial resources were belatedly deployed, the effort was a failure. The shambolic poet-psychiatrist-warlord-gambler managed to stay one step ahead of the enormous military and intelligence effort to find him, remaining at liberty for more than a decade.

In the early years of the millennium, something of an obsession grew up around the tiny village of Čelebići, high up in the mountains southeast of Foča near Montenegro. Rumors swirled in intelligence reports and in the press that Karadžić was being sheltered there. Correspondents frequently trekked up to the craggy hamlet and described the locals' distaste for outsiders, a form of journalism that was ultimately self-fulfilling. In February 2002, dozens of French and German troops blew holes in the walls around a farm and stormed in with armored cars and helicopters. There was no sign of any fugitives and no arrests were made.[27] NATO claimed to have found a large cache of weapons and insisted that the dramatic raid demonstrated the determination of the alliance.[28]

The Čelebići buzz and the recurrent waves of speculation pointing to a variety of Montenegrin monasteries turned out to be built entirely on false leads, many provided by US and British informants either for money or as deliberate disinformation. Similar misdirection eventually led to the biggest fiasco of the entire Karadžić manhunt, on April Fool's Day in 2004.

At about one o'clock that morning, Jeremija Starovlah, an Orthodox priest in Pale, was shaken awake by his wife, Vitorka. The phone was ringing and she was fearful it meant something had happened to their youngest son, who was away from home. Jeremija padded toward the living room, while Vitorka and the couple's eldest son, Aleksandar, stood in the hallway in their pajamas. As soon as the priest picked up the phone, the whole house was shaken by an almighty blast. Out of the darkness and the smoke, SFOR soldiers rushed in through doors and windows, shouting, with guns raised. Both Jeremija and Aleksandar were lying motionless on the floor. They were taken to the hospital in a coma.[29]

Vitorka, with the backing of the Serbian Orthodox church, accused NATO of beating the men senseless. The alliance apologized profusely but insisted their injuries had been the unintended consequences of the explosives used to blow off the front door in the course of a raid aimed at finding Karadžić. NATO had received a "credible" tip that the fugitive was being harbored by the priest, a vocal Karadžić fan, and was being guarded inside the house by armed men.

It was a debacle. Yet another false lead had been compounded this time by excessive force and the cavalier use of explosives. The version of events put out by Western officials was that while British and American troops had secured a perimeter around the priest's house, French commandos had blown up the door but miscalculated the amount of plastic explosive needed. The concrete interior had channeled and amplified the shock wave from the blast and grievously injured the Starovlahs.

The incident brought thousands of Bosnian Serbs into the streets in Karadžić masks, waving the Serb tricolor, and enhanced the fugitive's image as folk hero. A few months later, he completed the West's humiliation by publishing his latest collection of poems in Serbia. It was curiously titled *Under the Left Breast of History* and included a section headed "I Can Look for Myself," an apparently mocking reference to NATO's continuing failure to find him. In October 2004, his latest novel, *Miraculous Chronicles of the Night*, written while he was in hiding, sold out at the Belgrade International Book Fair. NATO was floundering while its quarry was hitting his literary peak.

In frustration, the focus of the pursuit turned toward Karadžić's money. The High Representative in Sarajevo at the time was Paddy Ashdown, a former Royal Marine commando and ex-leader of Britain's Liberal Democrats. The post gave Ashdown viceregal powers to run Bosnia as an international protectorate, and he used them to the utmost, cutting off public funding to the SDS on the grounds the money was being used to finance Karadžić's flight from international justice. Ashdown's office found that tens of millions of dollars were missing from the accounts of the Republika Srpska's forestry commission, electric power corporation, and other utilities. Ashdown was convinced that the missing money was used to fund the Preventiva, as Karadžić's bodyguards were colloquially known.

The flow of money was duly cut off. Judging by Karadžić's spartan lifestyle in Belgrade in his last years on the run, and the fact that the Dragan Dabić cover was at least partly self-financed through fees from his services as a spiritual healer, it is fair to assume Ashdown's efforts helped to cramp his style. But it brought the world no closer to capturing Karadžić.

Failure followed failure. After a tip-off that Karadžić was getting medical attention in Pale, Italian carabinieri and German troops closed down large areas of the town in March 2004 and went door to door in the driving snow, searching for wall cavities in Ljiljana's pink house.[30]

US troops picked up a Bosnian Serb general, Bogdan Subotić, on the suspicion that he was the channel to Stana Kojić, a Serb fortune-teller in Bijeljina whom Karadžić consulted in his constant quest to remain one step ahead of his pursuers.[31] The consultations with Kojić doubtless provided Karadžić with material that he ultimately incorporated into his spiritualist shtick as Dragan Dabić. But the questioning of General Subotić led nowhere.

As the years went by, the techniques used by the American military became increasingly heavy-handed to the point that Western diplomats in Sarajevo, including American embassy officials, began to worry that they were pushing at the borders of legality. That uneasiness reached a peak in July 2005 when Karadžić's thirty-three-year-old son, Saša, was picked up at home in Pale and led away in handcuffs with a flak jacket over his head to a helicopter that flew to the US base Camp Eagle in Tuzla. There he was held in solitary confinement for ten days, in the hope of sweating him into giving away his father's whereabouts.

"He knew we could hold him for seventy-two hours and he was as cool as a cucumber for those three days. But what he didn't know was that the commander could order another seventy-two hours, and then another. He started sweating and crying," a US official recalled.[32]

The interrogation was fruitless, but Saša Karadžić's treatment prompted the family to try to insulate themselves from the increasingly desperate search. After exploring the possibility of declaring her husband dead, Ljiljana made a dramatic appearance on Serb television on July 29, 2005, calling on him to give himself up.

> This is a message to my husband, Radovan Karadžić. I
> have to address you this way, because there is no other way.
> Our family is under constant pressure from all sides. We are
> being threatened in every way: through our lives and our
> property. We are living in a constant atmosphere of anxiety,
> pain and suffering. That is why, between loyalty to you
> and loyalty to our children and grandchildren, I had to
> choose and I have chosen. I find it painful and hard to ask
> you, but I beg you with all my heart and soul to surrender.
> That will be a sacrifice for us, for our family. In the hope
> that you are alive and that you are free to make the decision
> yourself, I beg you to make the decision and do it for all our
> sakes. In all my helplessness and my weakness, the only thing
> that I can do is beg you.[33]

By the time of this appeal, Karadžić was already cocooned in Belgrade and beginning to emerge in public as Dabić, using papers provided by the Serbian State Security Service, based on a personal history stolen from the real Dabić in Ruma.

"I think it was the conclusion of the secret police that it was safest to use the identity of a peasant who didn't move around," Bruno Vekarić, the deputy war crimes prosecutor in Belgrade, said.[34]

The first time anyone in the Serbian alternative therapy world came across the white-bearded wanderer was in late 2005, when he appeared in Belgrade at the house of Mina Minić. Minić advertised himself as a clairvoyant, but he failed to see through his visitor's disguise. His impression of Dabić was that he looked "like a monk who had done something wrong with a nun."[35]

Dabić told Minić that he had been living in New York but had come home after an ugly split with his wife, who was spitefully refusing to forward his medical credentials. Dabić was eager to learn the ways of the *visak*, a pendulum claimed by Balkan seers to identify disturbances in the energy fields around sick or troubled patients.

Dabić soon acquired his own *visak*, and his career as a mystic healer blossomed. He adopted the un-Serbian middle name of David and used it increasingly as a professional moniker. He also set up a website called Psy Help Energy which advertised the David Wellbeing Programme offering help from "experienced experts from pioneering areas of science where there are immense possibilities for interaction with natural forces in and around us."

Among other services available were acupuncture, homeopathy, "quantum medicine," and traditional cures. He also sold necklaces he called Velbing (well-being): lucky charms that he claimed offered health benefits and "personal protection" against "harmful radiation." He used elements of his training in psychiatric care and embellished them with Oriental-inspired theories of "the life force," "vital energies," and "personal auras."

He told his clients his topknot acted as a sort of spiritual radio receiver, drawing in energy from the environment. The website provided no address, and the two numbers it listed were prepaid mobile phones.

The showman and the man of destiny still craved a broader public, however. He pestered Goran Kojić, the editor of *Healthy Living*, for a writing slot.

"Here was this strange looking man. He said he was freelancing for a number of private clinics and he wanted to publish," Kojić said. "He said: 'I have a diploma but I don't have it with me. My ex-wife has it in the United States'. I said I can't publish you as a psychiatrist without a diploma, but I will take you on as a 'spiritual researcher'."[36]

His column was titled "Meditations," and it stressed the benefits of *tihovanje*, a form of meditation practiced through the centuries by Orthodox monks.

"If you use tihovanje, you will achieve higher states of being because it is from your own culture," Dabić wrote. He gave a public lecture on the subject in October 2007. By now he was a regular at seminars and panel discussions on alternative medicine. *Healthy Living*'s third annual festival in Belgrade advertised a presentation by David Dabić on "nurturing your inner energies." Videos of these occasions show a soft-spoken pensioner sitting the way Karadžić the warlord used to sit with his feet pointing inward and balancing on the outside edge of his soles.[37]

In his neighborhood, the kids called him Santa Claus, and the kindly old man used to stop and talk to them on the way home from the corner grocery store. He lived on the third floor of 267 Yuri Gagarin Street in apartment 19. The landlord, Maksimović, whose name was on the door, later insisted he had no inkling of his tenant's true identity. According to one visitor, there was a framed photograph on a table showing four boys all dressed in yellow L.A. Lakers T-shirts who Karadžić said were grandsons living in America. The picture was presumably provided by the secret police minders who initially presented him with the Dabić identity.

The neighbors said he had lived in the apartment since early 2007, at first alone and then he appeared to have found a woman companion in the last eight weeks there. Her name was Mila Cicak, a fifty-three-year-old unemployed nurse, but she angrily denied tabloid reports she had been Dabić's lover. She described herself as a friend who helped Dabić in his work. She too had no clue as to her friend's true identity.

It was hard to blame her. Another of Dabić's neighbors, who lived across the hall from him, was a woman who worked for Interpol and whose job it was coordinate the hunt for international fugitives like Karadžić.

"Every morning this woman switched on her computer and there was a picture of Radovan Karadžić and Osama bin Laden. And each morning she would say good morning to Dragan Dabić," Vekarić said.[38]

So convincing was Dabić in his role of healer that the closer people got to him, the more they believed in him and the more shocked they were when he was unmasked. Maja Djelić was an acupuncturist who was one of Dabić's closest friends. On the way back from a conference in October 2007, Djelić had a headache and Dabić had made it disappear by touching her temples with his hands.

"The people dealing with this stuff are usually charlatans, but not him. You could feel he had good bio-energy," she said later. The last time Djelić heard from her guru, in June 2008, just a few weeks before his arrest, he sent her an e-mail pondering the properties of the "magic number 11."[39] He had promised to teach her the secrets of transmitting bio-energy. Like many who knew Dabić, she had trouble coming to terms with the fact that he did not exist.

"I'm sorry I can't stay a friend to the man I knew," she said after the arrest. "I still believe in three days they're going to come back and say it's not him."

Many of Dabić's evenings were spent in the Luda Kuća (Madhouse) bar, a one-room establishment set among a few trees and a patch of grass under a cluster of tower blocks on Yuri Gagarin Street in a district known as Block 45.

In the heyday of Tito's Socialist Yugoslavia, Block 45 was a model suburb. It was near the Sava River and the blocks were interspersed with gardens. The well-to-do lived cheek by jowl with city workers. But the previous three decades had not been kind to the district, and its decline had sharpened since Serbia had been cut off by sanctions. By 2008, the gardens of Block 45 were unkempt, it was unsafe at night, and graffiti was climbing the walls of the apartment blocks like an implacable disease.

The Luda Kuća was a smoke-filled, rough-edged place that appealed to a shifting crowd of outsiders — impoverished war veterans, Bosnian Serbs, and Montenegrins. It served country wine, *šljivovica* (plum brandy), and pungent undiluted nationalism.

On the wood-paneled walls were pictures of the Serb modern nationalist pantheon: Slobodan Milošević, Vojislav Šešelj, Ratko Mladić, and, of course, Radovan Karadžić — each one a hero to the people, each one indicted for war crimes. For the clientele, there was no contradiction. When Karadžić was finally unmasked, the regulars felt honored rather than hoodwinked. Tales of Dragan Dabić passed overnight into legend.

One winter's night, during one of the bar's gusle jam sessions, Dabić turned up to listen and was eventually persuaded to join in. Rašo Vučinić, a young, black-haired, mustachioed national-ist who had been another of the gusle players that night recalled: "He was wearing a black hat and a black coat and he was standing at the threshold, listening."

"You young players are the greatest treasure of the Serbian people," the old man told Vučinić. "Sing with and through the gusle. Speak about the Serb traditions. Hold the banner of our glory high." Then he wrote out the lyrics of Serb songs about the war in Bosnia.[40]

When Dabić was cajoled into picking up the gusle himself, he played beautifully, according to Luda Kuća lore. After his arrest, the gusle he played was treasured as a relic. It was carved from elm with a large eagle at its head and portraits of national heroes on its body, including one of Vuk Karadžić, Radovan's nineteenth-century forebear and idol.

Those who witnessed the legendary gusle night shook their heads in disbelief at the memory. There was Radovan Karadžić, their hero and icon, playing the gusle for them under his own portrait, and no one had a clue who he was. The audacity!

Karadžić's lawyer, Sveta Vujačić, has his own Luda Kuća tale of sitting alongside Dabić while the whole bar broke into a bal-lad in Karadžić's honor. "Rašo, come down from the mountain," they sang, using an affectionate diminutive for Radovan.

"For Radovan and me it was hard not to show emotions. Everyone in Luda Kuća was singing," Vujačić recalled.[41]

Many Luda Kuća regulars claimed they had detected an oth-erworldly vibration emanating from the man they knew as Dr. David.

"Some might say he looked like a weirdo, but I looked at him as a living saint, and I didn't even know who it was," Vučinić, the gusle player, said.

The bar's owner, Tomas Kovijanić, another Montenegrin from a village close to Petnjica recalled: "There was something special about him, an aura or charisma. He had the appearance of a saint, a prophet, a magus."

"Every day I saw him, and not even remotely would I have recognized him," he said. One day, Kovijanić, a burly wisecracking fifty-four-year-old known to his customers as Miško, got talking to Dabić about the mountains of Montenegro, regaling his elderly customer about a childhood spent less than a mile away from the Karadžić home. They were family friends, he had bragged to his subsequent embarrassment.

"He was listening but said nothing nor made even a single gesture that gave away he knew the places I was talking about," the bar owner said.

In the summer of 2007, a swarm of bees had settled on a tree above the Luda Kuća and built a hive that grew so heavy it fell to the pavement. As Kovijanić remembered the incident: "People got worried about being attacked and somebody brought some insecticide, but Dr. David—Radovan—said, 'Don't kill the bees. Bees are blessed, living beings and deserve to be saved.' He brought a box and led the rescue effort. A friend of mine was a beekeeper and he came to take them away. Radovan wouldn't leave until they picked up every last bee."

Kovijanić said, "I am proud that he was here, that he felt safe and secure here. I am just sad because of what has happened and that he is going to a dungeon in The Hague."[42]

Vujačić first heard of Karadžić's arrest two days after the event but a day before it became public. He was traveling back from Kragujevac from the latest installment of Luka Karadžić's drunk-driving case, in which a twenty-one-year-old woman had been killed in a head-on collision with his car three years earlier.

The travails of the Bosnian Serbs' former first family seem likely to keep the lawyer busy for many years to come.

Karadžić's immediate circle of friends and supporters had not been able to get through to him for two days and were sufficiently concerned about his radio silence to break cover and call the lawyer.

"For Radovan not to be picking up his phone was really unusual," Vujačić said. "He always carried at least two phones and was always in contact... One of those numbers he'd had for two years."[43]

The reaction among Karadžić's friends to his disappearance speaks eloquently about the BIA's previous efforts to find him. It shows there was a close-knit support network constantly in touch with the fugitive and with each other. It also proved they did not bother to change phones or SIM cards very often. The Serbian spy agency's failure to track this chatter suggests that — prior to the change of management — it had not been trying very hard to find the fugitive.

Working for the Karadžić family does not appear to have made Vujačić rich. His office is a cramped apartment on the fifth floor of a central Belgrade block, reached by a creaking ascent in a vintage elevator through a dark, untended stairwell. The lawyer claims the office was burgled ten times in the years Karadžić was on the run, each time by BIA agents. They looked through his files and occasionally confiscated a bottle or two from his impressive whisky collection. Above replenished supplies of Teachers and Famous Grouse on his bookcase, one framed photograph now has pride of place: It shows Vujačić and Karadžić arm in arm, smiling for the camera. It was taken at four o'clock in the morning of July 22, 2008, the only picture to emerge from Karadžić's short stay at the Ustanička Street court.

It was also the first photograph to show Karadžić's face after his life on the run. Shorn of Dragan Dabić's woolly white beard, he is clearly older and gaunter, with hollow cheeks, but he is immediately recognizable as the Balkan warlord who had seemingly vanished a decade earlier.

Karadžić's arrest made headlines around the world. The UN secretary-general, Ban Ki-moon, hailed the arrest as a historic moment. Holbrooke declared "the Osama bin Laden of Europe" had been captured. The news brought people into the streets in central Sarajevo to celebrate a day Bosniaks thought would never come.

In Belgrade, ten thousand supporters were bused into town by the nationalist parties to chant and protest. It was the biggest demonstration against any of the war crimes arrests to date, but it altered nothing. Serbia had already changed course. The vote for Tadić and his modernizers reflected a popular desire to cast off old warlords like Karadžić.

Nine days later, shortly before four in the morning on July 30, Karadžić was driven to the Belgrade's international airport and flown to The Hague, where he made his first appearance before the tribunal the following day. The defendant waived his right to a defense lawyer claiming to have "an invisible adviser," presumably God. In court, he would represent himself.

His five-year performance before the International Criminal Tribunal for the former Yugoslavia was the realization of a long-held dream: to stand in the global arena and present himself as a mouthpiece for the Serb nation. Throughout his life in hiding he was pulled in two directions: horror at the thought of incarceration and a fierce desire to return to center stage. Several times, he tried in vain to engineer deals that would maximize his air time and minimize his jail time.

Once both had been thrust upon him, he seized the role of the Serb martyr in chief. While the prosecutor tried to focus on his individual responsibility, he presented his wartime actions as the expression of the national will of a long-suffering people. "The entire Serb people stand accused," he declared in his closing statement.

"Excellencies, the Serbs were cornered and they behaved far better than anyone else would have behaved if cornered in that way," Karadžić told the court. He spun an extraordinary inversion of wartime history in which the Serbs had been victims of aggression and there had been no systematic ethnic cleansing of Muslims and Croats.

"There is no example of a case when official authorities rounded people up and drove them out," he insisted, conceding that the occasional rogue individual might have acted differently. It was an extraordinary claim about a war that led to two million people being driven from their homes, more than half of them non-Serbs forced out of the Republika Srpska.

In the Karadžić version of history, these people "did leave their homes with a heavy heart but they left of their own free will." Had Karadžić not been involved, the bloodshed would have been far greater, but he "really was a true to friend to the Muslims."[44]

In the courtroom and in the public gallery on the other side of the bulletproof glass, mouths gaped at the sheer audacity of Karadžić's rhetoric. But he cared nothing for the ridicule or contempt of outsiders. He was spinning new myths for his people to help propel them forward for generations to come, just as he had been borne aloft by the old legends of Serb suffering, carrying him to greatness and justifying each step along the way.

# 12.
# THE OLD MAN IN THE FARMHOUSE: MLADIĆ ON THE RUN

Every time we got close to getting one of the people in his circle
to cooperate, they would go for a long session at the Russian embassy
and come out of it with cold feet about talking to us.

—*Miodrag Rakić, Serbian presidential aide*

**IN JULY 1997,** a Yugoslav army officer named Milan Gunj received
an urgent phone call at home in Belgrade. Something strange was
happening at work and he was needed immediately.

Staff Sergeant Gunj's job could best be described as an army
hotelier. He had risen through the ranks from barracks cook and
caterer to the rather pleasant task of looking after a string of
gated and guarded holiday homes the Yugoslav military had tra-
ditionally provided for its top brass. The man calling him on this
summer day was a soldier who worked in one of these bucolic
retreats, at a place called Rajac in the wooded hills of central Serbia. Some unexpected guests had arrived. The soldier dared not
say any more on the phone, but he was insistent Gunj come as
soon as possible.

Gunj was by now bemused and a little irritated, but any
doubts he may have had about the true urgency of the matter
were put to rest a few moments later when he received a second

call. This time it was from an aide in the office of the Yugoslav chief of the general staff, ordering Gunj to get to Rajac immediately and deal with his visitors. He would be told what he needed to know when he arrived. He got in his car and headed south out of Belgrade.

Sixty miles and two hours later, he arrived at Rajac after dusk to find a group of about a dozen armed men in civilian clothes milling around the entrance, and then the reason for all the subterfuge came striding out of the hotel lobby as if he had just commandeered the place, the unmistakable barrel-chested figure and blunt ruddy face Gunj had seen in a hundred news reports of the Bosnian war — General Ratko Mladić.

"I was somewhat surprised, scared, and confused by this turn of events," Gunj recalled. "First of all, because this happened in my compound, and I had no information that this would happen so it was a surprise event. And secondly, I know that Mr. Ratko Mladić has been accused of certain acts by the Hague Tribunal. And at that point in time I was in a state of panic. I was very afraid."[1]

Gunj was by no means the first or the last to feel terror in Mladić's presence. The "certain acts" the general stood accused of were the worst atrocities Europe had witnessed since the Nazi era. The Bosnian Serb general had overseen three years of the Sarajevo siege and the daily attrition of its residents by shelling and sniper fire. He was also there when the Muslim enclave of Srebrenica was overrun by his troops in July 1995.[2] Presenting himself as an instrument of national retribution, he declared the sacking of Srebrenica as payback against "the Turks" for a massacre of Serbs under the Ottoman Empire. He reassured panicked Muslim women captives that their loved ones would be safe at the same time his soldiers were rounding up and slaughtering eight thousand of their husbands and sons. The beetroot-faced

Three faces of Ratko Mladić: as the Republika Srpska's implacable general, disoriented and ailing at his arrest, and defiant once again in The Hague.

officer who had turned up to stay at Gunj's vacation home was the world's most wanted man.

Mladić and his entourage stayed for a month in Rajac before departing—again in the middle of the night—for another military resort, at Stragari, near the city of Kragujevac, a more elaborate sylvan hideaway with sports grounds, swimming pools, and table tennis. For the benefit of hunters, the surrounding woods were stocked with deer and mouflon, a species of wild sheep with flamboyantly curved horns.

General Djordje Ćurčin, an old family friend of Mladić, described a typical day with the fugitive: "We talked, we walked through the woods, we played some chess. We also played cards, table tennis. We had lunch. And then we walked some more."[3]

Such was the determination of the Yugoslav general staff to keep Mladić both comfortable and hidden that an entire department, the 30th Personnel Center, originally set up to oversee the social welfare of former Bosnian Serb officers, was tasked with looking after him.

According to Jovo Djogo, a former officer assigned to the center who went on to be Mladić's personal security chief, a substantial personal protection force was established around Mladić after the reward for his capture reached astronomical figures.

"There was a bounty of five million dollars on Mladić's head, and it was considered necessary to set up a unit that would protect him from various bounty hunters and criminals. This unit was attached to the 30th Personnel Center in Belgrade and consisted of Republika Srpska Army members, at times about a hundred of them," Djogo said.[4]

The Yugoslav government of Slobodan Milošević staunchly denied any responsibility for the mass atrocities committed by the Bosnian Serb military, but the elaborate measures taken in

Belgrade to tend to Mladić's safety and comfort after the war are a testament to close and organic ties. In the aftermath of the Bosnian war, the Yugoslav army was an overwhelmingly Serb force. And as far as its commanders were concerned, Mladić was one of them.

Along with a formidable phalanx of guards, Mladić had a driver, his own cook, even his own personal waiter who would travel with him back to Rajac in the late winter of each year. When the season was over and the deer hunters had departed, the entourage would return like a traveling court. During this period, Mladić also spent a considerable amount of time in Belgrade, at his family home on Blagoja Parović Street in the upmarket suburb of Košutnjak. He went out to restaurants and football matches in the Serbian capital. Video of these days shows a relaxed Mladić playing table tennis at Stragari, theatrically ruing a missed shot, and presiding over family celebrations.[5]

He was confident enough about his future to convince his family lawyer, Miloš Šaljić, to buy him a patch of land on the slopes of Mount Medvednica, where Mladić wanted to keep bees. He envisaged a peaceful, rustic retirement spent on grand-fatherly hobbies. Šaljić, an old army friend from Yugoslav army days, made the purchase in the name of Mladić's son, Darko.[6]

The men and women who helped keep the fugitive general in this contented bubble saw him as a national hero, embodying the martial virtues of Serb legends from other eras. Somehow they managed to persuade themselves that within this crude stub of a man was an echo of Serbia's heroic age. But just in case their loyalty should ever waver, they were shown photographs of their children—a characteristically direct reminder of the high price paid by informants.

In his fourteen years on the run, Mladić depended on a succession of institutions and groups to keep him from being captured: first the Serbian military establishment; then a closer coterie of his Bosnian Serb wartime lieutenants; and finally, when those concentric rings fell away like layers of a withered onion, his troubled family. But the common factor throughout was fear.

Like Milošević and Radovan Karadžić, Mladić was born into conflict. He was the wartime child of a Partisan family in the mountains southeast of Sarajevo. His father, Nedja, was killed in 1945 in a battle with forces of the Nazi-backed Ustasha, and after a short apprenticeship as a tinsmith, Mladić followed him into the military, going to officer school and commanding Yugoslav army units in Macedonia and Kosovo.

Unlike Milošević or Karadžić, Mladić had no interest in foreign languages or foreigners. He viewed them all with equal suspicion. During a lull in cease-fire talks toward the end of the Bosnian war, an American official asked him, for the purposes of small talk, if he had ever been abroad. "I went to Geneva once," the general replied. "I didn't like the beer." It was the end of the conversation.

By the time the country disintegrated in 1991, Mladić was a colonel and was sent to fight for the Yugoslav army against Croat separatist forces. There he won a reputation for courage bordering on recklessness — personally leading de-mining expeditions, for example. When the war spilled into Bosnia the following year, Mladić and his fellow Bosnian Serb officers changed uniforms and insignia, transferring formal allegiance overnight from Yugoslavia to the breakaway Republika Srpska. But the mission and ultimate leader remained the same, conquering territory for Serbs under a chain of command that led all the way up to President Milošević in Belgrade.

As a newly minted general, Mladić helped cut off and bombard his former neighbors in Sarajevo in May 1992, beginning the longest city siege in modern warfare. Three and a half years later, ten thousand of the city's residents would be dead. At Karadžić's side as the head of the Bosnian Serb army, he led a ferocious campaign to dismember Bosnia and establish an ethnically pure Republika Srpska. But General Mladić was never so busy with the war that he could not take the occasional weekend off for playing board games and relaxing with his wife and two grown children, Darko and Ana, whom he kept safe in Belgrade.

At these game nights, no one was allowed to mention politics or the war, but that did not stop the conflict from pulling the family apart. Ana was in her early twenties and had fallen in love with a young doctor — a human rights activist who believed his putative father-in-law was a war criminal. He would only marry Ana if she renounced her father. Unable to do that or give up her dreams of love and marriage, she took her father's favorite pistol from its display case after a night of board games in February 1994 and shot herself.[7]

Mladić could not accept his daughter's suicide. He found solace instead in conspiracy theories that put the blame on his enemies. It was a conviction that took the burden of guilt off his shoulders and deepened a reservoir of hatred toward non-Serbs.

The Serb generals in the Yugoslav military establishment stood ready to shelter Mladić no matter what appalling deeds he was accused of, but at the turn of the millennium, Serbia itself was undergoing rapid change. Milošević had been defeated in Slovenia, Croatia, and Bosnia, and then again in 1999, in Kosovo, supposedly the cradle of Serb civilization. The dream of a Greater Serbia had collapsed, leaving an impoverished rump.

Milošević's fall from power in October 5, 2000, and his delivery to The Hague the following June set Mladić on edge. He had been no fan of Milošević, but the regime had provided him with succor and protection, and now it was gone. Ćurčin recalled that "on the night when Mr. Milošević was arrested, he was in his own home, in his own apartment, and that night he left. When I saw him later on and spoke with him, he was visibly concerned for his security and the security of the people close to him. And he was determined not to surrender alive."[8]

Mladić was right to be worried. On the eve of Milošević's transfer to The Hague, Serbia's new liberal prime minister, Zoran Djindjić, offered the West a two-for-one deal. They could have Milošević and Mladić on the same day. His officials supplied Mladić's address to the CIA station chief and top MI6 official in Belgrade. There was just one condition — they had to send in their own soldiers to arrest him. But neither the Americans nor the British were prepared to dispatch troops into Serbia at such short notice on the base of an unconfirmed tip. Charles Craw-ford, the British ambassador to Belgrade at the time, steered the Foreign Office away from the idea.

"My conclusion, as the guy on the spot, was I didn't think it would be wise. We of course put the offer to London. But it would have meant SAS people getting on a plane and flying straight out; I didn't think it right to put British soldiers into a dangerous situation where they could not know for sure what was going to be happening or whom to trust," Crawford said.[9]

Mladić may not have known he had been offered up to the West as a goodwill token by Serbia's new rulers, but he was canny enough to realize he could no longer rely on the Belgrade gov-ernment to protect him. He hastily moved camp to yet another base, Krčmar, near Valjevo, a Tito-era refuge set in country-side every bit as pretty as Stragari but with stronger fortifica-tions and underground bunkers. From now on, Mladić would be in perpetual retreat, as the post-Milošević government in

Belgrade steadily asserted its authority over the country's security apparatus. It formally declared Mladić's retirement from the military in March 2002 and early the following month, a decree was issued legalizing cooperation with the ICTY. The era when Mladić could live out his time on the run in the army's luxury spas was fast coming to an end.

Reluctantly, the generals told Mladić he would have to leave Krčmar, but his initial response was defiance mixed with delusion. He ordered his bodyguards to hold their ground, triggering an uneasy standoff in May 2002, during which the army buzzed the base with helicopters in mock raids intended to rattle him into leaving. On June 1, Mladić finally bowed to the pressure and negotiated safe passage out of the base, while the army agreed to provide a convoy of staff cars to take him to his next hideout.

Mladić left behind him the comforts of full military protection and embarked on a steady descent into isolation and privation. His support network shrunk almost overnight from the entire Yugoslav military to a handful of old comrades from the Bosnian war.

Until his own arrest on war crimes charges in 2007, Zdravko Tolimir, a former Bosnian Serb general and assistant intelligence chief, oversaw the network, but it was run from day to day by Djogo. This former Bosnian Serb colonel and fervent Mladić loyalist was from the same Bosnian district of Kalinovik, and he managed the renting of a series of apartments for the general in the warren of tower blocks in New Belgrade. Green fields, woodland walks, and the life of a privileged military veteran were replaced by the concrete realities of urban Serbia.

"After the army said they would not look after him, he went to Jovo Djogo and a small team of people who cared for him," Mladić's lawyer, Miloš Šaljić, said. "In New Belgrade, he stayed inside the apartment and he was brought food and papers, and unlike in the military facilities, his family couldn't come to see him."[10]

"The rented apartments had very precise specifications," recalled Miodrag "Miki" Rakić, the Serbian presidential aide who coordinated the hunt. "They had to be in large buildings, but they could not be on the first floor, or on the top floor. He wanted nothing with security guards or security cameras."

One of the apartments that fit the bill was owned by a member of the clique of former Bosnian Serb officers, Marko Lugonja, who later admitted he had hid Mladić "for five or six days" in September 2002, but insisted he had done nothing wrong. "Mladić was my commander and I had no alternative," he told a Belgrade court.[11]

It was an unsettled existence for the first few months until the network found an apartment on Yuri Gagarin Street that Mladić felt safe in. He was living just a few doors down from Karadžić—two fugitives from genocide charges in the space of a few blocks. But despite the proximity, there is no evidence the two crossed paths. They could not bear each other by this time and investigators believe there was little or no overlap between their support networks.

The two men also approached the life of a fugitive with entirely different strategies. Karadžić hid in plain sight, under the flamboyant assumed identity of a New Age healer. Mladić hunkered down and maintained military self-discipline, banning the use of cell phones in the apartment and rarely venturing out except for an occasional evening walk along the Sava River with Darko, his only surviving child.

Meanwhile, for the handful of men and women in the general's inner circle, Mladić was a demanding guest. He wanted warm milk and honey early in the morning before his exercises. He required all his food to be fresh, bought the same day it was consumed. If it was uneaten by the evening, it was thrown away. Fruit and vegetables had to be bought from a range of stalls on the baffling grounds that their purchase from a single supplier would somehow arouse suspicion.

For most of his time in hiding, Mladić was careful about his appearance, shaving and grooming every day. One of his minders once asked him why he bothered. After all, it was not as if he was holding business meetings, she said. He replied that the way you looked at the moment of your death is the way you would look for the eternity of the afterlife. He was fastidious about his teeth too, but for more mundane reasons. He feared a trip to a dentist could inevitably compromise his security.

Such were the parameters of Mladić's life until March 12, 2003, when the whole country was plunged back into turmoil by sudden violence. Zoran Djindjić, Serbia's prime minister, was shot by a sniper as he walked into a government building in Belgrade, killed on the orders of a consortium of paramilitary gang leaders and crime bosses. They envisaged the murder as a preemptive strike against Djindjić's plans to smash organized crime and his readiness to cooperate with the Hague Tribunal.

The Djindjić shooting came as an ugly shock to a country craving normality after Milošević's years of turmoil and bloodshed, and there was a backlash from the mainstream security forces that his killers could not have foreseen. The wave of more than thirteen thousand arrests that followed came sufficiently close to Mladić's network for him to tighten his house rules still further. Up to this point, his close protection team had stayed with him, sometimes sleeping on the floor. After Djindjić's assassination, he changed apartments but did not take the bodyguards with him. They were kept a phone call away, with only one minder at a time knowing his address.

There were a handful of such minders, men and women who did stints of a few months at a time. It was made plain to them that if Mladić were discovered the suspicion would fall on them. They were presented with gift-wrapped portraits of their children or grandchildren and reminded that Mladić's associates knew where they lived and went to school. It was the most ruthless and effective threat imaginable, and Mladić's men used it liberally.

When threats came from the Mladić camp, there was every reason to take them seriously. The men who delivered them had an unquestionable history of violence, and there is evidence that people were killed to ensure that Mladić's whereabouts remained a secret.

On October 5, 2004, two soldiers, Dragan Jakovljević and Dražen Milovanović, were found shot dead at their posts at the barracks in Topčider, a district of Belgrade. The hasty military investigation that followed concluded that they had gotten into a fight in which one of them had shot the other and then committed suicide out of remorse. The absurdity of the army inquiry was underlined when the military prosecutor declared he had not bothered to carry out DNA testing because such forensic procedures were "an overrated thing."

Amid public uproar, a civilian commission of inquiry was set up but it kept running into a stone wall of hostility from the generals.

"The army destroyed everything at the scene of the shooting," recalled Božo Prelević, the Belgrade lawyer who headed the commission. "Under the excuse of looking for bullet casings, they dug up all the earth and destroyed the crime scene." When Prelević's commission persevered, the push-back from the military became more aggressive. "A colonel in military intelligence approached one member of the commission and said, 'You have two nice daughters. Why are you making trouble?' Once they forcibly entered my apartment and threatened me. The officers asked me, 'Did you really think we'd sit on our backsides and allow this?'"

In the end, the commission concluded that both soldiers had been shot by a third party, without any conclusions on who that third party was. Prelević believed the soldiers were shot because they had stumbled either on a drug deal or on a plot to hide Mladić. On balance, he leans toward the second option. "Why would they put so much energy into covering up a drug crime?" he asked.[12]

The victims' parents became convinced they had been murdered because they had come across across evidence that Mladić was being hidden in the labyrinth of underground tunnels beneath the barracks.

"Our sons were killed because they saw either Mladić or his security teams," Dragan's father, Janko Jakovljević, said, claiming that is what he was told by a sympathetic source inside the general's security detail.[13]

Topčider is a virtual underground city the Tito regime excavated in the bowels of a hill in central Belgrade, and it is where Milošević took shelter during the NATO bombing in 1999. After the Bosnian conflict, part of the complex was made the headquarters of the 30th Personnel Center, until it was formally disbanded in March 2002. Some investigators believe it continued to function off the books, as a shadow unit, long after that date.

In 2005, Sergeant Miroslav Petrović, a Serbian deserter, told the Belgrade daily Danas that the previous year he had met Serbian officers at the barracks for a discussion on improving Mladić's security.

"I attended a meeting at Topčider where I met many

members of the Bosnian Serb army, whose task was to secure the routes for the general if he traveled north of Serbia or to Bosnia," Petrović said. Of the two murdered soldiers he said, "Mladić was in Topčider last October. The unfortunate fellows saw him and were executed instantly."[14]

Petrović, who Danas said had spoken to the newspaper from a US base in the region, subsequently vanished. The Jakovljević and Milovanović families have since kept up their lonely search for the truth about their sons' deaths, making little progress until March 2013, when the constitutional court in Belgrade ruled that they had been denied justice and awarded them compensation, calling for a proper investigation.

The Topčider killings are not the only unsolved murders to have been linked to Mladić. In August 2005, another soldier who claimed to have seen the general died under mysterious circumstances. Srdjan Ivanović had completed his military service as a driver and was on his way from his Belgrade home to his barracks in Leskovac, Eastern Serbia, to drop off his gun and car keys, when he told his father that he was scared.

"Before he went back he said he was afraid for his life because as well as being a driver for his commander, he had also been a driver for Mladić," Miodrag Ivanović said. He offered to go with his son, but Srdjan reassured him it was only a day trip and he would be back soon. Miodrag never saw him alive again. He was informed the next morning that Srdjan had died of a heroin overdose, despite the fact that he was an athlete who had no history of alcohol or drug use.[15]

When the distraught father reached Leskovac, he was told he could not see the corpse as an autopsy was being performed, but the next morning he made his own way into the barracks clinic and came across a body bag. After unzipping it, he found himself looking down on the body of his son, which showed no signs that an autopsy had been performed. The only marks on the corpse were bruising on the head and shoulder. A legal analysis of the Ivanović case carried out by the reformist Center for Euro-Atlantic Studies in Belgrade found that the military coroner's report provided "no data on whether the soldier had consumed heroin or any other hard drugs, how the heroin got into the soldier's organism and whether there are any marks of intravenous injection of heroin on his body."[16]

As in the Topčider case, there is plenty of evidence that the official version is bogus, but so far there is no conclusive proof of the identity of the killers or their motives. The only certainty is that on his long flight from international justice, Mladić always left fear in his wake.

By mid-2005, he was back on Yuri Gagarin Street in a different apartment and feeling increasingly jumpy. In September, investigators later discovered, a policeman making routine inquiries about an incident in the tower block knocked on his door, adding to Mladić's paranoia. In December 2005, he was moved to Ljuba, a village near the northern Serbian town of Sremska Mitrovica, where one of his network of protectors had a country cottage. It seems to have been a desperate measure intended to salvage both his sanity and the mental health of his perpetually scared and harassed minders.

The rural interlude was short, probably because Ljuba was too small a community in which to hide at a time when the walls of Mladić's cloistered life were closing in. That month Djogo was arrested along with eight of the general's associates. Mladić abruptly dropped the network that had supported him until then, believing it was compromised. In the dead of night on February 4, 2006, he turned up on the outskirts of Belgrade at the apartment of his brother-in-law, Krsto Jegdić. Pressing the intercom, he announced himself only as "the guy from Bosnia." Jegdić assumed it was a brother who lived in eastern Bosnia and buzzed him in, only to find Mladić on his doorstep, carrying a backpack and a duffel bag, which contained his constant companions, a Heckler & Koch machine gun and two pistols.[17]

The general was clearly nervous and had aged dramatically since Jegdić had last seen him, but that didn't stop him from barking orders. He sent Jegdić's son down to dismiss the driver who had brought him there, and while the teenager was away, he made a comment that implied the boy's life might be in danger if Mladić was given away.

On this occasion, Mladić's customary menace backfired. Jegdić's wife was furious and insisted she would not share her home with a relative who made such threats. Instead, Jegdić offered to drive the unwanted visitor to the house of another Jegdić brother, Miroslav, who lived about thirty kilometers away, in the village of Mala Moštanica.

Mala Moštanica is a pretty settlement not far from the Sava River, its houses scattered across a few square miles of undulating woodland. Miroslav Jegdić's house is three unfinished stories of red brick and concrete balconies without railings. There are cherry trees in the back and a grapevine climbing up an improvised rickety trellis on the west wall. Its owner returned to his native Macedonia in 2011 to escape the notoriety of the Mladić connection, and since then the house has deteriorated to an empty shell, the latest piece of lifeless debris left in Mladić's wake.

When I visited in 2013, Miroslav's sister-in-law, Djuka Jegdić, emerged from a house just down the lane to quiz me, hoping my translator and I, notepads in hand, were realtors from Belgrade. The family had been trying to sell and leave for years.

Djuka denied accounts she used to cook meals for Mladić and Miroslav and take them across the lane in the evenings, insisting she had only found out about the general's presence years later, after his arrest. She conceded later in our conversation that her husband, Vukasin, had told her Mladić was hiding in Miroslav's house, but she did not believe him because his mind had become increasingly erratic.

"He started having hallucinations, and I thought this was just another hallucination. He would imagine he saw all sorts of people," Djuka said. In retrospect, she blamed the pressure of Mladić's presence and heavy-handed police tactics for his breakdown. "Once they came and took us both away and we couldn't warn our fifteen-year-old son, so he thought we had disappeared, waiting for us in the house on his own," she said, weeping at the memory.

In one incident in April 2006, men from BIA swept noisily into Mala Moštanica in an early-morning raid. Mladić, looking down through the wooden-slatted shutters of his second-floor window, must have thought his time had finally come, only to see the heavily armed BIA agents cluster around the wrong house, belonging to the wrong Jegdić — Vukasin.

"They turned our place upside down, leaving a terrible mess," Djuka recalled. "A couple of them walked around Miroslav's house, but he was away in Belgrade and they didn't go in. They just walked around and came back."

A Western investigator who was involved in the hunt said, "The 2006 raid was either monumentally stupid, or deliberate — a way of warning Mladić to move out, while looking busy for the benefit of Carla Del Ponte."

The ICTY tracking team and their Serbian counterparts blamed the BIA and its director, Rade Bulatović, who had proved so unhelpful in the search for Karadžić.

"Whenever we got close to getting an arrest, Rade Bulatović and the BIA created a diversion and arrested all the people in the concealment network," said Aleksandar Dimitrijević, a former head of military intelligence, who was serving as a Defense Ministry adviser at the time.[18]

"According to information we received later, a high-ranking Republika Srpska police officer delivered a piece of paper with eleven addresses where Ratko Mladić could have been been. He gave it directly to Rade Bulatović," Bruno Vekarić, Serbia's deputy war crimes prosecutor, said. "Had a police operation been conducted at those eleven addresses, Mladic would have been in The Hague immediately."[19]

Foul-up or conspiracy, the result was Mladić got away. He slipped out the back door into the woods to return the next morning. A couple of days later, he left Mala Moštanica for good.

With every passing month and each successive hiding place, however, the climate in Serbia was growing colder for Mladić. His friends in the army were retiring from the ranks, the public was forgetting about him, worrying more about Serbia's increasing isolation, and the political currents were turning against him. Djindjić's former deputy, Boris Tadić, was elected president in June 2004 by weary voters who saw hope in looking west toward the European Union, even at the price of surrendering Serb fugitives to The Hague. In the summer of 2008, new elections put reformists in the ministries and in charge of the security apparatus for the first time. Bulatović was replaced at the BIA, and within days Karadžić was arrested.

The resulting euphoria at the ICTY generated hopes that Mladić's capture would follow soon after. But the optimism was groundless. The general was far more careful and deeply hidden.

Even under new management, the BIA persisted with old sterile methods, cranking up the pressure on the Mladić family.

In November 2008, when Darko's computer systems firm tried to seal a €800,000 business agreement with a Serbian company, the would-be partner's factories in Valjevo were raided and searched for five hours by the police, scaring it away from the deal. Darko's wife, Biljana, found her career as a software expert in Serbia's telecommunications corporation starting to suffer, and she was demoted from the Belgrade headquarters to a suburban outpost.

In February 2010, the police raided Darko and Biljana's house and seized more than €14,000 in cash. The couple went to court to get the cash back and to have Biljana's job restored. Šaljić, the family lawyer, alleges the BIA tried to talk Biljana into divorcing Darko, telling her it would be in the interest of her children. She would get her job back and the pressure would lift if she complied.[20] Then in June 2010, the general's wife, Bosiljka, was charged with illegal weapons possession because of trophy pistols Mladić had left behind when he fled.

None of the pressure worked, nor was it ever likely to. No family member was going to betray the patriarch, especially since they had a protector that was far more powerful than the BIA—Russia's Federal Security Bureau (FSB). In Vladimir Putin's Russia, the spy agency—the successor to Putin's old employer, the KGB—took a protective interest in Mladić for a variety of reasons. Moscow saw him as a Slav military hero being hunted by Western powers trying to deepen their influence in Serbia, an old Russian ally. According to a zero-sum approach to world affairs, the West's gain in capturing Mladić would be Russia's strategic lost. Furthermore, the Russians were nervous of what Mladić might reveal about

Russian support for the Republika Srpska at the height of ethnic cleansing.

The BIA operatives tracking the Mladić support network found themselves increasingly playing spy versus spy with the FSB.

"Every time we got close to getting one of the people in his circle to cooperate, they would go for a long session at the Russian embassy and come out of it with cold feet about talking to us," recalled Rakić, the man entrusted with leading the manhunt during the Tadić presidency. He suspected that Russia was making regular payments to the Mladić family and entourage to relieve the financial pressure on them to give away the general's whereabouts.

Rakić also felt the unmistakable presence of the FSB looking over his own shoulder. In 2008, he and a colleague made a clandestine trip to the Hague Tribunal to discuss the Mladić case. They flew a roundabout route and Dutch protection officers drove them straight into the ICTY's underground car park. On his return, however, Rakić received a visit from one of Mladić's supporters in the security services warning him that his family would be in peril if he continued to cooperate with the court. Lest there be any doubt over the seriousness of the threat, he recited details of Rakić's young son's daily routine.

Shocked at the threat, Rakić angrily denied he was collaborating with the court, insisting he had never even been to The Hague. Without a word, the visitor took a piece of paper and drew a diagram of a conference table. Then he wrote out the name of every person who had attended his meeting in The Hague, indicating precisely where each of them had been sitting. Rakić described it as the most chilling moment of his life. From that moment on, until his death from cancer in 2014, he traveled with a two-man protection team.

There was little doubt in his mind that only the FSB had the sophistication to penetrate the Hague Tribunal so thoroughly. So in 2010, Rakić decided to confront the Russians head-on. At an international conference in Moscow he buttonholed Nikolai Patrushev, Putin's spymaster, a former head of the FSB, and the secretary of Russia's Security Council.

"I feel a very cold wind in our face coming from the east," Rakić told Patrushev. The Russian claimed the protection for Mladić had been sanctioned higher up, clearly meaning Putin himself. In the Kremlin, there was no one else higher than Patrushev.

"I will talk to my bosses and I'll do what I can," Patrushev offered. Whatever was said or done in Putin's security cabinet, it clearly made a difference. Russian support for the Mladić network dropped off. Even Moscow was cutting the general loose.

There is a difference of opinion among investigators on where Mladić went after Mala Moštanica. The official version says he made his way straight to Lazarevo, a village in northern Serbia where some of his cousins lived. There are suspicions, however, among some Serbian and Western investigators that he may have made a detour to another outpost of his in-laws, in the southeastern Bosnian village of Gacko.

There were a couple of credible sightings there, officials say, and some apparently conspiratorial activity by family members. They seemed to avoid using their mobile phones, and when they did make calls, they spoke in a stilted manner using what appeared to be a code. MI6 was sufficiently excited about the evidence to cajole its Bosnian counterpart in Sarajevo, the Intelligence and Security Agency (Obavještajno Sigurnosna Agencija–Obavještajno Bezbjednosne Agencija, or OSA-OBA), into sending agents into the area to sniff around. The British spies also suggested setting up extra electronic surveillance on the roof of the OSA headquarters. Week after week, the Bosnians insisted they would get this task done, until they returned after a long weekend to find the MI6 resident officers had run out of patience and done the job themselves, erecting the antennae and drilling an unsightly hole in the ceiling for the trailing wires.

After an OSA-OBA agent claimed to have sighted Mladić in Gacko, the BIA sent their own tracking team down from Belgrade in the summer of 2010 and began to pick up signs that someone could be hiding in a wooden shack by a small lake. But within days the local police started noticing the BIA presence and the surveillance was aborted without any definitive conclusion.

What is beyond doubt, whatever late twists it took, is that Mladić's life as a fugitive ended in Lazarevo, in the run-down farmhouse of his cousin Branislav. Living in a single cluttered room warmed only by a small electric heater, the old general's health took a steep plunge and Branislav found him sprawled on the floor one day after an apparent stroke. But Mladić, still more frightened of capture than of a lonely and squalid death, refused to be taken to a hospital. By now his isolation was almost total. He allowed neither his wife nor his son to visit. But despite all these precautions, it was family sentiment that gave him away in the end.

On May 6, 2008, Darko brought his children, Anastasija and Stefan, to visit the country cousins in Lazarevo for St. George's Day, a significant holiday in Serbia. The party was at another cousin's house but the family made a detour to Branislav's home, walking into the central courtyard and standing around with no apparent purpose for twenty minutes before leaving, to the puzzlement of the policemen trailing them. Only after Mladić's arrest did it become clear what they were doing.

"He was watching them through the window. He wasn't well.

He couldn't let the children see him but he had the desire to see them," Tadić said. "Then the Mladić family phoned Lazarevo twice in three days. Why two times? That is what eventually took us to that house."[21]

At dawn on May 26, 2011, plainclothes officers from a special war crimes unit of the Interior Ministry went to the village to raid the cousins' houses.

Two of them climbed the stairs in Branislav's house and found one door hard to open. There was something or someone behind it. When they pushed it open, they found an untidy room that was clearly being occupied. They glanced behind the door to see an old man in a black baseball cap standing behind it.

The officers asked for his identity card and the old man handed it over. It had the name Ratko Mladić on it, but the men still could not believe it. This wizened figure looked nothing like the swaggering general they had expected.

"Who are you?" they demanded.

"You have found who you're looking for," the man replied with a flash of defiance. "I'm Ratko Mladić."[22] It was the end of fourteen years on the run.

During that long odyssey, the fugitive had lost layer after layer of dignity and prestige, falling from VIP guest at military country clubs to a sickly and neglected old man hunched up among the cobwebs of a country cottage.

Mladić had at one point told his elderly cousin Branislav to shoot him rather than let him be taken alive. He even showed him the gun he was supposed to use. But Branislav was out on the morning of the arrest. Anyway, he told Šaljić, he could never have brought himself to pull the trigger. Neither, as it turned out, could Mladić. His Heckler & Koch was found lying among dirty socks at the bottom of a wardrobe.

President Tadić was doing his morning exercises when he got the call from Saša Vukadinović, the BIA chief who was on an official visit to Washington at the time but was being kept informed by his office.

"I think we got Mladić," Vukadinović said. The ailing captive was at that moment being driven from Lazarevo to Belgrade in a police car.

By now, the president was in a state of excitement. The hunt for Mladić had come to define his presidency. For more than five years he had been under pressure from the rest of the world to make this arrest. If this truly was the missing general, it would be the climatic moment of his career.

He asked if a DNA test could be done, but was informed the results could take days.

"What other evidence have you got?" Tadić wanted to know.

"The people who arrested him say it's him," Vukadinović replied. "And we'll send photos when he gets here."

Little more than an hour later, the mug shots were sent, downloaded, printed on a computer, and rushed into Tadić.

The president took one look at them and instantly declared, "This is Ratko Mladić!"[23]

Šaljić was summoned to the special war crimes court in Belgrade, to see his long-lost client. When he entered Mladić's cell, he was shocked.

"He actually looked blue and his mouth and face were twisted. I wouldn't have recognized him on the street," the lawyer recalled. On seeing him, the old man stood up and clung to Šaljić, sobbing.[24]

The next morning, Rakić brought the prisoner breakfast and family photos.

"He was terrified. He asked me if I was going to kill him. I said:

No — I'm just bringing you breakfast," Rakić said. He tried to use the moment of vulnerability to ask the captured fugitive about the networks that helped hide him. The prisoner snapped back: "You've got me. What do you want with these people? These people sacrificed themselves for me. Let them go."

Šaljić's attempts to forestall Mladić's transfer to The Hague on health grounds failed, but a Belgrade judge did grant the defeated general his last request on Serbian soil, to visit the grave of his daughter, Ana, the fragile young woman who had killed herself seven years earlier with his favorite pistol.

Mladić was given forty-five minutes at the grave and his minders withdrew a respectful distance, forming a somber ring around him.

"You could see his lips move," Rakić recalled. "He was speaking to her."[25]

# 13.
# THE LEGACY

After these verdicts, it's very difficult
to speak about justice in the region.
—*Nataša Kandić, Serbian human rights activist*

**THERE WERE 161 NAMES** on the list of indicted war crimes suspects drawn up by the International Criminal Tribunal for the former Yugoslavia. Ten died before they ever got to The Hague. Another twenty had their indictments withdrawn. Of the remainder, sixty-five fugitives were tracked down and arrested.

According to the official records, the rest handed themselves in. But the real number taken to the Dutch capital against their will was much higher. Many arrests were dressed up as "voluntary surrenders" so the indictees could salvage some dignity and receive cash benefits offered by their governments for coming out of hiding.

Almost no one would have submitted to justice willingly if the likely alternative had not been apprehension. Without the Balkan manhunt, the cells in Scheveningen prison would still be empty and the Hague Tribunal would have been no more than a hollow gesture in the general direction of international justice.

The three men most responsible for unleashing carnage on the people of the former Yugoslavia, the three master butchers, Slobodan Milošević, Radovan Karadžić, and Ratko Mladić, were brought one by one to stand before the Hague Tribunal. But the triumvirate was never reunited there. Milošević — Yugoslavia's kamikaze pilot who brought his country and its people down in flames — ultimately cheated final legal judgment. In March 2006, four years into his turgidly long trial, he died in his cell of a heart attack, well before Karadžić or Mladić were even caught.

The two Bosnian Serb leaders, both indicted for genocide, did meet again in the tribunal's Courtroom Number One in a moment of farce in January 2014. Like the revival of an old double act after twenty years in the wilderness, the two pensioners dressed in their Sunday best and struggled to recover their swagger. Karadžić had called Mladić to the stand to testify for him, but proceedings had to be suspended because the old general had left his dentures in his cell. Even with his teeth in, he refused to answer the questions put to him, insisting on reading a prepared statement instead.

When the judges refused to admit the seven-page soliloquy as evidence, Mladić snarled at the bench: "Thanks for preventing me from stating what I wanted to say. You have confirmed to me that the Hague Tribunal is not a court of law but a Satanic court."

At the height of their power, Karadžić and Mladić could never have been described as friends, but they had complemented each other. Mladić had done the dirty, bloody work that was necessary to make Karadžić's vision of an ethnically pure Serb republic a reality. Karadžić's bloviation and clunky poetry provided the gossamer veil of romanticism and deniability for Mladić's slaughter.

In the glare of global scrutiny in the Hague courtroom, the two men found common cause. Karadžić addressed Mladić respectfully as "General, sir," and on his way out of the court, Mladić could be heard to tell Karadžić, "Thanks a lot, Radovan. I'm sorry these idiots wouldn't let me speak. They defend NATO bombs."[1]

In the course of their trials, the two men sought to keep alive the cult of exclusive victimhood they had used first to rationalize, then to obscure the mass killings for which they stood accused. Their strategy was to play the martyr and fill the court with noise, in the hope that the tens of thousands killed at their behest were kept silent, without a compelling voice in the courtroom.

The trials have ground on at a glacial pace in the tribunal's bid to be comprehensive and fair beyond reproach. The lawyers in court, their billing meters ticking, have little interest in stepping up the tempo. The court has made many of them rich. And meanwhile the defendants bide their time inside the walls of the old Dutch prison in The Hague's beach suburb of Scheveningen, where the Nazis once locked up members of the Dutch resistance. In 2005, a new state-of-the-art facility was built inside the complex to house prisoners from the ICTY and indictees of the International Criminal Court, all of them so far African.

The prison wardens at Scheveningen witness a daily phenomenon that many of citizens of the former Yugoslavia could have predicted. The warlords, militiamen, and ultranationalists from all sides, who were once ready to kill in the name of ethnic distinctions, have found they get along famously when locked up together. They play in mixed football teams, cook each other meals, and even swap clothes. In this Dutch prison, a thousand miles from the Balkans, Tito's dream of Brotherhood and Unity has achieved a strange afterlife, providing an esprit de corps among war crimes defendants from Yugoslavia's constituent nations.

Wry post-Yugoslav jokes often imagined a scene in heaven or hell where the three main nationalist leaders — Serbia's Slobodan Milošević, Croatia's strongman Franjo Tudjman, and the Bosnian Muslim leader Alija Izetbegović — meet, chat, and spar. In the tastefully designed Dutch purgatory at Scheveningen, only Milošević turned up to act out the joke for real. The other two nationalist presidents died while under investigation by the ICTY: Tudjman for ethnic cleansing in central Bosnia and the killing of Serb civilians in Croatia's Krajina region, and Izetbegović for importing Arab mujahideen, who fought and allegedly committed war crimes outside the Bosnian army's chain of command.[2]

In the absence of other erstwhile heads of state, Milošević played the role of the boss of bosses, requiring people to address him as Mr. President, remaining largely aloof from the crowd. He never joined in the football games, just the occasional bit of volleyball, in which he participated in the same condescending manner as an elder statesman on the campaign trail.

"He always acted like he was the boss, with his chin held up in the air," recalled Naser Orić, a Bosnian army officer. "Someone was bringing him in brandy and whisky in milk or juice cartons. He always smelled of alcohol."[3]

Orić was tried, and eventually acquitted on appeal, for alleged war crimes committed in raids mounted from the Srebrenica enclave. I met him in February 2014 in the café of a Sarajevo gas station. He came in a black leather bomber jacket, and chewed on a Cuban cigar as he told me about the security precautions he had to take to avoid abduction by Serbian intelligence. He also explained how his earlier career was intertwined with

Milošević in a manner that embodied the complexities of Yugo-slavia's collapse.

By a twist of Balkan fate, Orić had once served in Milošević's security detail. He stood guard in June 1989 when the then Serbian president unleashed the forces of nationalism with his speech marking the six-hundredth anniversary of the Battle of Kosovo. As the young Yugoslav policeman stared out at the crowd he could see bands of Serb Chetniks dressed in the same fur hats and death's-head badges their forefathers had worn when they slaugh-tered Bosnian Muslims like him in the Second World War.

Orić grew even more uneasy in the run-up to the war in 1991 when he was ordered to take part in the smuggling of arms from Belgrade to Serb separatists in Croatia.

"We were told that if any civilians saw the guns we had to kill them. Not even a chicken can see the weapons. That was another sign of what was going to happen," Orić recalled. He fled his police post soon after, moving to Bosnia with warnings of the approaching catastrophe that few of his fellow Bosniaks could bring themselves to believe.

Orić was finally reunited with Milošević in Schevenin-gen, where he witnessed the last days of the leader who had unchained Yugoslavia's demons. He believes Milošević's death was the suicidal act of a lonely and broken man. "Milošević was always longing for his wife, Mira. When she went to Moscow, he starting trying to get sent there for treatment for his heart condi-tion. He was taking blood pressure pills and other pills to coun-ter the effect of the blood pressure pills. When he was refused permission to go to Moscow and see Mira, he just stopped taking his pills."[4]

When Karadžić arrived in Scheveningen in July 2008, he also sought a leadership role in the cell block, albeit in a more garrulous, convivial manner than Milošević, playing the gracious host at visiting times, assiduously remembering the names of fellow inmates' wives and children.

He continued to pursue his obsession with maps, putting up a large city plan of Sarajevo on the wall of his cell, on which he stuck pins marking alleged locations of Bosnian army positions. His defense was that the Bosnian military was using the city as one huge human shield.

Mladić is on a different floor of the facility and hardly sees Karadžić. By all accounts, he cuts a more reclusive and curmudgeonly figure, spending long spells alone in his cell.

The rest of Schveningen's Balkan population has sorted itself into groups according to shared interests rather than ethnicity. For a while, a five-a-side football club developed around the more athletic of the professional soldiers, including Orić, as well as the Croatian general Ante Gotovina, the Montenegrin colonel Veselin Šljivančanin, and Ramush Haradinaj, a former prime minister of Kosovo and commander in the Kosovo Liberation Army.

"We mostly played in mixed teams, but on at least one occasion there was a Serbs versus Croats game. Gotovina was marking me, but I have to say, he was very correct," said Šljivančanin, who was jailed for ten years for his role in the executions of more than 260 Croat prisoners near Vukovar.[5]

When he was released in July 2011, Šljivančanin sought out Gotovina to say goodbye and the two officers embraced. The Montenegrin also got on well with Orić.

"He loved sport. He was very proud and very correct. We had no conflict. He just wanted to do sport," Šljivančanin recalled of Gotovina.

Orić agreed there was a group of inmates who coalesced around a type of military-sporting code. "Gotovina and I always got along, and Šljivančanin and I were on the same team. He played on the right wing. I was on the left wing."

"All the people there were always very pleasant and they always wanted to help. We looked out for each other. If someone looked from outside at us they would say: These people are friends. Why did they go to war?" said Momčilo Krajišnik,[6] Karadžić's closest associate and one of the architects of Bosnia's ethnic cleansing. "We had very close relationships. We had friendly relations. Our common problem brought us close together. I had better conversations with some Muslims and Croats than with some Serbs simply because these men were more compatible with me. If you go to trial and you don't have a suit, someone lends you a suit. If someone makes a nice meal, you wouldn't say I will give it just to Serbs, you would give it to Croats and Muslims. We all ate together. When we talked we discussed different things, business, sports, and so on. It was civilized."

The one exception to the prison bonhomie was Vojislav Šešelj, the leader of the Serbian Radical Party, who had recruited the ultranationalist paramilitary groups responsible for atrocities in Croatia and Bosnia. He was at least consistent in his snarling irascibility, showing no signs of mellowing once he was in custody. He swore constantly at the guards. He took no part in team sports and refused to be in the gym at the same time as Orić. He tormented Šljivančanin for having once been Tito's bodyguard, "Tito's piglet" Šešelj called him.

Orić told the story of a chess match between Šešelj and Mladen "Tuta" Naletilić, a Bosnian Croat crime boss who commanded a "convicts' battalion" in the war and was sentenced to twenty years in prison for torture and forced labor. Šešelj was perpetually angry anyway, but the white-haired bewhiskered Croat wound him up further.

"Tuta was saying to Šešelj, 'Your great-grandfather was a Croat, but was caught stealing an egg and was excommunicated.' Šešelj got furious and ranted at Tuta, but whenever he lost his focus, Tuta would steal one of his pieces," Orić said.

It could be a scene from any village square in the Balkans. Two aging men squabbling over a chessboard. But Schveningen is a far more comfortable place to grow old than the war-ruined countries they left behind. It is half prison, half spa. It has yoga classes, top-flight medical care, language-study rooms, a library, classes on pottery and painting, musical instruments, personal trainers, public sculpture and murals in the courtyard. There is an extensive cafeteria, but the prisoners are allowed to order in groceries and do their own cooking, using a €15 weekly stipend. Families can spend seven consecutive days per month with the detainee, and even girlfriends are allowed conjugal visits. According to the prison authorities, quite a number of babies have been conceived at Scheveningen.[7]

Haradinaj told an acquaintance: "In Pristina, you could stick three stars on this place and charge money."

"I honestly expected it was going to be like Guantánamo," Orić said. "But if our children had been looking for a retirement home for us, they couldn't have done better. No retirement home has such conditions."

The dissonance is jarring. Punishment for some of the worst crimes humanity has witnessed is being handled by the Dutch penal system, one of the most liberal on the planet. While most of the inmates tend to mellow in such conditions, few have shown genuine remorse.

Krajišnik, who played a pivotal role in organizing the ethnic cleansing of Bosnia from his comfortable perch in Pale, now claims to be a humanist at heart. "I never made distinctions between people on the basis of their ethnicity and religion. I have always believed that God made all men so I hate none," he said.[8]

Krajišnik is now back in Pale after having served two-thirds of his twenty-year sentence, most of it in British jails. He runs various businesses from a suite of offices above a gas station on the road into town from Sarajevo. Pale itself is as picturesque as ever: serene, alpine, small. At the time Karadžić and Mladić strutted through its streets, it was Bosnia's Berchtesgaden, a tranquil hideaway from which to plan the ethnic purification of nations.

Krajišnik says he found Zen-like equanimity while in prison, but he does not acknowledge having personally committed any wrong over the course of the Bosnian war. All the bad things were done by other people, whom he will not name. "I don't know what happened during the war. It was clear that it takes just a few of those pathological murderers to set a whole city on fire." One man in prison, he recalled, would wake up in the middle of the night sweating, convinced he could see the faces of all his victims at the window in the dark. Not Krajišnik. He sleeps peacefully.

It is probably too much to ask of justice that it drives the guilty to remorse. A spartan prison regime of bread and water and bucket toilets probably would not have made any of the perpetrators any sorrier but rather just fed the cult of victimhood that is the lifeblood of the nationalist cause.

Most of the surviving victims and families of the dead are appalled at the cushy conditions at Scheveningen, but the imbalance between the horror visited on them and the redress offered by any system of justice is unbridgeable anyway. For such crimes there will never be any such thing as closure and it was ever thus. In 1946, after the forty-seven minutes it took to sentence the convicts at Nuremberg, the American journalist Martha Gellhorn observed: "Justice seemed very small suddenly. Of course it had to be, for there was no punishment great enough for such guilt."[9]

The same was true more than sixty years later in the Balkans. A better measure of value of the Hague arrests is to contemplate the awfulness of the alternative, if the perpetrators had been left to walk free, an outcome that would have assigned no value at all to the tens of thousands of lives they took away.

The states that emerged from Yugoslavia are finding it hard enough to escape its debris. The task would be immeasurably harder if the demagogues and their regiment of butchers had been left at liberty after the war. This was probably the greatest contribution of the manhunt. It extracted the likes of Milošević, Karadžić, and Mladić from the Balkan arena and in so doing removed a powerful force for conflict and instability.

The assumption of the NATO generals after the Dayton Accords that peace and justice were alternatives, that the arrest of war criminals would bring an instant return to fighting, was proved wrong. What is striking about the post-Dayton period in Bosnia is an almost total absence of reprisals. Given the gory horrors of the conflict in which the killers were often neighbors well known to the victims' families, that lack of vengeance is an astounding phenomenon. It is explained, at least in part, by the faith Bosnians put in the Hague Tribunal's capacity to dispense justice.

The fact that the killing came to a halt so abruptly, as if a switch had been flicked, also demonstrates the decisive role of political leadership in creating the conditions for the mass murders of the 1990s. The nationalist leaders who assumed power at the breakup of Yugoslavia were not struggling to contain the murderous impulses of their people. On the contrary, they created circumstances for psychopaths and sadists to kill with impunity.

Once the leadership was removed and that permissive climate came to an end, the blood stopped flowing. So the manhunt for the architects of ethnic cleansing and their transfer to The Hague was not a trigger for renewed conflict. Quite the reverse. It was vital to prevent a return to bloodshed. The lesson taught by the pursuit of the Yugoslav war criminals is that there can be no sustainable peace without some measure of justice.

The effort to deliver justice was sprawling and complex. It brought together prosecutors from across the globe, led in turn by South African, Canadian, Swiss, and Belgian prosecutors. It was spearheaded by a maverick American diplomat, a handful of Polish commandos, Britain's SAS, and later the special forces of the Netherlands, the United States, Germany, and France. For a few years at least, the manhunt was the top priority of the CIA, MI6, and the DGSE. Finally it was the work of officials, human rights activists, and journalists in the region who defied the *omertà* and denial enforced by nationalist propaganda.

Only on occasion was this a concerted international effort. For the most part, the manhunt was driven forward fitfully by the domino effect of separate actions. The perseverance of the ICTY prosecutors ultimately bore fruit with the arrival of sympathetic officials like Madeleine Albright, Wesley Clark, Jacques Klein, and Robin Cook. Their decision to enforce the tribunal's indictments ultimately shamed others into following suit. They created a new norm. Fear of capture by armed commandos provoked voluntary surrenders. Once the cells in Scheveningen were being filled and the ICTY's credibility was beyond doubt, it became easier for prosecutors to demand that Western aid and European Union membership be made conditional on states handing over the wanted men. That in turn emboldened pro-Western and democratic politicians in Serbia and Croatia to make a stand against the nationalist orthodoxy of denial.

The ultimate success of the Hague manhunt was not the outcome of some grand master plan. Nor were its many failures along the way. The eighteen lost months between the Dayton Accords and the first arrests by the international community were not signs of conspiracy but of timidity. NATO governments and their generals judged the peace in the region to be far more fragile than it was in reality. The people of the former Yugoslavia were weary of war and contemptuous of their leaders' venality. Once Western policy-makers realized that there would be no backlash, and it was clear there would not be reprisals against their soldiers for carrying out detentions, they poured substantial resources into the hunt.

France was an exception. The French military dragged its feet throughout the process. It was the last of the five powers in Operation Amber Star to carry out arrests and was more of a hindrance than a help in tracking down Karadžić. To some extent, this reticence was a product of bitter experience. More French soldiers had been killed during the Bosnian war than peacekeepers from any other nation. Army commanders were not in a hurry to sacrifice more of their troops for an enterprise they believed would jeopardize the peace. But sentimentality about France's historical ties with Serbia led some French officers to turn a blind eye to the atrocities committed in Serbia's name. As to a secret deal with Karadžić, it may not be hard to imagine President Jacques Chirac purring assurances of immunity to the Bosnian Serb leader, particularly at a time French servicemen were being held hostage. But Karadžić never produced documentary proof to back such claims.

Nor is there any concrete evidence for Bosnian Serb claims of similar guarantees from the US diplomat Richard Holbrooke.

America's hesitancy to commit to the manhunt was a consequence of the Pentagon's risk-averse culture after the Black Hawk Down disaster in Somalia. But that complex was eventually shrugged off. By the end of the Clinton administration, the pursuit of Karadžić in Bosnia represented the biggest mission deployment of US special forces anywhere in the world. Its failure reflected the fact, to be demonstrated later in the hunt for Osama bin Laden, that finding fugitives in their natural habitat is diabolically hard and strength in numbers is not necessarily an advantage to the pursuers. On the contrary, it can make it easier for the quarry to see them coming. That is why the ICTY's own tracking team, for all its faults, proved a better value on an arrest-per-dollar basis than the far more formidable spy agencies deployed by the Western powers.

By saving the ICTY from oblivion, the manhunt changed legal history. Throughout the twentieth century, idealists had talked about a permanent international court that would hold accountable those responsible for the worst crimes, including political leaders and heads of state. There was a burst of enthusiasm for such a court in the immediate aftermath of the Nuremberg trials, but it subsided as the Cold War set in and such universalist idealism faded.

The end of the Cold War, however, set in motion a new drive to create institutions dispensing international justice. The examples set by the ICTY and its ad hoc African twin, the International Criminal Tribunal for Rwanda, showed such institutions could work and offered at least the hope of deterring future atrocities. The creation of the International Criminal Court (ICC) in 2002, not far from the ICTY's headquarters in The Hague, marked a historic and significant transfer of legal authority from sovereign states to an international institution.

More than 120 states now give the ICC the power to initiate proceedings against high functionaries suspected of serious crimes, including genocide, crimes against humanity, war crimes, and aggression.[10]

As was the case with the ICTY at its inception, few initially gave the ICC much chance of survival. It was designed to operate independently of the great powers in the UN Security Council. Its judges and prosecutor are elected on a one state, one vote principle. Without a dominant say, the major powers have distrusted the new court, fearing it might one day turn its attention to them. They have tried to suffocate it in the cradle. Clinton belatedly decided to sign the Rome Statute establishing the ICC on New Year's Eve 2000, one of the last days of his presidency. His successor, George W. Bush, spent his first months in office seeking to reverse that decision and "unsign" the document. The bare-knuckle, legally dubious methods the United States and its allies employed in their post-9/11 war on terror only deepened the reluctance to risk scrutiny by a foreign court.

The Bush administration could not stop the ICC from coming into being, however. A rush of ten ratifications of the Rome Statute in April 2002 brought it over the threshold of the sixty member states necessary to bring it to life. It was formally born on July 1, 2002. Nations joined up faster than anyone had expected, in part because the court came to be seen as a counterweight to the Bush administration's unilateralist leanings. Unlike most international institutions, it was the creation of mostly small and midsize nations* rather than the permanent five Security Council members.

*The ICC's supporters in the UN called themselves the "like-minded group" and included several European and Latin American states, as well as Australia, Canada, and New Zealand.

In the long term, however, it is hard to run an international institution without Security Council support. The lack of US endorsement, along with India's and China's refusal to join, have hobbled the workings of the ICC, which depends on state contributions to function. It does not have an agency like the tracking team that is empowered and willing to carry out international arrests,[11] and it can investigate war crimes against the wishes of the government involved only if it is armed with a referral from the UN Security Council. In practice that means that all eight ICC indictments up to 2014 have been against Africans. Washington, Moscow, and the other competing powers have less at stake in Africa, so have less reason to veto investigations. But the focus on African crimes has inevitably drawn accusations of racism and threats of a boycott from the African Union.

In the face of the slaughter in Syria and Iraq, the ICC has been powerless. With a return to sharp-edged great-power rivalry following the post–Cold War lull, there is a real danger of the ICC stalling. To this day, the ICTY is still the high-water mark of international justice for crimes against humanity.

That is not surprising. The conditions that permitted the pursuit and capture of the Hague indictees were unique. The crime scene was in Europe and was patrolled in the immediate postwar period by a substantial NATO force, which eventually agreed to act as the ICTY's arresting officer. Furthermore, the governments of the region sorely wanted something that Europe had to offer, EU membership, giving Western capitals the sort of leverage that is hard to reproduce elsewhere.

The ICTY's great achievement, pushing back the culture of impunity for mass atrocities, was born of a particular set of circumstances. Now, in the absence of those circumstances, its legacy is in danger of unraveling.

It was always going to be a fragile legacy, vulnerable to erosion. The justice on offer in The Hague was destined to be incomplete. More than 130,000 people were killed in the course of Yugoslavia's disintegration, most of them civilian victims of war crimes. Across large swaths of Bosnia and Kosovo, there were atrocities in almost every town. In the face of murder on this scale, the Hague indictment list of 161 suspects was illustrative rather than comprehensive. Originally intended to net the worst offenders and architects of ethnic cleansing, the Hague list ended up a mixed bag, involving plenty of small-fry prison guards and soldiers simply because they were easy to indict when the court was fighting for survival. Even after all the suspects on the list had been rounded up and transferred to The Hague, or otherwise accounted for, it left a lot of killers at large in the Balkans and many atrocities ignored and forgotten by justice.

In Serb eyes, the justice meted out by the Hague Tribunal was partial in more ways than one. Crimes against Serbs, they say, have largely gone unpunished. They point in particular to the killings of hundreds of mostly elderly Serbs in Croatia in the aftermath of Operation Storm in August 1995, and the murder of Serb civilians at the hands of the Kosovo Liberation Army (KLA) guerrillas after the 1999 war. There was outrage over the acquittal of Orić, the Bosniak commander in Srebrenica, and of Haradinaj, the former KLA commander. The latter's trial was marked by the death and disappearance of several of the witnesses.

The Serbs are right to think that crimes against their countrymen have gone unpunished but incorrect to think they are alone in being so wronged. There are too many graves containing the bones of all ethnicities for international justice to cope with, given finite resources. Such inadequacy does not discriminate against Serbs in favor of Bosniaks, Croats, and Kosovars. It discriminates against victims in favor of perpetrators.

Some of the deficit has been made up by national war crimes courts established in the former Yugoslav states — another legacy of the ICTY. The parallel courts in Serbia, Croatia, and Bosnia have been able to cooperate better than expected and have mounted hundreds of prosecutions. However, they lack political support and have on occasion stumbled spectacularly. In 2013, the court in Sarajevo was forced to release twelve men who had been indicted for war crimes, including six allegedly involved in the Srebrenica massacres, because the European Court of Human Rights in Strasbourg ruled they had been tried under the wrong criminal code.[12]

The Serbian Special War Crimes Court in Belgrade, established in 2003, convicted seventy people in its first ten years of existence, but an Amnesty International report in June 2014 found that, largely due to government support that was tepid at best, "the number of completed prosecutions remains low, and the rate at which indictments are brought is too slow."[13]

The record of the Croatian Special War Crimes Chamber is even worse. An Amnesty International report in 2010 found that the system completed on average only eighteen war crimes trials a year, with seven hundred cases awaiting prosecution. Three-quarters of these cases were targeted at ethnic Serbs. War crimes committed by Croats have gone largely unpunished and un-investigated.

The hardest irony to accept for the prosecutors and investigators who led the Hague manhunt has been the ICTY's own role in undoing their legacy. After all the suspects had been successfully rounded up, the tribunal's judges reversed a string of convictions of high-ranking defendants on appeal, including the Croatian generals Ante Gotovina and Mladen Markač in November 2012, and then the Serbian chief of staff, General Momčilo Perišić.

Even more controversially, at the end of May 2013, the tribunal acquitted Jovica Stanišić and Franko Simatović, two senior state security officials from the Milošević era who had been instrumental in arming, equipping, and training Serb paramilitary groups responsible for wholesale abuses in Croatia and Bosnia.

The series of acquittals represented a sharp about-face for the tribunal, which had hitherto held senior officers and officials accountable for the mass atrocities committed by their underlings on the grounds that they were involved in a "joint criminal enterprise." Under the leadership of an American judge, Theodor Meron, an eighty-three-year-old Holocaust survivor and former Israeli diplomat, the new judgments significantly raised the threshold of proof needed to convict political leaders. It was no longer enough to demonstrate that senior officers had control over the units who committed mass murder. The prosecution now had to be able to show evidence of specific orders to carry out particular crimes. So although the court had evidence that Stanišić had made reference to mass killings and had declared "we'll exterminate them completely," that seemingly damning remark was judged "to be too vague to be construed as support for the allegation that Stanišić shared the intent to further the alleged common criminal purpose."[14]

The decisions caused a rift at the heart of the tribunal. Michèle Picard, a French judge on the panel that acquitted Stanišić and Simatović, delivered her dissenting verdict, arguing, "If we cannot find that the accused aided and abetted those crimes, I would say we have come to a dark place in international law indeed."[15]

A Danish judge on the tribunal, Frederik Harhoff, went further in his dissent, circulating a letter to fifty-six friends and lawyers suggesting Meron had put pressure on his colleagues to acquit the high-profile defendants. Harhoff also questioned whether the tribunal president was himself under the influence of the US and Israeli governments, concerned that the principle of "joint criminal enterprise" could one day put them in the dock for backing armed groups in places like Lebanon, Syria, Iraq, or Afghanistan. "You would think that the military establishment in leading states (such as USA and Israel) felt that the courts in practice were getting too close to the military commanders' responsibilities," Harhoff wrote. "In other words: The court was heading too far in the direction of commanding officers being held responsible for every crime their subordinates committed. Thus their intention to commit crime had to be specifically proven."[16]

Harhoff was subsequently removed from the tribunal's bench on the grounds the letter reflected bias, and he was criticized for singling out Meron for his US and Israeli identity. But it was hard to escape the conclusion that some of the tribunal's judges had taken fright at the consequences of its work for all states waging proxy wars through allied militias. They had wanted to bring some justice to the former Yugoslavia, not change the world. Their strongest critics argued that, in acquitting the generals and the spy chiefs, they had done neither.

The acquittals, wrote Eric Gordy, a lecturer in the politics of Southeast Europe at University College London, marked "a sad end to the story of a court that was founded with little hope, encouraged some, then jettisoned it all."[17]

When Meron went to Sarajevo to mark the tribunal's twentieth anniversary in May 2013, the mothers of the Srebrenica victims turned their backs to him as he began to speak, while other activists walked out holding aloft a banner declaring "RIP Justice." Nataša Kandić, a veteran human rights activist from Belgrade, said, "The consequences of these rulings are clear. You cannot expect indictments based on command responsibility. After these verdicts, it's very difficult to speak about justice in the region."[18]

For Hasan Nuhanović, a Srebrenica survivor, the tribunal's apparent about-face was the last veil to be lifted on an illusion of justice. Nuhanović's mother, father, and brother were killed by Bosnian Serb forces. His mother's burned remains were found on a trash dump. The bodies of his father and brother were buried in a mass grave and then dug up with hundreds of others and reburied in a second pit, where they were finally identified.

"We wanted the reconstruction of our homes. Hundreds of villages just disappeared from the map, and we wanted to be somehow compensated, along with getting the arrest of war criminals. We lived an illusion, thinking that if someone lived through something like that, they would be rewarded," Nuhanović said. "We realize now that package will never be delivered. And what did we get for living through all that? We got the absence of war."[19]

A short-lived Balkan Spring broke out in February 2014, bringing demonstrators onto the streets of Bosnian towns to protest against the country's economic and political stagnation. It produced a generational divide between the mostly young activists, who wanted more from life, and their parents, who vividly remembered the war and were still grateful they were no longer under fire and their children were no longer being killed.

Even that single irreducible achievement, the absence of war, seems under threat. The youth of different ethnicities mix less now than at any time in the region's history, and each is taught a different version of history. Reconciliation has never seemed so far off.

The sense of foreboding has grown every time a protagonist in the Yugoslav carnage has been set free. It is not just the ICTY's acquittals that have fed this dread. Thanks to the liberal sentencing guidelines under which many of the war criminals were jailed, men convicted of dozens or even hundreds of killings are benefiting from early release, having served two-thirds of their sentences. They are returning home, to be welcomed as heroes by their communities.

Krajišnik was greeted in Pale by thousands of people waving flags and placards bearing nationalist slogans. Always under Karadžić's shadow during the war, he had never previously received such adulation. A former Bosnian Croat separatist leader, Dario Kordić, who had been convicted of orchestrating the massacres of Muslims in central Bosnia, was released in June 2014 after serving two-thirds of his twenty-five-year sentence. He too was met by cheering crowds, flags, and slogans, as well as a Catholic bishop who conducted a thanksgiving mass. Slavo Kukić, a Bosnian Croat university professor who criticized Kordić's welcome, was beaten up with a baseball bat.[20]

The return of the Hague Tribunal's convicts has been accompanied by a drive to erase memories of the slaughter. After survivors and bereaved families put up a memorial to the mass murder of Muslims in Višegrad, the response of the local Serb authorities was as unsubtle as it was symbolic. They arrived with an angle grinder and removed the word "genocide" from the stone monument. A group of Višegrad widows tried to restore it in lipstick, only for it to be obscured by municipal white paint a few days later.[21]

In Višegrad, and at the sites of other mass killings of Bos-niaks, Serb nationalists have not only prevented memorials to the victims; they have made a point of erecting monuments to fallen Serb soldiers instead.

"Those who committed the war crimes against us are still winning. They are killing our truth," said Bakira Hasečić, a Višegrad survivor who was raped multiple times by Serb para-militaries at her home and in the local police station in 1992. Her sister was raped and killed. Her eighteen-year-old daughter was raped in front of her and had her head smashed by a rifle butt, yet survived.

In western Bosnia, where the most notorious concentration camps were situated, the story is the same. On the grounds of one of these camps, at Trnopolje, where torture and rape were rife and where hundreds of Bosniaks and Croats were killed, a concrete memorial to fallen Serb soldiers has been placed at the entrance and inscribed with an ode to freedom.

Omarska, an iron ore mine that served as a death camp during the war, is now run by a Luxembourg-based multinational steel corporation, ArcelorMittal. The firm says it is perfectly ready to put up a memorial on the site, just as soon as the local authority in Prijedor gives its consent. That is something the town council, run by Serb nationalists, has declined to do.

When he was thirty, Kasim Pervanić spent a few months in Omarska, along with hundreds of other Bosniak men. Every night, the guards would read out a list of names. The men on the list were taken away and never came back. Most were killed in a large shed known as the White House. The guards called Pervanić's name one night but he hid and the guards left empty-handed. More than twenty years on, he still wakes up sweating at 2:30 a.m., the same time they came for him.

After failing to settle abroad, in the United Kingdom or Holland, Pervanić returned to Kevljani, his village, which is a mile or so from Omarska and the site of a massacre of its Bosniak residents.[22] When he got back in 2003, there was nothing left of the settlement. It had been obliterated and its foundations were submerged in tall grass. He spent nine years building a new house, with a traditional square, double-decked roof—a singular act of determination and defiance. He lives alone but the memories come calling every day. The postman was one of the Omarska guards. The man who sells Pervanić metal wire for his construction work was a camp commandant.

He never talks about the past unless they mention it first. Then he cannot help himself. They dwell on the people they saved, not the people that were killed. "So who killed all these people then?" Pervanić asks. "It looks like no one is responsible.

"As time goes by you become numb. You lose your feelings," he said. "It is nineteen years since the war and fourteen years since I came back here. No Serb has spent the night in a Muslim village, and no Muslim has ever spent the night in a Serb village... If there was a new war, no one would survive. No one would be spared."

The war criminals are walking free again. Nationalism is on the rise and the memories of the dreadful past are being physically erased. Victims are being made to cower once more. For those who stood by while the crimes were committed and waved their flags on cue, it is more comfortable to imbibe the familiar nationalist bromides, reassuring themselves they were the true victims. The sound of the slogans blocks out the murmurs of the bones buried under their feet.

So after such an extraordinary achievement—the relentless pursuit of the accused until all 161 names on the Hague list had been checked off and the mission completed—what is there left as a legacy?

Some justice was done. A few score of the guilty stood before the dock and were made to listen while the survivors recounted the bare facts. The convicted were deprived of some years of liberty. It is not justice's fault that this appears so paltry in face of such atrocious crimes. This is all it has to offer. That and a reasonable stab at the truth.

"Without the tribunal there wouldn't be a database of seven million documents which very clearly gives the history of the conflict, so that no one can deny that crimes have taken place, and that genocide has been committed," Serge Brammertz, the ICTY's last chief prosecutor, said.[23]

Resurgent nationalists in the states of the former Yugoslavia are covering over the truth of what happened with a thick layer of revisionism and denial, but the meticulous record of the tribunal, with its seven million documents, cannot be buried forever. Nor can the demand for justice for humanity's worst crimes. The Yugoslav manhunt showed that the judgments of an international court could be enforced. It showed that, given time, resources, and political will, war criminals could ultimately be tracked down and held to account. It set a benchmark against which all future efforts will be judged.

# ACKNOWLEDGMENTS

**IF I HAD NOT SET OUT** to write this book, I would never have known the depth and extent of the generosity of my friends and colleagues. I was constantly surprised by the time and effort they contributed, without which it would have been a much poorer, thinner piece of work.

Nerma Jelacic and David Rohde opened doors that allowed me to get started. Nerma gave me my first crucial introductions in The Hague while David kindly persuaded Sarah Chalfant at the Wylie Agency to act as my agent. Sarah's belief and enthusiasm took the idea to both sides of the Atlantic and luckily brought it to Judith Gurewich at Other Press, whose sound instincts and advice carried me the rest of the way.

The experience has reinforced my faith in journalism and journalists. Peter Bergen, a writer and analyst I have long looked up to, went well beyond the call of collegiality to introduce me to people who do not usually talk to reporters. Tara McKelvey was also extraordinarily generous with her contacts, as was Susanne Koelbl at *Der Spiegel*. Both put me in touch with protagonists in my story I would never have found on my own. The same is true of Eugeniusz Smolar. Michael Smith bestowed on me an unsolicited act of kindness that lifted my spirits in the early stages.

## ACKNOWLEDGMENTS

Fergal Keane and Gordon Corera at the BBC made suggestions that ended up having a dramatic impact on the book, as did Tim Judah, the most knowledgeable and thoughtful British journalist covering the Balkans for as long as I can remember. Chuck Sudetic gave me a lot of ideas about people to track down. In Paris, Christophe Boltanski gave advice on the structure that saved me lot of angst and wasted time.

Three historians I very much admire gave me invaluable guidance. I am grateful to Robert Donia for being so generous with his time and helping me rethink my approach, especially to the introduction. Lara Nettelfield gave wise counsel and heartening encouragement when I needed it most. Marko Attila Hoare talked me through some of the knottier issues I was wrestling with.

I am extremely lucky to have fantastic colleagues at *The Guardian* who make it such a pleasure to work there. Malik Meer and Max Benato edited my original feature article on the manhunt and were the first to suggest it could be the kernel for a book. Jamie Wilson, the foreign editor, was understanding and supportive throughout, and Ian Cobain gave me some early expert advice. Arnel Hecimović was considerate and supportive, and Ed Vulliamy is a lifelong inspiration.

Researching the book became an excuse to travel and see old friends from Balkan days who have deep reservoirs of knowledge. In Washington, Vlatka Mihelić-Landay and Samantha Power provided unvarnished views based on long experience and commitment, and supplied an extensive list of people to contact. Ethan Carson, Katty Kay, Tom Carver, Caitriona Palmer, and Dan De Luce kindly gave me a place to stay and wonderful company on my research trips.

In Brussels, Alexandra Stiglmayer and Chris Riley looked after me and gave me the benefit of their expertise on the former

Yugoslavia and the British military, respectively. Dejan Anastasijević, a courageous and hugely respected journalist, talked me through the intricacies of the Serbian security apparatus.

In The Hague, Serge Brammertz was encouraging and open-minded about the project. Among former ICTY folk, Louise Arbour and Jean-Daniel Ruch provided me with important insights into the tribunal. As for former United Nations officials who played a role in the manhunt, I would particularly like to thank Jacques Klein, Alex Ivanko, and Colonel David Jones for help and advice.

In Bosnia, Enes Zlatar took time out of his music career to be a great colleague, translator, and travel companion in the latter stages of the research. Kasim Pervanić was a gracious host in Kevljani, after his brother Kemal was kind enough to recommend me. Boba Lizdek in Sarajevo delved back through twenty-year-old memories and came up with priceless details.

In Belgrade, Milan Dinić took me to see people I would never have been able to meet on my own, and supplied excellent translations and analysis. Aleksandar Vasović drew on his encyclopedic knowledge of modern Serbian history and was patient with me as I struggled to take it all in. In Zagreb, Gordan Malić has a similarly profound grasp of detail, and took time to talk me through some of the Croatian side of the drama.

Back in London, Carl Newns at the Foreign and Commonwealth Office cajoled a reluctant bureaucracy into declassifying some of the documentation on the manhunt, and Arminka Helić (now Baroness Helić), a Bosnian-born British foreign policy-maker, gave me a unique insight. Karen Pierce and the former ambassador Charles Crawford were especially helpful with suggestions and recollections in the early stages of writing.

A host of people were kind enough to read through chapters and make suggestions or point out embarrassing blunders. They include Dejan Anastasijević, Neven Andjelić, Milan Dinić, Arnel Hecimović, Nerma Jelacic, Jasmina Kuzmanović, Adam LeBor, Gordan Malić, Monika Stedul, David Rohde, Ian Traynor, and Ed Vulliamy. Keenan McCracken at Other Press went through all of it numerous times at the end and was a very sensitive editor, significantly improving the quality of the text. The managing editor, Yvonne Cárdenas, has a forensic attention to detail in the copyediting stage that was awe-inspiring. Any remaining errors are entirely my own.

Many people who had been involved in the manhunt gave me a huge amount of help, guidance, and information but cannot be named, mostly because they are former members of the special forces or intelligence services, or are still working in government or in the ICTY. Without them this book really would not have been possible. They talked to me in most cases because they believed that it was a story worth telling and that its lessons were in danger of being forgotten.

I am heavily indebted to Miodrag Rakić, who put his trust in me and gave me extensive help even as he struggled with cancer. He was one of the heroes of the story, confronting the layers of protection around the war criminals head-on, braving death threats along the way, so that his country's future would no longer be held hostage by a handful of mass murderers. He died in May 2014.

Without the patience and understanding of my wife, Monika, I would never have been able to spend all the time on the road and in the library necessary to get this book done. She made some telling comments and saved me from some grievous errors. For all that, I owe her a huge debt of gratitude. As for my son, Benjamin, he is the inspiration for this book, and for much else besides.

# CHRONOLOGY

## ARRESTS AND TRANSFERS TO THE ICTY IN THE HAGUE

**1995**

Duško Tadić: April 24, Bosnian Serb, arrested by police in Germany
in 1994

**1996**

Djordje Djukić: February 12, Bosnian Serb, arrested January 30
in Bosnia and Herzegovina by Bosnian Army
Dražen Erdemović: March 30, Croat, arrested by Yugoslav police
Tihomir Blaškić: April 1, Bosnian Croat, voluntary surrender
Zdravko Mucić: April 9, Bosniak, arrested by Austrian police
Zejnil Delalić: May 9, Bosniak, arrested by German police
Hazim Delić: June 13, Bosniak, arrested by Bosnian police
Esad Landžo: June 13, Bosniak, arrested by Bosnian police

**1997**

Zlatko Aleksovski: April 28, Bosnian Croat, arrested in 1996 by
Croatian police
Slavko Dokmanović: June 27, Croatian Serb, captured by Polish
UN soldiers
Milan Kovačević: July 10, Bosnian Serb, arrested in Bosnia by
British soldiers
Mario Čerkez: October 6, Bosnian Croat, voluntary surrender
Drago Josipović: October 6, Bosnian Croat, voluntary surrender
Dario Kordić: October 6, Bosnian Croat, voluntary surrender

Mirjan Kupreškić: October 6, Bosnian Croat, voluntary surrender

Zoran Kupreškić: October 6, Bosnian Croat, voluntary surrender

Dragan Papić: October 6, Bosnian Croat, voluntary surrender

Vladimir Šantić: October 6, Bosnian Croat, voluntary surrender

Vlatko Kupreškić: December 18, Bosnian Croat, arrested in Bosnia
   by Dutch troops

Anto Furundžija: December 19, Bosnian Croat, arrested in Bosnia
   by Dutch troops


## 1998

Goran Jelisić: January 22, Bosnian Serb, arrested in Bosnia by US troops

Miroslav Tadić: February 14, Bosnian Serb, voluntary surrender to
   US troops in Bosnia

Milan Simić: February 15, Bosnian Serb, voluntary surrender to
   US troops in Bosnia

Simo Zarić: February 25, Bosnian Serb, voluntary surrender to US troops
   in Bosnia

Dragoljub Kunarac: March 5, Bosnian Serb, voluntary surrender to
   French troops

Mladjo Radić: April 8, Bosnian Serb, arrested in Bosnia by British troops

Miroslav Kvočka: April 9, Bosnian Serb, arrested in Bosnia by
   British troops

Zoran Žigić: April 16, Bosnian Serb, voluntary surrender

Milojica Kos: May 29, Bosnian Serb, arrested in Bosnia by British troops

Milorad Krnojelac: June 15, Bosnian Serb, arrested in Bosnia by
   German troops

Stevan Todorović: September 27, Bosnian Serb, seized in Serbia by
   US-hired gang

Radislav Krstić: December 2, Bosnian Serb, arrested in Bosnia by
   US troops


## 1999

Dragan Kolundžija: June 7, Bosnian Serb, arrested in Bosnia by
   British troops

Radoslav Brdjanin: July 6, Bosnian Serb, arrested in Bosnia by
   British troops

Radomir Kovač: August 2, Bosnian Serb, arrested in Bosnia by
   German troops

Vinko Martinović: August 9, Bosnian Croat, arrested in 1997 by
   Croatian police

Momir Talić: August 25, Bosnian Serb, arrested by Austrian police

Damir Došen: October 25, Bosnian Serb, arrested in Bosnia by
   British troops

Stanislav Galić: December 21, Bosnian Serb, arrested in Bosnia by
   British troops

Zoran Vuković: December 24, Bosnian Serb, arrested in Bosnia by
   French troops


## 2000

Mitar Vasiljević: January 25, Bosnian Serb, arrested in Bosnia by
   French troops

Dragoljub Prcać: March 5, Bosnian Serb, arrested in Bosnia by
   British troops

Mladen Naletilić: March 21, Bosnian Croat, arrested in 1999 by
   Croatian police

Momčilo Krajišnik: April 3, Bosnian Serb, arrested in Bosnia by
   French troops

Dragan Nikolić: April 21, Bosnian Serb, seized in Serbia by US-hired gang

Duško Sikirica: June 25, Bosnian Serb, arrested in Bosnia by
   British troops


## 2001

Biljana Plavšić: January 10, Bosnian Serb, voluntary surrender

Blagoje Simić: March 12, Bosnian Serb, voluntary surrender

Milomir Stakić: March 23, Bosnian Serb, arrested by Serbian police

Dragan Obrenović: April 15, Bosnian Serb, arrested in Bosnia by
   US troops

Slobodan Milošević: June 29, Serbian, arrested by Serbian police
Rahim Ademi: July 25, Kosovar in Croatian army, voluntary surrender
Mehmed Alagić: August 4, Bosniak, arrested by Bosnian police
Amir Kubura: August 4, Bosniak, arrested by Bosnian police
Enver Hadžihasanović: August 4, Bosniak, arrested by Bosnian police
Vidoje Blagojević: August 10, Bosnian Serb, caught in Bosnia
    in British–US operation
Dragan Jokić: August 15, Bosnian Serb, voluntary surrender
Sefer Halilović: September 25, Bosniak, voluntary surrender
Pavle Strugar: October 21, Serbian, voluntary surrender
Nenad Banović: November 9, Bosnian Serb, arrested by Serbian
    special forces
Predrag Banović: November 9, Bosnian Serb, arrested by Serbian
    special forces
Miodrag Jokić: November 12, Serbian, voluntary surrender
Paško Ljubičić: November 21, Bosnian Croat, voluntary surrender

## 2002

Dušan Fuštar: January 31, Bosnian Serb, voluntary surrender
Momir Nikolić: April 2, Bosnian Serb, arrested in Bosnia by US troops
Dragoljub Ojdanić: April 25, Serbian, voluntary surrender
Momčilo Gruban: May 2, Bosnian Serb, voluntary surrender
Nikola Šainović: May 2, Serbian, voluntary surrender
Milan Martić: May 15, Croatian Serb, voluntary surrender
Mile Mrkšić: May 15, Croatian Serb, voluntary surrender
Dušan Knežević: May 18, Bosnian Serb, voluntary surrender
Darko Mrdja: June 13 or 14, Bosnian Serb, arrested in Bosnia by
    British troops
Ranko Češić: June 17, Bosnian Serb, arrested by Serbian police
Miroslav Deronjić: July 8, Bosnian Serb arrested in Bosnia by US troops
Radovan Stanković: July 10, Bosnian Serb, arrested in Bosnia by
    French troops

# CHRONOLOGY

## 2003

Milan Milutinović: January 20, Serbian, voluntary surrender

Haradin Bala: February 18, Kosovar, arrested by Kosovo Force

Isak Musliu: February 18, Kosovar, arrested by Kosovo Force

Vojislav Šešelj: February 24, Serbian, voluntary surrender

Fatmir Limaj: March 4, Kosovar, arrested by Slovenian police

Mladen Markač: March 11, Croatian, voluntary surrender

Naser Orić: April 11, Bosniak, arrested in Bosnia and Herzegovina
by US troops

Miroslav Radić: May 17, Serbian, voluntary surrender

Franko Simatović: May 30, Croat serving in the Serbian security
apparatus, arrested by Serbian police

Jovica Stanišić: June 11, Serbian, arrested by Serbian police

Ivica Rajić: June 24, Bosnian Croat, arrested by Croatian police

Veselin Šljivančanin: July 1, Montenegrin, arrested by Serbian police

Željko Mejakić: July 4, Bosnian Serb, voluntary surrender

Mitar Rašević: August 15, Bosnian Serb, voluntary surrender

Vladimir Kovačević: October 23, Montenegrin, arrested by
Serbian police

Milan Babić: November 26, Croatian Serb, voluntary surrender

## 2004

Ivan Čermak: March 11, Croatian, voluntary surrender

Valentin Ćorić: April 5, Bosnian Croat, voluntary surrender

Milivoj Petković: April 5, Bosnian Croat, voluntary surrender

Slobodan Praljak: April 5, Bosnian Croat, voluntary surrender

Jadranko Prlić: April 5, Bosnian Croat, voluntary surrender

Berislav Pušić: April 5, Bosnian Croat, voluntary surrender

Bruno Stojić: April 5, Bosnian Croat, voluntary surrender

Mirko Norac: July 8, Croatian, arrested by Croatian police

Ljubiša Beara: October 10, Bosnian Serb, arrested by Serbian police

Miroslav Bralo: November 10, Bosnian Croat, voluntary surrender

Dragomir Milošević: December 3, Bosnian Serb, voluntary surrender

## 2005

Savo Todović: January 15, Croatian Serb, voluntary surrender

Vladimir Lazarević: February 3, Serbian, voluntary surrender

Milan Gvero: February 24, Bosnian Serb, voluntary surrender

Rasim Delić: February 28, Bosniak, voluntary surrender

Radivoje Miletić: February 28, Bosnian Serb, voluntary surrender

Momčilo Perišić: March 7, Serbian, voluntary surrender

Idriz Balaj: March 9, Kosovar, voluntary surrender

Lahi Brahimaj: March 9, Kosovar, voluntary surrender

Ramush Haradinaj: March 9, Kosovar, voluntary surrender

Mićo Stanišić: March 11, Bosnian Serb, voluntary surrender

Gojko Janković: March 14, Bosnian Serb, voluntary surrender

Johan Tarčulovski: March 16, Macedonian, arrested by
    Macedonian police

Drago Nikolić: March 17, Bosnian Serb, voluntary surrender

Vinko Pandurević: March 23, Bosnian Serb, voluntary surrender

Ljube Boškoski: March 24, Macedonian, arrested in 2004 by
    Croatian police

Ljubomir Borovčanin: April 1, Bosnian Serb, voluntary surrender

Sreten Lukić: April 4, Bosnian Serb, voluntary surrender

Milorad Trbić: April 7, Bosnian Serb, voluntary surrender

Vujadin Popović: April 14, Bosnian Serb, voluntary surrender

Nebojša Pavković: April 25, Serbian, voluntary surrender

Ante Gotovina: December 10, Croatian, arrested on December 7
    in Spain

## 2006

Milan Lukić: February 21, Bosnian Serb, arrested in 2005 by
    Argentinean police

Dragan Zelenović: June 10, Bosnian Serb, arrested in 2005 by
    Russian police

Sredoje Lukić: September 16, Bosnian Serb, voluntary surrender

# CHRONOLOGY

**2007**

Zdravko Tolimir: June 1, Bosnian Serb, seized by Serbian police, deported to Bosnia

Vlastimir Djordjević: June 17, Serbian, arrested by Montenegrin police

**2008**

Stojan Župljanin: June 11, Bosnian Serb, arrested by Serbian police

Radovan Karadžić: July 21, Bosnian Serb, arrested by Serbian police

**2011**

Ratko Mladić: May 26, Bosnian Serb, arrested by Serbian police

Goran Hadžić: July 20, Croatian Serb, arrested by Serbian police

## TWENTY INDICTMENTS WITHDRAWN

Mirko Babić, Nenad Banović, Zdravko Govedarica, [*first name unknown*] Gruban, Marinko Katava, Dragan Kondić, Predag Kostić, Goran Lajić, Zoran Marinić, Agim Murtezi, Nedeljko Paspalj, Milan Pavlić, Milutin Popović, Draženko Predojević, Ivan Šantić, Dragomir Šaponja, Željko Savić, Pero Skopljak, Nedjeljko Timarac, Milan Zec

## TEN REPORTED DECEASED BEFORE TRANSFER TO THE TRIBUNAL

Stipo Alilović, Janko Bobetko, Goran Borovnica, Simo Drljača, Dragan Gagović, Janko Janjić, Nikica Janjić, Slobodan Miljković, Željko Ražnatović, Vlajko Stojiljković

# ABBREVIATIONS

**BIA**   Bezbednosno-Informativna Agencija
(Security Information Agency), Serbia

**CIA**   Central Intelligence Agency, United States

**COS**   Commandement des Opérations Spéciales
(Special Operations Command), France

**DGSE**   Direction Générale de la Sécurité Extérieure
(General Directorate for External Security), France

**DIA**   Defense Intelligence Agency, United States

**DRM**   Direction du Renseignement Militaire
(Directorate for Military Intelligence), France

**DST**   Direction de la Surveillance du Territoire
(Directorate for Territorial Surveillance), France

**FCO**   Foreign and Commonwealth Office, United Kingdom

**FIST**   Fugitive Intelligence Support Team, ICTY

**FSB**   Federal Security Bureau, Russia

**GCHQ**   Government Communications Headquarters,
United Kingdom

**GIGN**   Groupe d'Intervention de la Gendarmerie Nationale
(National Gendarmerie Intervention Group), France

**GROM**   Grupa Reagowania Operacyjno-Manewrowego
(Operational Mobile Response Group), Poland

**HDZ**   Hrvatska Demokratska Zajednica
(Croatian Democratic Union)

**HIS**   Hrvatska Izvještajna Služba (Croatian Information Service)

# ABBREVIATIONS

| | |
|---|---|
| **HVO** | Hrvatsko Vijeće Obrane (Croatian Defense Council), Bosnian Croat |
| **ICC** | International Criminal Court |
| **ICTY** | International Criminal Tribunal for the Former Yugoslavia (the Hague Tribunal) |
| **IFOR** | Implementation Force, NATO |
| **JNA** | Jugoslavenska Narodna Armija (Yugoslav National Army), Yugoslav |
| **JSO** | Jedinica za Specijalne Operacije (Unit for Special Operations), Serbian |
| **JSOC** | Joint Special Operations Command, United States |
| **JUL** | Jugoslovenska Levica (Yugoslav Left) |
| **KLA** | Kosovo Liberation Army |
| **KSK** | Kommando Spezialkräfte (Special Forces Command), Germany |
| **NATO** | North Atlantic Treaty Organization |
| **NSA** | National Security Agency, United States |
| **OSA-OBA** | Obavještajno Sigurnosna Agencija–Obavještajno bezbjednosne agencija (Intelligence and Security Agency), Bosnia |
| **PIFWC** | Person Indicted for War Crimes, NATO |
| **RSK** | Republika Srpska Krajina (Republic of Serbian Krajina), Croatian Serbia |
| **SAS** | Special Air Service, United Kingdom |
| **SDS** | Srpska Demokratska Stranka (Serb Democratic Party), Bosnian Serb |
| **SEAL** | Sea, Air, Land Teams, United States Navy |
| **SFOR** | Stabilization Force, NATO |
| **SIS** | Sigurnosno-Informativna Služba (Security Information Service), Croatia |
| **ST6** | SEAL Team Six, United States Navy, Joint Special Operations Command |
| **TIFU** | Tracking, Intelligence, and Fugitives Unit |
| **UNPROFOR** | United Nations Protection Force |

# NOTES

## INTRODUCTION: THE ECHO OF NUREMBERG

1. Former DGSE agent Pierre Martinet said that one of his colleagues earned an award for undercover service in the Balkan art world. The possession of high-quality art in the hands of thugs like Hadžić and his circle is not as far-fetched as it might appear on the surface. Art theft was a lucrative sideline of ethnic cleansing. A senior Serbian official told me that in some cases, when looted artifacts fell into the hands of Yugoslav intelligence officials who realized what they were worth, they set out to track down the owners, not to return their property but to kill them, eliminating a potential obstacle to selling the work on the global art market. See Pierre Martinet, *DGSE Service action: Un Agent sort de l'ombre* (Paris: Editions Privé, 2005).

2. It was literally a manhunt. There was just one woman on the list of indictees, Biljana Plavšić, and she turned herself in.

3. For a comprehensive history of the long quest for international justice, see Gary Jonathan Bass, *Stay the Hand of Vengeance: The Politics of War Crimes Tribunals* (Princeton, NJ: Princeton University Press, 2000).

4. Ibid., 12.

5. Britain's prime minister at the time, John Major, bizarrely blamed the Bosnian war on "the collapse of the Soviet Union and of the discipline that that exerted over the ancient hatreds in the old Yugoslavia." As Noel Malcolm pointed out in his book *Bosnia: A Short History* (London: Macmillan, 1994): "The 'discipline' exerted by the Soviet Union on Yugoslavia

came to an abrupt and well-publicized end in 1948, when Stalin expelled Tito from the Soviet-run Cominform organization."

6. A question attributed to Kiro Gligorov, Macedonia's first president after independence.

7. The figures given in this paragraph are according to Mirsad Tokaca, *The Bosnian Book of the Dead* (Sarajevo: Research and Documentation Centre and Humanitarian Law Center of Serbia, 2013).

8. David Rieff, *Slaughterhouse: Bosnia and the Failure of the West* (New York: Simon & Schuster, 1995), 27.

9. Julia Preston, "UN Security Council establishes Yugoslav War Crimes Tribunal," *Washington Post* (February 23, 1993).

10. Bass, *Stay the Hand of Vengeance*, 215.

11. Ibid., 220.

12. Louise Branson, "Serbian Killer Turned Away by US Embassy," *The Sunday Times* (March 17, 1996).

13. In return for his testimony Erdemović wanted to move his family to the West and be given immunity from prosecution. The tribunal was unwilling to guarantee the latter. On March 2, 1996, perhaps in the hope of forcing events, he and another soldier arranged to meet a correspondent for the French newspaper *Le Figaro*. They sat down to talk in a small country hotel near the Hungarian border. Erdemović was just twenty-five with a face still pockmarked by acne. He had been drafted into the black-uniformed Tenth Sabotage Detachment, which performed some of the gory labor in executing the eight thousand Muslim men and boys captured at Srebrenica. The Serbian security services stopped the journalist at the airport and confiscated the tapes of her interview with Erdemović. He was arrested half an hour later but prosecutors intervened quickly to ensure he was given up to the Hague Tribunal. Erdemović was flown to The Hague but was not granted immunity.

14. Ultimately, the judges reduced his sentence to five years because they accepted his argument that he had taken part in the executions on threat of death. His commander told him, "If you do not wish to do it, stand in the line with the rest of them and give others your rifle so that

they can shoot you." ICTY transcript, Erdemović trial, November 19, 1996.

15. On July 15, 2014, a civil court in The Hague held the Netherlands accountable for the deaths of the men and boys the Dutch UN battalion handed over to the Bosnian Serbs at Srebrenica. "Dutch State Liable for 300 Srebrenica Massacre Deaths," Associated Press (July 16, 2014).

16. Skeptics still doubt the official story that Bormann committed suicide after a failed attempt to flee Berlin in 1945. The Nazi hunter Simon Wiesenthal always believed that Bormann and his entourage managed to escape to South America.

17. A 2008 internal Department of Justice history of the OSI, "Striving for Accountability in the Aftermath of the Holocaust," was obtained by the National Security Archive at George Washington University and is available on its website at http://nsarchive.gwu.edu/NSAEBB/NSAEBB331/DOJ_OSI_Nazi_redacted.pdf.

18. The ICTY also looked into possible violations by NATO in its 1999 bombing campaign against Serbia, which was aimed at forcing Belgrade to withdraw its troops from Kosovo, but prosecutors decided there was insufficient evidence that civilian casualties were intentional.

## 1. OPERATION AMBER STAR

1. David Scheffer, *All the Missing Souls: A Personal History of the War Crimes Tribunals* (Princeton, NJ: Princeton University Press, 2012), 124.

2. Ian Black, "Blair Bowls Yeltsin Over," *The Guardian* (May 28, 1997).

3. Clinton was being sued by Paula Jones, an Arkansas state employee.

4. John F. Harris, "Russia-NATO Pact Gives Moscow a Voice on European Security," *Washington Post* (May 28, 1997).

5. The White House, Office of the Press Secretary (Paris) May 27, 1997. Remarks by President Clinton, French President Chirac, and Secretary General Solana at NATO/Russia Founding Act Signing Ceremony.

6. This account was provided by a US official who attended the event.

7. In its first year of operation, it was known as the Implementation

Force and was supposed to be in the country for only twelve months to implement the Dayton Accords. In fact, NATO would end up running Bosnia's security for seven years, until 2004, when the baton passed to the European Union.

8. Charles Crawford, interview with author, July 7, 2011.

9. Samantha Power, *A Problem from Hell: America and the Age of Genocide* (New York: Basic Books, 2002), chapter 13.

10. Robert Gelbard, interview with author, April 1, 2013.

11. Scheffer, *All the Missing Souls*, 144.

12. Ibid., 130.

13. United Nations Security Council Resoutions 827, 1031, and 1088, respectively.

14. Scheffer, *All the Missing Souls*, 149.

15. It was later expanded to include Spain and Italy, and renamed Operation Fervent Archer. Despite the aspirational title, however, neither of the two new members ever carried out any arrests.

16. UK Cabinet Office paper 5, "International Policy Towards War Crime Indictees in Bosnia," May 7, 1997, Freedom of Information disclosure.

17. For more about Mladić's hideout, see http://www.telegraph.co.uk/news/worldnews/europe/bosnia/1481773/Well-break-some-bones-in-pursuit-of-war-criminals.html.

18. William Stuebner, interview with author, April 1, 2013.

19. Ibid.

20. John Pomfret, "Bosnian Serbs' Leader Stages Show of Defiance; Karadžić Tour Ends Months of Seclusion," *The Washington Post* (February 10, 1996).

21. General Meigs, interview with author, April 2, 2013.

22. Foreign and Commonwealth Office paper, "War Criminals: Background Note," Freedom of Information disclosure.

23. Ibid.

24. In January 2012 Darroch was named the UK's national security adviser.

25. Foreign and Commonwealth Office paper 2a, Kim Darroch to Peter Ricketts, "War Crimes Indictees: Karadžić," June 17, 1997, Freedom of Information disclosure.

26. Ibid.

27. Cabinet Office paper 5.

28. Jean-Dominique Merchet, "Gourmelon, Commandant en eaux troubles. En Bosnia, l'Officier aurait eu des relations 'contestables' avec les Serbes," *Liberation* (April 24, 1998). The exact term used was *"une sombre histoire de cul"*—"a dark-ass story."

29. Jacques Massé, *Nos chers criminels de guerre: Paris, Zabreb, Belgrade en classe affaires* (Paris: Flammarion, 2006), 137.

30. Foreign and Commonwealth Office background note, "'War Criminals', Karadžić," undated but probably July 1997, Freedom of Information disclosure.

31. Scheffer, *All the Missing Souls*, 148.

32. Ibid., 155.

## 2. OPERATION LITTLE FLOWER

1. John Pomfret, "Polish Agents Rescued 6 US Spies from Iraq; Scotch Lubricated Escape During Gulf War," *Washington Post* (January 17, 1995).

2. Jacek, interview with author, February 7, 2014, on condition of anonymity; he is still in the security trade where anonymity is a virtue.

3. Confidential memo, from Clint Williamson to John Ralston, June 19, 1997.

4. Ibid.

5. "Detention and Arrest of Slavko Dokmanović," UN restricted document, July 15, 1997.

6. "Dokmanovic Case: Tribunal Update 35: Last Week in The Hague," Institute for War and Peace Reporting (June 30 – July 5, 1997).

7. "Detention and Arrest of Slavko Dokmanović."

8. ICTY document, "Dokmanović Case—Trial Chamber Denies the Motion for Release by the Accused," October 27, 1997, available at http://www.icty.org/sid/7458.

9. ICTY document, "Completion of the Internal Inquiry into the Death of Slavko Dokmanović," July 23, 1998, available at http://www.icty.org/sid/7458.

### 3. A HIGH EXPECTATION OF VIOLENCE: THE SAS IN BOSNIA

1. Ed Vulliamy recounts a brandy-fueled conversation with Kovačević in 1996 in Ed Vulliamy, *The War Is Dead, Long Live the War: Bosnia: The Reckoning* (London: Vintage Books, 2012), 49.

2. Human Rights Watch, "Who's Who in Prijedor," *Bosnia and Hercegovina: The Unindicted: Reaping the Rewards of "Ethnic Cleansing,"* Vol. 9, No. 1 (January 1997).

3. Ibid.

4. Ibid.

5. Ibid.

6. Ibid.

7. Elizabeth Neuffer, "Bosnia's War Criminals Enjoy Peacetime Power," *The Boston Globe* (October 29, 1996).

8. Ibid.

9. ICTY Case Information Sheet, "Prijedor," IT-97-24.

10. From an ICTY source.

11. "Prijedor Detention: Possible Misuse of Red Cross Symbol," from the private secretary of the secretary of defence to his opposite number in the Foreign Office, August 5, 1997, Freedom of Information disclosure.

12. Ed Vulliamy, "Comment: Anthrax Follies; 'Planted' Intelligence Is a War Correspondent's Nightmare," *The Guardian* (March 25, 1998).

13. In a 2013 interview with the author, the official also said, "I have clearly seen changes in the conservatives over the last twenty years, but Bosnia constantly haunts them." A guilty conscience left over from the Bosnia experience arguably informed David Cameron's decision that Britain should take a leading role in the military intervention in Libya and Foreign Secretary William Hague's advocacy of human rights issues, particularly in Bosnia.

14. Charles Crawford, interview with author, July 7, 2011. The Foreign

Office has refused to declassify Crawford's notes.

15. "International Policy Towards War Crime Indictees in Bosnia," Cabinet Office draft policy paper, May 7, 1997, Freedom of Information disclosure.

16. Ibid.

17. Memo from Kim Darroch to Peter Ricketts, June 9, 1997, Freedom of Information disclosure.

18. Memo from Darroch to the Ministry of Defence, June 11, 1997, Freedom of Information disclosure.

19. Memo from Darroch to Ricketts, June 17, 1997. Freedom of Information disclosure.

20. Cees Banning and Petra de Koning, "De Droom van Joris Voorhoeve," *NRC Handelsblad* (June 18, 2005).

21. Arthur ten Cate and Martijn van der Vorm, *Callsign Nassau: Het moderne Korps Commandotroepen 1989–2012* (Amsterdam: Boom uitgevers Amsterdam, 2012).

22. Ibid.

23. The committee was called BLC(O), for Balkan—official. It had a subcommittee devoted to the pursuit of the war criminals.

24. ICTY document, judgment summary, December 5, 2003.

25. Misha Glenny, "The Death of Djindjić," *The New York Review of Books* (July 17, 2003).

26. Boris Tadić, interview with author, March 2013.

27. *Pad Ratka Mladića* [The Fall of Ratko Mladića], television documentary by Slaviša Lekić, Prva Srpska Televizija, January 27, 2015.

28. Tim Judah, "The Fog of Justice," *The New York Review of Books* (January 15, 2004).

29. Nemanja Mladenovic, "The Failed Divorce of Serbia's Government and Organized Crime," *Journal of International Affairs* 66, No. 1 (Fall/Winter 2012).

30. Ibid.

31. Tom Walker and Milorad Ivanovic, "Vengeful Serbs Betray Top MI6 Man," *Sunday Times* (August 16, 2014).

## 4. MANHUNTING THE PENTAGON WAY

1. David Scheffer, *All the Missing Souls: A Personal History of the War Crimes Tribunals* (Princeton, NJ: Princeton University Press, 2012), 136.

2. Mark Bowden, "Raring to Get Started, Delta Learns Its Limits," *The Philadelphia Inquirer* (November 16, 2000). The hunt for Escobar, widely regarded as the wealthiest criminal in history, ended in December 1993, when he was shot dead in a gunfight with Colombian forces.

3. Ltg. (Ret.) William G. Boykin with Lynn Vincent, *Never Surrender: A Soldier's Journey to the Crossroads of Faith and Freedom* (New York: Hachette Book Group, 2008).

4. Francona recorded his experiences in *Chasing Demons: My Hunt for War Criminals in Bosnia* (Carmel, CA: Francona Advisers, 2012).

5. Ibid.

6. Ibid.

7. "Bosnian Serb Woman Sentenced for War Crimes," Agence France-Presse (May 17, 2013).

8. Francona, *Chasing Demons*.

9. Ibid.

10. Ibid.

11. Ibid. The CIA discovered that it had been spotted by agents of Iran's Islamic Revolutionary Guard Corps and warned Francona that his team was under hostile surveillance.

12. Richard J. Newman, "Hunting War Criminals: The First Account of Secret US Missions in Bosnia," *US News & World Report* (June 28, 1998).

13. Francona, *Chasing Demons*.

14. Ibid.

15. Blagoje Simić, the Bosanski Šamac mayor, also fled soon after. He surrendered in Serbia on March 12, 2001.

16. Daniel Voll, "Radovan Karadžić, a Deeply Misunderstood Mass Murderer," *Esquire* (December 1997).

17. At the start of the war at least, that was not unusual. As the conflict went on and bitterness deepened, the Serbs who stayed behind in

Sarajevo were increasingly discriminated against, often sent first and more often to the front lines.

18. Todorović later claimed that he had recognized his assailants as members of a ring of mercenaries whose pictures he had seen in the newspapers. The Spiders, as they were called, were allegedly led by a dual French Serbian national, Jugoslav Petrušić, who had long-standing links with both French and Serbian intelligence. He led a Serb mercenary force fighting for Mobutu Sese Seko in Zaire in the mid-nineties. US intelligence sources say the Spiders were not involved and that their team was recruited from Bosnian Serbs loyal to the Sarajevo government. The next time this CIA-hired snatch team went into action, in April 2000, the Spiders had an alibi. They were on trial for an alleged assassination plot against Slobodan Milošević.

19. "War Crimes Suspect Hands over Archive to Hague Tribunal," Associated Press (August 21, 1998).

20. ICTY document, "Dragan Nikolić, Sušica Camp," IT-94-2.

21. Eight men were sentenced to jail for their part in the abduction, some of them in absentia, including Amir Mirankic, the alleged ringleader who had gotten away. "Serbian Court Sentences Eight Serbs for Kidnapping War Crimes Suspect," Associated Press (November 24, 2000).

22. ICTY document, "Prosecutor vs Dragan Nikolić. Decision on Defense Motion Challenging the Exercise of Jurisdiction by the Tribunal," October 9, 2002.

## 5. THE HUNT IN CROATIA

1. Carla Del Ponte and Chuck Sudetic, *Madame Prosecutor: Confrontations with Humanity's Worst Criminals and the Culture of Impunity* (New York: Other Press, 2008), 242–45.

2. Peter Galbraith, interview with author, December 11, 2014.

2. Ian Traynor, "Franjo Tudjman: Authoritarian Leader Whose Communist Past and Nationalist Obsessions Fuelled His Ruthless Pursuit of an Independent Croatia," *The Guardian* (December 13, 1999).

4. Senior aides to both leaders claimed the partition of Bosnia and

Herzegovina was the primary topic of discussion. Tudjman and Milošević denied it, but their subsequent actions give the claims credibility.

5. "Bosnia 'Carve-up Planned over Dinner,' " *BBC News* (March 19, 1998).

6. The Brijuni islands are a beautiful archipelago in the Adriatic that Tito made his official summer residence. Tudjman met his generals there in the days before Operation Storm, and like most of his meetings it was recorded. After his death, the transcripts found their way to the ICTY, which judged them to be genuine.

7. Vjeran Pavlaković, "Better the Grave Than a Slave: Croatia and the International Criminal Tribunal for the Former Yugoslavia," in Sabrina P. Ramet, Konrad Klewing, and Reneo Lukić, eds., *Croatia since Independence: War, Politics, Society, Foreign Relations* (Munich: Oldenbourg Verlag GmbH, 2008), 6.

8. Cable from US embassy in Zagreb to the State Department, May 26, 2003.

9. ICTY document, evidence of Marko Prelec, tribunal analyst, November 20, 2000.

10. Del Ponte and Sudetic, *Madame Prosecutor*, 245.

11. Military Professional Resources Inc., which boasted of having "more generals per square foot than in the Pentagon," helped train both the Croatian and the Bosnian armies; see Leslie Wayne, "America's For-Profit Secret Army," *The New York Times* (October 13, 2002).

12. Tudjman's favorite strategic theorist was Samuel P. Huntington, an American conservative and the author of the 1996 landmark tome *The Clash of Civilizations and the Remaking of World Order* (New York: Simon & Schuster, 1996).

13. Peter Galbraith, interview with author, December 11, 2014.

14. Philip Shenon, "Croatian General Plans to Surrender to Hague Tribunal," *The New York Times* (March 31, 1996).

15. ICTY transcript, October 1, 1997, trial of Tihomir Blaamir.

16. Ivan Violic, "Dario Kordić, a War Criminal Indicted by the Hague Tribunal, Lives Undisturbed in Zagreb," *Globus* (July 12, 1996).

17. Interview with author, December 11, 2014.

18. The others on the plane that day were Mario Čerkez, Drago Josipo-vić, Marinko Katava, Zoran and Mirjan Kupreškić, Dragan Papić, Vladimir and Ivan Šantić, and Pero Skopljak.

19. Chris Hedges, "10 Bosnian Croats Surrender to War Crimes Tribunal," *The New York Times* (October 7, 1997).

20. ICTY document, trial chamber judgment, Prlić et al., May 29, 2013.

21. Comments that follow here are from Stjepan Mesić, interview with author, February 4, 2013.

22. Del Ponte and Sudetic, *Madame Prosecutor*, 249.

23. Ibid., 251.

24. Ibid.

25. Ibid., 252.

26. In a dispatch to Washington on the trial, the US embassy speculated what the country would be like "if all Croatian judges were like Sarić" before concluding she was probably unique. "Without intensive and sustained reform to overcome biased judges, witness intimidation, deliberate obstruction of justice, political opposition and a flawed criminal code, the Gospić case likely will remain the exception, not the rule." (US embassy cable to State Department, March 26, 2003.)

27. Del Ponte and Sudetic, *Madame Prosecutor*, 251.

28. Gordan Malić, "Razgovor s Bobetkom," (September 20, 2002): 27.

29. Anonymous source, interview with author, March 14, 2014.

30. Account given by Ostojić to US embassy according to May 26, 2003, cable, Wikileaks.

31. Ranko Ostojić, interview with author, February 4, 2014.

32. Jean-Arnault Derens, "TPI: le général croate fugitif Ante Gotovina est un citoyen français," *Le Monde Diplomatique* (March 1, 2005).

33. Vjeran Pavlaković, "Croatia, the International Criminal Tribunal for the Former Yugoslavia, and General Gotovina as a Political Symbol," *Europe-Asia Studies* 62, No. 10 (December 2010).

34. Ian Traynor, "The Fugitive Who Stands in the Way of Croatia's EU Entry," *The Guardian* (March 18, 2005).

35. "British Spies at Large in Croatia," *Nacional* (August 24, 2003).

36. ICTY document, Del Ponte's address to the UN Security Council, June 13, 2005.

37. Del Ponte and Sudetic, *Madame Prosecutor*, 269.

38. The Croatian police had even made a public announcement in May 2005 that he had been traveling on a passport under the name of Horvat when he first fled Croatia after his 2001 indictment; see "Officials Say Gotovina Fled Croatia Under Name of Kristian Horvat," Croatian News Agency HINA (May 3, 2005).

39. Del Ponte and Sudetic, *Madame Prosecutor*, 269.

40. Karl Laske, "Le Croate Ante Gotovina aurait bénéficié d'un soutien français," *Liberation* (September 7, 2009).

## 6. GORILLAS AND SPIKES

1. Pete Blaber, *The Mission, the Men, and Me: Lessons from a Former Delta Force Commander* (New York: The Berkley Publishing Group, 2008), 44. Blaber's book does not specify that Karadžić was the target, describing him only as "a high-ranking PIFWC"; I confirmed independently that it referred to Karadžić.

2. Ibid., 43.

3. Ibid., 53.

4. Ibid., 63.

5. ICTY transcript, trial of General Krstić, November 1, 2000. The radio intercept was recorded by the Bosnian army on August 2, 1995. It was ultimately not admitted as evidence because the prosecution had introduced it during hearings of defense witnesses. Krstić always denied its authenticity.

6. Ibid., testimony of witness DD, July 26, 2000. Also described in Ed Vulliamy, *The War Is Dead, Long Live the War: Bosnia: The Reckoning* (London: Vintage Books, 2012), 92.

7. Anonymous source, interview with author, April 9, 2013.

8. Florence Hartmann, *Paix et chatiment: Les Guerres Secrètes de la Politique et de la Justice Internationales* (Paris: Flammarion, 2007), 196.

9. Anonymous source, interview with author, April 2013.

10. Ruth Sullivan, "NATO Berated Over KaradBer," *Financial Times* (August 22, 2000).

11. The details of this operation come from a US special forces officer involved in its planning on condition of anonymity, interview with author, April 2013.

12. See Paula Broadwell with Vernon Loeb, *All In: The Education of General David Petraeus* (New York: Penguin Books, 2012).

13. Ibid.

14. Robert J. Donia, *Radovan Karadžić: Architect of the Bosnian Genocide* (New York: Cambridge University Press, 2015), 289.

15. Nick Hawton, "Love on the Run: Secret Letters of Europe's Top War Crimes Suspect," *The Times* (June 14, 2005).

16. Telephone interview with author, April 10, 2014.

17. Interview with author, April 9, 2013.

18. Broadwell, *All In*.

19. It remains unclear what happened to Kafgia and Jamalah once they returned to their home countries. There are no records of their cases.

20. In June 2011, Petraeus became the ultimate embodiment of the new hybrid of paramilitary-led intelligence operations and intelligence-led special forces, when he went straight from the Afghan battlefield to CIA director. He did the job for little more than a year before resigning because of an extramarital affair with his biographer, Paula Broadwell.

## 7. THE TRACKING TEAM

1. The job also involved heading the prosecution office in the International Criminal Tribunal for Rwanda, an unfeasible dual task that involved frequent flights to Kigali, Rwanda, and Arusha, Tanzania, the court's headquarters. In 2003, the UN Security Council voted to split the job, appointing a separate ICTY prosecutor.

2. Del Ponte gives her own account of the fight against Western apathy and Balkan obstructionism in her memoir, written with Chuck Sudetic,

*Madame Prosecutor: Confrontations with Humanity's Worst Criminals and the Culture of Impunity* (New York: Other Press, 2008).

3. John Hagan, *Justice in the Balkans: Prosecuting War Crimes in the Hague Tribunal* (Chicago: Chicago University Press, 2003), 72.

4. ICTY case information sheet, Čelebići Camp, reference number IT-96-21.

5. The following quotes, unless otherwise noted, are from Louise Arbour, interview with author, November 20, 2012.

6. Hagan, *Justice in the Balkans*, 5.

7. Michaela Schäuble, *Narrating Victimhood: Gender, Religion and the Making of Place in Post-War Croatia* (New York: Berghahn Books, 2014), 226.

8. Del Ponte and Sudetic, *Madame Prosecutor*, 268.

9. Foreign and Commonwealth Office document 10, "Yugoslav War Crimes Tribunal: Support for Unit to Trace Indictees," January 10, 1997, Freedom of Information disclosure.

10. Raymond Carter, telephone interview with author, April 10, 2015.

11. Christian Axboe Nielsen, interview with author, November 27, 2013.

12. Arbour, interview with author.

13. Veselin Šljivančanin, interview with author, October 31, 2013.

14. Anonymous source, interview with author, September 11, 2012.

15. Ed Vulliamy and Nerma Jelacic, "The Warlord of Višegrad," *The Guardian* (August 11, 2005).

16. Ibid.

17. Jacques Massé, *Nos chers criminels de guerre: Paris, Zabreb, Belgrade en classe affaires* (Paris: Flammarion, 2006), 175.

## 8. THE STRANGE DEATH OF DRAGAN GAGOVIĆ

1. The Chetnik atrocities are detailed in Marko Attila Hoare, *Genocide and Resistance in Hitler's Bosnia: The Partisans and the Chetniks* (Oxford University Press. 2006), 331–32.

2. The account of events in Foča are drawn from Dragan Gagović,

Himzo Selimović, and other former residents, interviews with author, mostly conducted in October and November 2006.

3. Himzo Selimović, interview with author, November 22, 1996.

4. I went to Foča on that occasion with a colleague, Alexandra Stigl-mayer of *Time* magazine, who later edited the book *Mass Rape: The War Against Women in Bosnia-Herzegovina*, translated by Marion Faber (Lincoln, NE: University of Nebraska Press, 1994).

5. *Public Eye*, CBS News (January 15, 1999).

6. Two suspects from the French zone had previously been transferred to The Hague. On March 4, 1998, Dragoljub Kunarac, on the same indictment as Gagović, handed himself over to French soldiers after negotiating a price (see chapter 9). Milorad Krnojelac was arrested on June 15, 1998, but his capture was carried out by German special forces, officially under French SFOR command.

7. Jacques Massé, *Nos chers criminels de guerre: Paris, Zabreb, Belgrade en classe affaires* (Paris: Flammarion, 2006), 182.

8. "The Death of Indictee Dragan Gagović," Institute for War and Peace Reporting (January 10, 1999).

9. International Crisis Group, "War Criminals in Bosnia's Republika Srpska" (November 2, 2000).

10. Massé, *Nos chers criminels de guerre*, 184.

## 9. THE SPYMASTER OF THE HÔTEL DE BRIENNE

1. Philip Short, *Mitterrand: A Study in Ambiguity* (London: The Bodley Head, 2013), 525.

2. Emma Daly, "The Day the Serbs Went a Bridge Too Far," *The Independent* (June 7, 1995).

3. Rémy Ourdan, "Six années de liaisons dangereuses franco-serbes," *Le Monde* (November 4, 1998).

4. "Sarajevo on the Spot," *Newsweek* (December 17, 1995).

5. Chuck Sudetic, "The Reluctant Gendarme," *The Atlantic* (April 2000).

6. Pierre Martinet, *DGSE Service action: Un Agent sort de l'ombre* (Paris: Editions Privé, 2005), 239.

NOTES

7. Ibid., 241.

8. Stéphane Durand-Souffland, "Rondot, un maître espion au procès Clearstream," *Le Figaro* (October 5, 2009).

9. Jacques Massé, *Nos chers criminels de guerre: Paris, Zabreb, Belgrade en classe affaires* (Paris: Flammarion, 2006), 180.

10. R. Jeffrey Smith, "Secret Meetings Foiled Karadžić Capture Plan; US Says French Jeopardized Mission," *Washington Post* (April 23, 1998).

11. Massé, *Nos chers criminels de guerre*, 180.

12. Anonymous German officer, e-mail interview with author, March 27, 2014.

13. Ibid.

14. Ibid.

15. Massé, *Nos chers criminels de guerre*, 185.

16. Vasiljević was sentenced to twenty years, reduced to fifteen years on appeal, for his part in the execution of seven Muslim men lined up along the Drina and shot. After six years in an Austrian prison, he was released early in March 2010 and received a hero's welcome in Serb-run Višegrad.

17. Richard Holbrooke, *To End a War* (New York: Random House, 1998), 255.

18. Momčilo Krajišnik, interview with author, February 2014.

19. An account of this incident is provided in Massé, *Nos chers criminels de guerre*, 161.

20. Ibid., 163.

21. Krajišnik, interview with author.

22. Ibid.

23. Roger Faligot, Jean Guisnel, and Rémi Kauffer, *Histoire politique des services secret français: De la seconde guerre mondiale à nos jours* (Paris: Éditions La Découverte, 2013), 536.

24. Massé, *Nos chers criminels de guerre*, 80, 82.

25. Carla Del Ponte and Chuck Sudetic, *Madame Prosecutor: Confrontations with Humanity's Worst Criminals and the Culture of Impunity* (New York: Other Press, 2008), 204.

26. Massé, *Nos chers criminels de guerre*, 102.

27. Durand-Souffland, "Rondot, un maître espion au procès Clear-stream."

## 10. SLOBODAVIA: THE FALL OF MILOŠEVIĆ AND THE UNRAVELING OF SERBIA

1. Adam LeBor, *Milošević: A Biography* (London: Bloomsbury, 2002), 315.

2. Ibid., 295.

3. Alexandra Niksic, "Serbia's Notorious Couple Apart for the First Time," Agence France Presse (April 7, 2001).

4. Jonathan Steele, Pazit Ravina, and Peter Beaumont, "Cornered Dictator Is Left with Nowhere to Run: The Disgraced Serbian Leader Is Under Siege," *The Observer* (April 1, 2001).

5. LeBor, *Milošević*, 302.

6. Vidosav Stevanovic, *Milosevic: The People's Tyrant*, translated by Zlata Filipovic (London: I. B. Tauris, 2004), 196.

7. Dragan Bujosevic and Ivan Radovanovic, *The Fall of Milosevic: The October 5th Revolution* (London: Palgrave Macmillan, 2003), 28.

8. Ibid., 128.

9. Ibid., 130.

10. Ibid., 171.

11. Stevanovic, *Milosevic*, 206.

12. Toma Fila, interview with author, October 29, 2013.

13. LeBor, *Milošević*, 37.

14. Dragiša Blanuša, *Čuvao sam Miloševića* (Belgrade: NIGP, 2001), 21.

15. Ibid., 22.

16. Ibid., 155.

17. Alexandra Niksic, "Yugoslav Cabinet Split over Move to Extradite War Criminals," Agence France Presse (June 23, 2001).

18. Carlotta Gall, "Belgrade Begins Process of Sending Milošević to The Hague," *New York Times* (June 25, 2001).

19. Blanuša, *Čuvao sam Miloševića*, 182.

20. Ibid., 183.

21. Kevin Curtis, interview with author, April 4, 2013.

22. See www.airliners.net/aviation-forums/general_aviation/read.main
/508790/.

23. "Milošević Jailed in The Hague," CNN.com World (June 29, 2001).

24. ICTY official statement, June 29, 2001.

25. Patrick Lopez-Terres, interview with author, May 15, 2015.

## 11. RADOVAN KARADŽIĆ: THE SHAMAN IN THE MADHOUSE

1. At the time of writing, Luka Karadžić was still defending himself from the same charges from the same incident. In February 2012 the Serbian appeal court sentenced him to more than two years in prison for driving under the influence of alcohol, but his defense team argued successfully that the manner some of the evidence had been introduced violated the Code of Criminal Procedure, and had the case declared a mistrial. A new trial began in April 2015.

2. I approached Luka Karadžić for comment during the research for this book, but after initially agreeing to speak, he changed his mind and demanded money, saying the book would "make millions" and he was entitled to a share.

3. Jack Hitt, "Radovan Karadžić's New-Age Adventure," *The New York Times Magazine* (July 22, 2009).

4. Miodrag Rakić, interview with author, October 30, 2013. Rakić died of cancer in May 2014.

5. Sveta Vujačić, interview with author, October 30, 2013.

6. Nick Hawton, *Europe's Most Wanted Man: The Quest for Radovan Karadžić* (London: Arrow Books, 2009), 1.

7. This account is by an ICTY official briefed on the event.

8. Robert J. Donia, *Radovan Karadžić: Architect of the Bosnian Genocide* (New York: Cambridge University Press, 2015), 24.

9. See Mirko Klarin, producer and screenwriter, *Život i priključenije Radovana Karadžića* (Sense Agency, 2005).

10. Stacy Sullivan, "To His Home Town, Serb Karadžić Is a Local Hero Who Made Good," *Washington Post* (August 21 1996).

11. Tom Gjelten, "Karadžić Was Once Considered a Moderate by Many," NPR (July 24, 2008).

12. Ibid.

13. "Karadžić's Wife says West Misunderstands Radovan," Reuters (May 4, 1996).

14. Tim Judah, *The Serbs: History, Myth and the Destruction of Yugoslavia* (New Haven, CT: Yale University Press, 2009), 165.

15. Donia, *Radovan Karadžić*, 50.

16. Ibid.

17. Ibid., 72.

18. Ibid.

19. See Pawel Pawlikowski, director, *Serbian Epics* (BBC, 1992).

20. Ibid.

21. ICTY transcript, intercepted conversation between Radovan Karadžić and Gojko Djogo, October 12, 1991.

22. Michael A. Sells, "The Construction of Islam in Serbian Religious Mythology and Its Consequences," in *Islam and Bosnia: Conflict Resolution and Foreign Policy in Multi-Ethnic States*, edited by Maya Shatzmiller (Montreal: McGill-Queens University Press, 2002), 58.

23. Hawton, *Europe's Most Wanted Man*, 133.

24. Richard Holbrooke, *To End a War* (New York: Random House, 1998), 339.

25. Hawton, *Europe's Most Wanted Man*, 135.

26. Yeltsin's remarks are according to French officials speaking off the record.

27. The wild-goose chase in the Bosnian highlands is satirized in the 2007 film *The Hunting Party*, starring Richard Gere as a down-at-the-heels American journalist convinced he can track down the elusive Karadžić-like figure known as "The Fox." The film begins with the words "Only the most ridiculous parts of this story are true" and ends with the reflection: "In theory, the official hunt for war criminals in Bosnia continues to this day . . . However, the two most wanted men—Radovan Karadžić and Ratko Mladić—continue to elude the US, the United Nations, the

European Union, NATO, The Hague, and all in the civilized world who claim to be looking for them. In the ten years that Radovan Karadžić has been on the run, he has published two books and one play. Perhaps if the international community opened a summerstock theater...But they're probably too busy 'searching' for Osama Bin Laden."

28. "Hunt for Karadžić: Raid to Net Prime Suspect Botched by NATO: Recriminations Follow French-led Assault on Mountain Hideaway," *The Guardian* (March 1, 2002).

29. Information Service of the Serbian Orthodox Church, April 9, 2004.

30. Hawton, *Europe's Most Wanted Man*, 80.

31. "Bogdan Subotić dao SFOR-a vrijedne informacije o Radovanu Karadžiću," *Slobodna Bosna* (March 12, 2004).

32. Anonymous source, interview with author, February 2013.

33. "Karadžić's Wife Urges Surrender," *BBC News* (July 29, 2005).

34. Hitt, "Radovan Karadžić's New-Age Adventure."

35. Ibid.

36. Julian Borger and Ian Traynor, "The Healer on the 73 Bus, Europe's Most Wanted Man," *The Guardian* (July 23, 2008).

37. Ibid.

38. Hitt, "Radovan Karadžić's New-Age Adventure."

39. Julian Borger, "The Night Karadžić Rocked the Madhouse," *The Guardian* (July 23, 2008).

40. Ibid.

41. Sveta Vujačić, interview with author, October 30, 2013.

42. Borger, "The Night Karadžić Rocked the Madhouse."

43. Sveta Vujačić, interview with author, November 30, 2013.

44. ICTY transcript, October 1, 2014.

## 12. THE OLD MAN IN THE FARMHOUSE: MLADIĆ ON THE RUN

1. ICTY, transcript of testimony, Milan Gunj, March 2, 2009.

2. ICTY, video footage of Mladić entering Srebrenica, July 11, 1995.

3. ICTY, transcript of testimony, Djordje Ćurčin, March 23, 2009.

4. "Srbi Showdown: Djogo o Bivši Komšija i podržavanje Nivoi Mladića—Mladića ozbiljne optužbe protiv Koštunice," *Slobodna Bosna* (September 6, 2007).

5. Michael Dobbs, "Mladić—the Family Man," *Foreign Policy* (July 20, 2012).

6. Miloš Šaljić, interview with author, March 18, 2013.

7. Erich Follath, "Portrait of a Man Possessed: A Search for the Real Ratko Mladić," *Der Spiegel* (September 30, 2011).

8. Transcript of testimony, Ćurčin.

9. Charles Crawford, interview with author, July 7, 2011.

10. Šaljić, interview with author.

11. "Two Alleged Aides to Mladić Plead Not Guilty to Providing Shelter for the Fugitive," AP (November 20, 2006).

12. Božo Prelević, interview with author, October 29, 2013.

13. Janko Jakovljević, interview with author, October 2013.

14. "Serb Army 'Shielding Mladić from War Crimes Court,'" *The Independent* (April, 12 2005).

15. Miodrag Ivanović, interview with author, October 2013.

16. "Political, Media-Related and Legal Analysis of the Cases of RTS, Topčider and Leskovac," Center for Euro-Atlantic Studies (June 29, 2009).

17. *Pad Ratka Mladića* [The Fall of Ratko Mladića], television documentary by Slaviša Lekić, Prva Srpska Televizija, January 27, 2015.

18. Ibid.

19. Bruno Vekarić, interview with author, March 19, 2013.

20. Šaljić, interview with author.

21. *Pad Ratka Mladića*, January 27, 2015.

22. Ibid.

23. Boris Tadić, interview with author, March 17, 2013.

24. Šaljić, interview with author.

25. Miodrag Rakić, interview with author, March 18, 2013.

## 13. THE LEGACY

1. "Mladić Refuses to Testify for Karadžić at ICTY Trial," BBC News (January 28, 2014).

2. According to anonymous sources within the ICTY prosecutors.

3. Naser Orić, interview with author, February 13, 2014.

4. A Dutch investigation in April 2006 found Milošević died of natural causes. Although there had been evidence that he had been taking unprescribed, smuggled medicines in the preceding months, there was no evidence of them in his cell when he died.

5. Veselin Šljivančanin, interview with author, October 31, 2013.

6. Momčilo Krajišnik, interview with author, February 11, 2014.

7. "Scheveningen—a Far from 'Normal' Prison," Balkan Investigative Reporting Network (November 27, 2013).

8. Krajišnik, interview with author, February 11, 2014.

9. James Owen, *Nuremberg: Evil on Trial* (London: Headline Review, 2006).

10. For an account of the International Criminal Court's genesis, see David Bosco, *Rough Justice: The International Criminal Court in a World of Power Politics* (New York: Oxford University Press, 2014).

11. The former US war crimes envoy David Scheffer suggested a legal framework for the ICC's own tracking team in 2014 ("Proposal for an International Criminal Court Arrest Procedures Protocol," *Northwestern Journal of International Human Rights*, Vol. 12, Issue 3), but it remains very much a theoretical exercise.

12. "Euro Court Rules Bosnia War Crimes Sentences Unjust," Balkan Investigative Reporters Network (July 18, 2013).

13. "Serbia: Ending Impunity for Crimes Under International Law," Amnesty International (June 2014).

14. ICTY document, trial chamber judgment, "Prosecutor v. Jovica Stanišić and Franko Simatovic," vol. II (May 30, 2013).

15. Ibid.

16. "ICTY Judge Frederik Harhoff's Email to 56 Contacts, June 6, 2013," published online by Danish newspaper *BT*: http://www.bt.dk/sites/default/files-dk/node-files/511/6/6511917-letter-english.pdf

17. Eric Gordy, "What Happened to the Hague Tribunal," *New York Times* (June 2, 2013).

18. Nataša Kandić, interview with author, October 29, 2013.

19. Hasan Nuhanović, interview with author, February 10, 2014.

20. "Bosnian Professor Beaten for Criticising War Criminal," Balkan Investigative Reporters Network (June 24, 2014).

21. Julian Borger, "War Is Over—Now Serbs and Bosniaks Fight to Win Control over a Brutal History," The Guardian (March 23, 2014).

22. Kasim's younger brother, Kemal, who he helped keep alive in Omarska, has made a film about Kevljani called *Pretty Village*.

23. Serge Brammertz, interview with author, October 3, 2011.

# SELECT BIBLIOGRAPHY

## WAR CRIMES AND INTERNATIONAL JUSTICE

Armatta, Judith. *Twilight of Impunity: The War Crimes Trial of Slobodan Milosevic*. Durham, NC: Duke University Press, 2010.

Bass, Gary Jonathan. *Stay the Hand of Vengeance: The Politics of War Crimes Tribunals*. Princeton, NJ: Princeton University Press, 2000.

Bosco, David. *Rough Justice: The International Criminal Court in a World of Power Politics*. New York: Oxford University Press, 2014.

Del Ponte, Carla, and Chuck Sudetic. *Madame Prosecutor: Confrontations with Humanity's Worst Criminals and the Culture of Impunity*. New York: Other Press, 2008.

Hagan, John. *Justice in the Balkans: Prosecuting War Crimes in the Hague Tribunal*. Chicago: Chicago University Press, 2003.

Hartmann, Florence. *Paix et Châtiment: Les Guerres Secrètes de la Politique et de la Justice Internationales*. Paris: Flammarion, 2007.

Hawton, Nick. *Europe's Most Wanted Man: The Quest for Radovan Karadžić*. London: Arrow Books, 2009.

Hazan, Pierre. *Justice in a Time of War: The Truth Story Behind the International Criminal Tribunal for the Former Yugoslavia*. Translated by James Thomas Snyder. College Station, TX: Texas A&M University Press, 2004.

Honig, Jan Willem, and Norbert Both. *Srebrenica: Record of a War Crime*. New York: Penguin, 1996.

Massé, Jacques. *Nos chers criminels de guerre: Paris, Zagreb, Belgrade en classe affaires*. Paris: Flammarion, 2006.

Neier, Aryeh. *War Crimes: Brutality, Genocide, Terror, and the Struggle for Justice.* New York: Times Books, 1998.

Neuffer, Elizabeth. *The Key to My Neighbor's House: Seeking Justice in Bosnia and Rwanda.* New York: Macmillan, 2002.

Power, Samantha. *A Problem from Hell: America and the Age of Genocide.* New York: Basic Books, 2002.

Rohde, David. *Endgame: The Betrayal and Fall of Srebrenica, Europe's Worst Massacre Since World War II.* New York: Farrar, Straus and Giroux, 1997.

Scheffer, David. *All the Missing Souls: A Personal History of the War Crimes Tribunals.* Princeton, NJ: Princeton University Press, 2012.

Stephen, Chris. *Judgement Day: The Trial of Slobodan Milošević.* New York: Atlantic Books, 2004.

## THE BALKANS AND THE FALL OF YUGOSLAVIA

Almond, Mark. *Europe's Backyard War: The War in the Balkans.* New York: Mandarin, 1994.

Andrić, Ivo. *The Bridge Over the Drina.* Translated by Lovette F. Edwards. London: The Harvill Press, 1994.

Bujosevic, Dragan, and Ivan Radovanovic. *The Fall of Milosevic: The October 5th Revolution.* London: Palgrave Macmillan, 2003.

Donia, Robert J. *Radovan Karadžić: Architect of the Bosnian Genocide.* New York: Cambridge University Press, 2015.

Glenny, Misha. *The Balkans 1804–2012: Nationalism, War and the Great Powers.* London: Granta Books, 2012.

——. *The Fall of Yugoslavia: The Third Balkan War.* London: Penguin Books, 1992.

Goldstein, Slavko. *1941: The Year That Keeps Returning.* Translated by Michael Gabe. New York: New York Review of Books, 2013.

Holbrooke, Richard. *To End a War.* New York: Random House, 1998.

Job, Cvijeto. *Yugoslavia's Ruin: The Bloody Lessons of Nationalism.* Lanham, MD: Rowman & Littlefield Publishers, 2002.

Judah, Tim. *Kosovo: War and Revenge.* New Haven, CT: Yale University Press, 2000.

——. *The Serbs: History, Myth and the Destruction of Yugoslavia*. New Haven, CT: Yale University Press, 2009.

LeBor, Adam. *Milosevic: A Biography*. London: Bloomsbury, 2002.

Maass, Peter. *Love Thy Neighbor: A Story of War*. New York: Knopf, 1996.

Magaš, Branka. *The Destruction of Yugoslavia: Tracking the Break-Up 1980–92*. London: Verso, 1993.

Malcolm, Noel. *Bosnia: A Short History*. London: Macmillan, 1994.

Oliver, Ian. *War & Peace in the Balkans: The Diplomacy of Conflict in the Former Yugoslavia*. London: I. B. Tauris, 2005.

Rieff, David. *Slaughterhouse: Bosnia and the Failure of the West*. New York: Simon & Schuster, 1995.

Robertson, Geoffrey. *Crimes Against Humanity: The Struggle for Global Justice*. London: Penguin Books, 2012.

Sell, Louis. *Slobodan Milosevic and the Destruction of Yugoslavia*. Durham, NC: Duke University Press, 2002.

Silber, Laura, and Allan Little. *The Death of Yugoslavia*. London: Penguin/BBC Books, 1995.

Simms, Brendan. *Unfinest Hour: Britain and The Destruction of Bosnia*. London: Allen Lane, 2001.

Stevanovic, Vidosav. *Milosevic: The People's Tyrant*. Translated by Zlata Filipovic. London: I. B. Tauris, 2004.

Tanner, Marcus. *Croatia: A Nation Forged in War*. New Haven, CT: Yale University Press, 2010.

Thompson, Mark. *A Paper House: The Ending of Yugoslavia*. London: Vintage Books, 1992.

Vulliamy, Ed. *Seasons in Hell: Understanding Bosnia's War*. New York: Simon & Schuster, 1994.

——. *The War Is Dead, Long Live the War: Bosnia: The Reckoning*. London: Vintage Books, 2012.

## MILITARY AND INTELLIGENCE

Blaber, Pete. *The Mission, the Men, and Me: Lessons from a Former Delta Force Commander*. New York: The Berkley Publishing Group, 2008.

# BIBLIOGRAPHY

Boykin, Ltg. (Ret.) William G., with Lynn Vincent. *Never Surrender: A Soldier's Journey to the Crossroads of Faith and Freedom.* New York: Hachette Book Group, 2008.

Corera, Gordon. *MI6: Life and Death in the British Secret Service.* London: Phoenix, 2010.

Faligot, Roger, Jean Guisnel, and Rémi Kauffer. *Histoire politique des services secrets français: De la seconde guerre mondiale à nos jours.* Paris: Éditions La Découverte, 2013.

Francona, Rick. *Chasing Demons: My Hunt for War Criminals in Bosnia.* Carmel, CA: Francona Advisers, 2012.

Jennings, Christian. *Midnight in Some Burning Town: British Special Forces Operations from Belgrade to Baghdad.* London: Cassell Military, 2004.

Martinet, Pierre. *DGSE Service action: Un Agent sort de l'ombre.* Paris: Editions Privé, 2005.

# INDEX

# INDEX

Bachelet, Jean-René, 200

Bair, Andrew, 7, 9

Balkan Spring, 328

Balkan wars, West's slowness to
respond to, xxiii–xxiv, xxix, 3

Bambiland, 224

Banja Luka metal factory
atrocities at, 174
Dutch-British intelligence cell
at, 61–62, 67, 69–70

Banović, Predrag and Nenad,
63–64, 72–73

Barriot, Patrick, 200

Beara, Ljubiša, 171–172

Belarus, 268

Belgrade, 280
Mladić in, 287, 289
organized crime in, 91–93, 225
Ražnatović and football clubs of,
175–176

Berger, Sandy, 139

Bijeljina, Bosnian war starting in, 184

bin Laden, Osama, 130

Blaber, Pete, 128–130, 148, 358n1

Blagojević, Vidoje, 69–70

Blair, Tony, 1–2, 59, 70, 159
effects of election of, 55, 159
increasing willingness to pursue
war criminals, 49–50, 159

Blanuša, Dragiša, 236, 238, 240, 242

Blaškić, Tihomir, 105, 107–108, 110

Blot, Jacques, 200

Bobetko, Janko, 114–115

Bolivia, 6–7

Bormann, Martin, xxix, 349n16

Bosanski Šamac, 86–87, 96–97

Bosnia and Herzegovina, xxii, 18, 149,
303–304
arrests in, 58, 94, 173, 205–209
Balkan Spring in, 328
ethnic cleansing in, xxii, 103

ethnic relations in, xix, 257, 261,
328–329
faith in Hague Tribunal in, 318
French zone of, 205–209
Karadžić as Serb leader in, 212, 261
Milošević and, xx, 74, 243
Milošević losing territory of,
222, 289
NATO's roles in, 3, 160, 270,
349n7
plans to dismember, 104, 183–184,
289, 355n4
Republika Srpska and, 263, 266
Serb separatists in, 183–184, 263
split by Dayton Accords, 11
US roles in, 3, 78, 80
war crimes courts in, 325
war criminals in, 48, 152, 156, 209
war criminals' influence on
governability of, 5, 8, 15, 54
western, 62, 330

Bosniak-Croat Federation, Bosnia
split into Republika Srpska
and, 11

Bosniaks. See Muslims

Bosnian Serbs, xxii, 17, 19, 288
atrocities by, xvii, xxvii, 286
Karadžić as leader of, 261, 270
NATO airstrikes on, 199, 201, 216

Bosnian war, 3, 277, 347n5
casualties in, xxii, xxvi
French fighting back in, 198–199
international response to, xxiv,
49, 200, 247, 352n13
Milošević orchestrating, xxii, 184

Boykin, William G. "Jerry," 80–83

Brammertz, Serge, 153, 154, 167, 332

Brandić, Anto, 86

Brashich, Deyan, 95, 96

Brčko, detention camps near, 85–86

Brdjanin, Radoslav, 65

# INDEX

# PHOTO CREDITS